The Family Business Map

Assets and Roadblocks in Long-Term Planning

The Family Business Map

Morten Bennedsen
INSEAD

and

Joseph P.H. Fan
The Chinese University of Hong Kong

palgrave
macmillan

First published 2014 by
PALGRAVE MACMILLAN

Palgrave Macmillan in the UK is an imprint of Macmillan Publishers Limited, registered in England, company number 785998, of Houndmills, Basingstoke, Hampshire RG21 6XS.

Palgrave Macmillan in the US is a division of St Martin's Press LLC, 175 Fifth Avenue, New York, NY 10010.

Palgrave Macmillan is the global academic imprint of the above companies and has companies and representatives throughout the world.

Palgrave® and Macmillan® are registered trademarks in the United States, the United Kingdom, Europe and other countries.

ISBN 978–1–137–38235–1

This book is printed on paper suitable for recycling and made from fully managed and sustained forest sources. Logging, pulping and manufacturing processes are expected to conform to the environmental regulations of the country of origin.

A catalogue record for this book is available from the British Library.

Library of Congress Cataloging-in-Publication Data
Bennedsen, Morten.
The family business map : assets and roadblocks in long term planning / Morten Bennedsen and Joseph P.H. Fan.
pages cm
ISBN 978–1–137–38235–1
1. Family-owned business enterprises.   2. Family-owned business enterprises—Succession.   I. Fan, Joseph P. H. II. Title.
HD62.25.B457   2014
658'.04—dc23   2014021915

Typeset by MPS Limited, Chennai, India.

Table of Contents

List of Figures and Tables

Case List

ver the world. For
...ny businesses in Europe,
symbolically, we first met a decade ago
...where Asia and Europe come together. The more we
our research and our findings, the more we realized that family
firms in East and West had much in common. And given similarity of the
opportunities and challenges they face, there is a lot they can learn from
each other.

While constantly amazed by the prevalence of family firms and the
similarity of their experiences, we are just as impressed by the different
approaches used to solve problems when they arise. In Europe, some
established family enterprises have been working for over 100 years to
keep the family and the business moving forward together. In China, the
average private firm is not even 20 years old, while Indian families at the
helm of some of the world's biggest conglomerates are already looking to
transfer their wealth to second and third generations.

After many years spent teaching owner-managers, families and heirs on
every continent, we felt there was a need for a global perspective on long-
term planning both for families and their firms. Talking to people 'on the
ground', we realized that the industries serving family businesses are very
much experience based, and that knowledge of the field is fragmented.
For these reasons we decided to write a book devoted to family firms,
their opportunities, challenges and sustainability.

Starting out with a mission to provide a framework for long-term planning
based on experiences from East and West, South and North, the book

offers a blend of case studies and research insights designed to provide a blueprint for families in business, drawing on the many commonalities that unite them, while emphasizing the need to implement strategy and governance according to the specific cultural and business environment.

The family is the most basic social and economic unit in human society. The tradition of family-organized production has persisted throughout the history of mankind, from hunting and gathering to the development of agriculture, the industrial revolution and the modern era. Even today, there are still more family firms than any other type of business organization, and they generate much of the economic output and value of most of the nations on the planet.

But the sustainability of each individual family firm can never be taken for granted. Simply continuing the success and prosperity of a complex business beyond the current generation's lifespan is a challenge. To both the casual observer and the academic it's apparent that inter-generational transitions are difficult. The saying 'Wealth does not survive three generations' was borne out by our research in Europe and Asia, where we found multiple examples of family firms that failed to flourish when handed on to the next generation. Indeed, for publicly traded companies in Hong Kong, Singapore and Taiwan, we estimate that more than half of the business's value is lost in transition.

In Europe, as the baby-boomers reach retirement age, thousands of small- and medium-sized family firms are anticipating such a transition in the coming decade. In China, where private companies have existed only since the 1980s, a majority of founders are now in their fifties, many of them with sizeable businesses employing numerous workers. In another ten years, they too may be thinking of retirement. Moreover, they are the first generation to have accumulated private wealth with no prior succession experience. In India, where many family firms are in first- and second-generation hands, there is pressure to design succession models in accordance with culture values as well as often complex family structures. In the Middle East, thanks to the oil wealth accumulated since the 1970s, a huge number of first- and second-generation family firms are approaching transition. Conversely, in many African countries the absence of long-term planning around business and families often has catastrophic consequences for business development.

With so many impending transitions, this book is designed to improve long-term planning and overcome some of the challenges of growing the family firm over generations. We firmly believe that learning from mistakes as well as successes is the most effective way forward. In sharing the fruits of our research and proposing a practical planning tool, we hope it will be embraced by all those who care about the sustainability of family businesses.

Why read this book?

The contents are derived from courses, interventions and research that we have conducted over the years. We present a unique framework for family firms as well as a novel hands-on approach to planning that has successfully been used with hundreds of family firms on every continent. Unlike books based simply on Western experience, our global comparative approach encompasses family businesses worldwide, be they in Africa, America, Asia, Europe or Latin America. The methods and tools proposed here are transferable, because while every family business is unique, it shares many features with other family firms in other cultures. Both our framework and our recommendations are based on large-scale research, much of which has been published in leading academic journals over the last two decades. The use of a large sample size ensures that our cases and examples are truly representative of family firms in general, and thus constitute a reliable source of information.

The planning framework and cases presented here will be useful for any owner-manager or family in search of inspiration. Beyond that readership, it will also be of benefit to professionals who are part of the ecosystem around family firms – family business managers, advisors, consultants, private wealth managers, investment bankers and family and corporate lawyers.

Writing the book has been a wonderful journey through which we have met and received help from many people. Special thanks are due to the authors and colleagues with whom we have worked on related topics over the last 15 years. To make the book more reader friendly we have chosen not to include citations within each chapter and to use the word 'we' on all research where one of us was a co-author without mentioning the whole set of co-authors. Similarly, we often discuss other researchers' work without in-text citations. In the 'Discover more' section at the end of each chapter we list relevant cases and research, including work by Mario Amore, Pramuan Bunkanwanicha, Deborah Cadbury, Yann Cornil, Robert J. Crawford, Andrew Ellul, Ray Fismann, Francisco Pérez-González, Rolf Hoefer, Sterling Huang, Ming Jian, Li Jin, Winnie Leung, Vikas Mehrotra, Randel Morck, Kasper M. Nielsen, Marco Pagano, Fausto Panunzi, Margarita Tsoutsoura, Hannes Wagner, Yupana Wiwattanakantang, Daniel Wolfenzon, Yinhua Yeh and Stefan Zeume.

We wish to thank the co-authors of many of Joseph's Chinese business cases: Yiwei Gu, Jun Huang, Lisa Qian, Tian Jian Zhang and Guannian Zhou. Their contributions enabled us to overcome the cultural and language barriers and to bring China closer to the rest of the world. We also want to acknowledge the help and insight provided by the following colleagues and experts during the writing process: John Chan, Philip Chan, Ling Chen, Carolyn Chou, Toshio Goto, Aleksandra Gregoric, Denis Gromb, Julia Hieber, Roger King, Philip Koh, Xinchun Li, Xiaowei Rose Luo, Joachim Schwass and Christian Stewart.

Over the last decade, we have met many owner-managers and families whose lives and stories have inspired us. Among these we wish to thank Christian and Tim Brorsen (Vordingborg Lumber Yard), Demu Chen (Jie Holding Group Co., Ltd), Luc and Charles Darbonne (Daregal), Kerong Du (Tianjin Xinmao Science & Technology Co., Ltd), Jeroen and Willem van Eeghen (van Eeghen Group, Peter Foss (FOSS), Xianghijan He (Midea Group), André Hoffmann, Zengoro Hōshi and his wife, the Hottinger family, Jinghui Jian (Hong's Foundation for Education & Culture), Bob and Mark de Kuyper (De Kuyper), Eddy W.M. Lee (Lee Kum Kee Co., Ltd Group), Jihui Li (Yangjiang Shibazi Group), Gérard Lipovitch (les HENOKIENS), Joseph Lo, (Shui-Mu International Co., Ltd), Lixiang Mao (Ningbo Fotile Kitchen Ware Co., Ltd), Antonio and Francisco Monzini (Monzini), Priscilla de Moustier (Wendel Family), Mario Pelino (Confetti Pelino), Stan Shih (Acer Group), Eva Fischer Hansen and Michael Staal (Brunata), M.Y. Sze (Airland (Holdings) Co. Ltd), Jean Thiercelin and the Thiercelin family (Thiercelin), Søren Thorup Sørensen (KIRKBI), Frederick Chavalit Tsao (International Maritime Carriers Ltd (IMC) Group), Junhao Wang (JuneYao Group), Linda Wong (Yihai Group) and Xiaoguang Zhou and Jiangbo Yu (Neoglory Group).

Special thanks to Hazel Hamelin at INSEAD, who edited the entire manuscript three times and without whose dedication the book would not have been finished. Also to our publisher, especially Tamsine O'Riordan and Josephine Taylor, who stood by for the book's completion with great patience. And to MBA, EMBA and PhD students at the Chinese University of Hong Kong (CUHK) and INSEAD who read early rough drafts and offered many suggestions, stories and feedback that greatly enriched the contents.

We wish to thank the Institute of Economics and Finance (IEF) of CUHK as well as the Wendel International Centre for Family Enterprise, Nathalie Bogacz and Carole Guillard at INSEAD for their generous support of the project. We are especially grateful to Maggie Lau of IEF for her diligent secretarial services and efficient coordination of all the people who provided input. The following former CUHK PhD students read and checked the manuscript: Yashu Dong, Sammy Fung, Shufang Lai, Sifei Li, Xin Liu, Yang Liu, Joyce Yu, Ru Zhang and Nancy Zheng. Also CUHK students, Vincent Ballack, Yakun Luo, Danni Xie and Tiffany Zhang gave us valuable assistance in preparing many details of the book, particularly the graphic illustrations. Vincent Ballack provided excellent research assistance in the process of operationalizing the applications of the family business map.

Morten dedicates the book with love to his wife Birthe and their children, Sigrid, Aslak and Astrid, and looks forward to making up for the many days of travelling and writing when he should have been spending time with them.

This book is dedicated by Joseph to his beloved wife Tina, whose love and sacrifice throughout 25 years of marriage made his long career in research endurable, and to their children, Joseph and Alice, whose cheerful support made it possible to finish the book.

chapter **1**

Building Blocks

There are more family firms than any other type of business in the world. This book is about their uniqueness, their opportunities and their challenges. It explains how owners and families can develop business strategies to make the most of their opportunities, and governance strategies to minimize the cost of the challenges. Chapter 1 provides a first insight into the *Family Business Map*, a powerful analytical tool to guide families in their strategic choices.

We begin with two families: the Mulliez family and the Wang family. Their stories illustrate how family ventures in very different societies and settings share common features and challenges. One story is set in northern France, the other in Taiwan. One started a business 100 years ago and it is now in the fourth generation; the other was controlled by the founder until his death in 2008. Both reveal how successful entrepreneurs, regardless of industry, culture or continent, based their business strategies on a unique family contribution, and how they overcame the limitations of family ownership with creative governance solutions. These two stories introduce the importance of family assets and roadblocks, the pillars of our long-term planning framework.

The Mulliez family

The Mullliez family stands out in France's business landscape. Founders of one of the largest retail distribution groups worldwide, they have refined a unique model of family venture capital and have nurtured entrepreneurial talent through four generations.

Louis Mulliez, a self-made man, started a small textile manufacturing business around 1900, which eventually became known as Phildar, working with his eldest son almost from the beginning. By the time his second son, Gerard, joined the retail sector in 1946, the brand was well known for its textiles and sewing material. The company turned to franchising to expand its distribution network – the first Phildar franchise store was licensed in 1956 – ultimately becoming one of the largest textile distributors in the world, with 1,500 stores by the end of the 20th century. It was at Phildar that Gerard Mulliez learned the retail business. He never finished high school. In the early 1960s he decided to strike out on his own. In 1961, aged 29, he opened a grocery store in Roubaix in a neighborhood known as the *haut champs* (high fields) – the origin of what ultimately became the mighty Auchan retail empire.

That first store failed but the family was willing to give him a second chance – this time to set up a supermarket in northern France. There was one condition – that the new business must succeed within three years. Inspired by Edouard Leclerc, the former priest and founder of the E. Leclerc retail chain, Gerard Mulliez, himself a devout Catholic, adopted the discount self-service formula.

It was an instant success. During its first year Auchan reported sales of €10 million and significant profits. In less than 30 years, Gerard Mulliez built Auchan into one of the France's top retailers, an international retail chain and a multinational corporation. Today it is one of the principal distribution groups in the world, with a presence in 12 countries and 175,000 employees. And his relatives have been spectacularly successful in founding other retail and distribution companies: in sports and leisure (Decathlon), catering (Flunch, Pizza Pai), do-it-yourself (Leroy Merlin), electrical appliances (Boulanger), rental equipment (Kiloutou), and hard discount (Simply Market). Today, the firms owned by the Mulliez family together employ 366,000 people and have a turnover of €66 billion.

The Mulliez family has grown since the founder married Marguerite Lestienne in 1900 and had 11 children. Their eldest son, Louis Jr, was even more 'productive', with 13 children. Of these, Ignace and Jeanne had seven each, and Gerard six. As of 2011, there were 780 direct descendants, 550 of whom belong to the *Association Famille Mulliez* (AFM) the organization that control the business interests of the family.

Before launching a business or joining one of the firms belonging to Cimovam – the holding company that ultimately owns all the Mulliez firms – each family member undergoes a strict initiation from the age of 22, led by Antoine Mayaud, grandson of Louis Mulliez, fondly known as 'Mr Human Resources'. This is one way in which the Mulliez are unique: they favor in-house training over business school diplomas. Once trained, they can become members of AFM with the approval of the supervisory board and receive shares in Cimovam. Only then are they entitled to ask for financial and advisory support for their pet projects and each must prove the viability of any prospective project. A private equity fund, CREADEV, has been set up to support enterprise creation, though it is not reserved exclusively for family members. Growth is mostly financed internally. The Mulliez despise speculation and stock markets; once referred to as 'corporate prostitution' by André Mulliez, one of Gerard's brothers. Consistent with family values – that money should be reinvested in production – dividend pay-outs have remained low throughout the firm's history.

The Mulliez have made a unique contribution to their businesses for more than 100 years. First, their strong family values are transmitted in the way they do business. The family motto, *tous dans tout* (everyone in everything), reflects the core values of solidarity, family heritage and responsibility towards future generations. These are based on Catholic principles such as the requirement to work rather than live off the labor of others, that wealth and property are the fruits of hard work, and that inequality is part of the natural order of things. They instill a strong sense of discipline and meritocracy. Second, they have nurtured entrepreneurship within every generation, allowing them to open up new companies (or chains) within the retail sector. The legacy and experience of over 100 years of successful business ventures provide a solid platform to develop existing firms and to invest in new ventures. Finally, the size of the family creates a deep pool from which qualified and willing talent can be drawn, unlike smaller families which have a limited number of potential successors.

It is fascinating to observe how these key family contributions have become the foundations of Mulliez business strategies, and how the value of family assets is transferred and enlarged through specific governance mechanisms, including the internal education of new generations of entrepreneurs and the private equity model of finance – all members in principle own the same portfolio of businesses (even if they manage only one of them).

But the Mulliez family has faced some major roadblocks over the generations. The most obvious one stems from the rapid expansion of the family, growing to almost 800 members in a little more than 100 years. The main challenges are how to reconcile the need to accumulate resources to finance new entrepreneurial ventures with the need to pay dividends to ensure family members can enjoy a high standard of living; how to provide incentive structures for the most talented family entrepreneurs without sacrificing the interests of the family as a whole; and how to kindle an interest in developing entrepreneurial skills among the younger generation.

The Mulliez have implemented a unique governance structure to eliminate the cost of these roadblocks. First, the board of the AFM ensures that the family's interests prevail over personal ambitions, and the AFM is systematically represented on the boards of the individual firms. Second, each member of the family holds shares in the holding company rather than in the operating companies, hence they all have the same share portfolio. One share in Cimovam entitles them to ownership of all the family firms in a fixed proportion, ensuring that less promising companies won't lose out to the benefit of a cash cow like Auchan, which for decades has accounted for more than half the group's dividend.

The Mulliez are a brilliant example of how families form business strategies based on their unique contribution, and implement governance mechanisms that both enlarge the value of that contribution while mitigating current and potential roadblocks – a combination that is also illustrated by the following classic rags-to-riches tale from Taiwan.

The Wang family and Formosa Plastics Group

Wang Yung-ching, the son of a poor tea farmer, was born in northern Taiwan (then Formosa) in 1917. Despite a love of learning, he only completed elementary school. Having started work as an apprentice in a rice store at the age of 15, a year later, with the experience he had accumulated as well as support from his father who helped raise NT$200 (about US$1,000 today) and from friends and relatives, he set up his own rice store. To build his business he worked over four hours longer every day than his fellow tradesmen, eventually becoming the top-selling store in the neighborhood. Forced to close down during the Second World War, he subsequently quit the rice business and turned to lumber.

In 1954, he and his younger brother, Yung-tsai, co-founded Formosa Plastics Corporation. It was the dawn of a new era. At start up, Formosa Plastics Corporation was the smallest PVC factory in the world. Two years later, it began constructing downstream facilities and established Nan Ya Plastics Corporation. Today, after more than 50 years of development and expansion, the conglomerate has subsidiaries in the US, China, Vietnam, the Philippines and Indonesia, and over 90,000 employees around the world. It is the largest private sector enterprise in Taiwan.

Wang Yung-ching's unique contribution gained him a reputation as a 'god of management' and made him a national hero. He devoted his whole life to the business until his death in 2008, at the age of 92. A man of strong principles who worked extremely hard, he planned every detail of each production process, living by the motto 'get down to the root of the issue' and transmitting his entrepreneurial skills and values to his children, many of whom became successful business men and women in their own right.

Wang Yung-ching had three wives: Guo Yue-lan (his first and legitimate wife), Liao Chiao (his second wife) and Li Bao-zhu (a third wife with whom he spent his later years). Altogether he had two sons, seven daughters, and three more children out of wedlock. Some worked for the family business, others ran their own companies. His younger brother had eight children. There were 20 in the second generation and ultimately six branches of the family.

Wang spent three decades planning business succession, not least to mitigate potential conflict within the family. In addition to the complex family set-up, which was prone to infighting, his estate was subject to 50 percent inheritance tax. Concerned for the continuity of the business empire, he conceived an elaborate succession model with the aim of constructing a stable ownership and management structure that would keep the group from being dissolved.

The group includes ten companies listed on the Taiwan Stock Exchange, including the four core companies: Formosa Plastics Corporation, Nan Ya Plastics Corporation, Formosa Chemicals & Fibre Corporation, and Formosa Petrochemical Corporation. Many of these are part of a stock pyramid system. The Wang family has both direct and indirect ownership stakes in the four traded companies. In addition, the group has adopted a cross-shareholding structure among the four core companies – a mechanism commonly used by family firms to leverage their control.

Unlike many family firms, ultimate controlling shares in Formosa Plastics Group are not concentrated in the hands of the family but held by a charitable foundation, the Chang Gung Memorial Hospital, set up by Wang Yung-ching in 1976 in memory of his father. Transfer of these shares is prohibited by law. Dividends can only be used for charitable purposes rather than distributed to family or non-family members. The Hospital foundation is governed by a board of directors comprised of five family members, five distinguished community leaders (most of them related to the Wangs) and five professionals (all on the staff of the hospital).

No management power was vested in the next generation. Instead, in 2006, the founding brothers handed management of the business group to a seven-member strategic committee (established in 2002) whose members included Wang Wen-yuan and Wen-chao, sons of Wang Yung-tsai; Wang Rui-hua and Rui-yu, daughters by his third wife; and three non-family managers who hold key positions in the group.

Wang Yung-ching died intestate. The absence of a will might be assumed to have created a major roadblock for the family and the business, but other concerns had to be considered. Death duty on his huge estate would clearly have been massive – with a fortune of US$5.5 billion he was the world's 178th richest man and Taiwan's second-richest in 2008 – the highest tax band (50 percent) would inevitably have been applied and the remainder split between the surviving spouses and his blood relatives. According to Taiwan's civil code, if Wang's second and third wives had evidence to support the validity of their marriages (a public ceremony with at least two witnesses), they would have the same rights as the first wife and an equal share of the inheritance. Besides the nine legitimate children, his three illegitimate children would also be regarded as blood relatives if they could prove linear descent. Perhaps Wang Yung-ching knew that no matter what he wrote in a will, disputes were bound to arise given the family's convoluted structure. His first priority was the continuity of the business, as apparent from a letter written to his children and published after his death: 'With your recognition and support, I would appeal to you to leave my wealth to the public for the sake of the society, so that the enterprise to which I devoted my life can perpetuate and benefit the staff and the community forever …' His intention was seemingly to do his best to continue the empire while leaving the rest to the courts.

What can we learn from the Mulliez and the Wang families?

The business ventures founded by Louis Mulliez in Europe and Wang Yung-ching in Asia exemplify the essence of what makes family businesses competitive. It is values and heritage which form the foundation of the Mulliez's hugely successful five-generation business venture. The interests of the family come first (*tous pour tout*) and responsibility towards future generations is enhanced by a strong work ethic, strict discipline and a focus on merit – each family member must prove their worth and undergo in-house training before being allowed to a launch new business venture. They have developed a unique ability to transfer entrepreneurial spirit and talent down the generations. Their track record and knowledge of the French, European and global retail and distribution sectors is extraordinary, and their ability to cultivate *esprit de famille* in addition to knowledge and discipline, makes them a role model for families in business around the world.

The story of the Wangs and Formosa Plastics Group has things in common with the Mulliez family despite the different industry, culture and family structure. The two brothers also demonstrated the power of value-driven leadership and became role models for their children. Leading by example, they transferred the will to succeed to their descendants, many of whom are now successful entrepreneurs in other major companies. Unlike their own parents, who had been too poor to pay for an education, the brothers bought the best international education for their offspring as a springboard to future business careers.

But with 21 legitimate children and three children outside marriage, the proliferation of different branches and diverging interests stood to threaten the family's future ownership and control. So, unlike the Mulliez, Wang Yung-ching abandoned the idea of conserving family governance and instead focused on business continuity and social responsibility. He demonstrated a commitment to the wider stakeholder community including his employees and society as a whole. Like the Mulliez, he encountered roadblocks to succession: how his estate could be transferred intact and preserved from potential family squabbles. Since the group had a poor environmental track record (and a history of related court cases), perhaps he wanted to give something back to society.

The Mulliez family faced a similar issue back in the 1950s, when the fast-growing family was already several hundred strong: How to keep the family and the business together and provide incentives for future generations to get involved. They too created innovative governance structures to deal with the roadblocks of ownership and control dilution and to achieve the goals they had set. The Mulliez formulated guiding principles for future involvement and set up a unique governance structure based on the family association, the holding company and an investment vehicle, which kept the family together, transmitted the entrepreneurial spirit across generations, and provided funds for expansion.

Wang Yung-ching's solution was to transfer ownership of Formosa Plastics Group to a hospital foundation. Free from tax obligations, it was another way of giving back to the society that had allowed his business to flourish by providing the resources to improve public health, somewhat akin to the 'polluter pays' principle. Given the complex family structure, this was a crucial vehicle in concentrating and protecting family control since most of the shares were locked into the charitable foundation and could not be sold in the foreseeable future. Today, no single member has a dominant ownership stake, nor can they be appointed to the seven-member management team without the support of the board, thereby preventing potential squabbles among the branches from undermining business continuity.

We still do not know the final outcome of Wang Yung-ching's succession model. In making the transition from family to charitable institutional ownership he apparently wanted the business to belong to society, but this choice also allowed him to 'rule from the grave', by perpetuating his contribution and enabling him to avoid choosing a successor who might undermine his reputation. It is too early to say how successful the model will be in the long run. How long can the ownership structure resist diverging family interests? How competent will the healthcare experts and community leaders prove to be as trustees of a large industrial group. Meanwhile, legal actions are still being pursued by family members to resolve the uncertainty over the exact distribution of Wang Yung-ching's fortune.

The Family Business Map (*FB Map*)

The Mulliez and Wang stories highlight some of the major questions to be addressed in this book:

- What are the special contributions of families to their businesses, that is, family assets?
- How can families build business strategies based on their unique contributions that allow companies to thrive in a competitive environment?
- What are the specific constraints 'roadblocks' unique to family businesses?
- How can families develop governance strategies that mitigate the corporate (and family) costs of such roadblocks?

The differing experiences discussed in this book provide contrasting answers to these questions. Every family firm has its own variations. For example, the reappearance of the Toyoda and Ford families in the top management of their eponymous automobile firms raises the question of how and what families contribute to the business, and in what ways family managers are different from external managers. In-fighting among the Reliance brothers in India, the Ho family in Macau, and the Pritzker family in the US (to name a few) underline the challenge of designing succession and governance to avoid corporate as well as family meltdowns. LVMH's takeovers of many old European family firms in the luxury industry, including its attempts to wrestle control from the iconic luxury company Hermès, underline the importance of designing ownership to balance family control with business growth. The American food company Kraft's controversial and hostile takeover of the famous British chocolate empire Cadbury, after more than 180 years of family involvement, raises issues about how family firms protect themselves after going public and the role of institutional investors, including hedge funds, in designing sustainable ownership structures for family firms.

Our aim here is to help family stewards and other stakeholders answer the above questions by identifying the unique contributions (family assets) and specific constraints (roadblocks) and to match these with appropriate business and governance strategies to get the most out of their ventures without sacrificing the family or destroying value in the business.

Family assets

Successful business families have discovered how to exploit their family assets as the foundation of their business strategy. Such assets might include strong values, which may be the values and vision of the founder, as in the case of Wang Yung-ching, or the ability to instill family values across generations, as in the Mulliez example.

Another example, Forever 21, a global chain of low-price fashion stores for young women, started out as a Korean family business in Los Angeles. It exploited the Korean cultural and work ethic and the network that dominates the cheap clothing industry in that city. Indeed, Chinese family businesses abroad have for centuries proved to be highly proficient at doing business using one set of values in a very different business culture. Values instilled in childhood and early adulthood are more easily transferred by parents than by external managers – one reason why family businesses have a clear advantage when it comes to strategies based on values.

Political and business networks are another powerful family asset, since connections can more easily be maintained within the family than passed on to non-related managers. In longstanding businesses, the family legacy may also be an asset. Recent examples include Akio Toyoda's promotion to top manager at Toyota, which was well received by the financial markets. The legacy effect was also obvious in public concerns about the ability of Cyrus Mistry to replace the much-admired Ratan Tata as the first non-family CEO of the 144-year-old Indian conglomerate Tata.

As detailed in Chapter 2, family assets are the key reason for family management on a long-term basis. It is easier to exploit networks and connections when family members are involved in day-to-day operations and can make the important phone call themselves, just as it is easier to assimilate family values into business strategy when they actively manage the firm. Since each family has a different set of assets, it is important that they identify, preserve and expand these if current and future members are to continue managing the family business.

family assets are the key reason for family management

Roadblocks

We have seen several obstacles encountered by the Mulliez family and by Wang Yung-ching's family. In the latter there were 21 children in the second generation alone; the Mulliez grew to 780 members in just over 100 years. We refer to this phenomenon, common to business families around the globe, as the *power of numbers*. As the family grows, ownership is diluted by the repeated division and distribution of shares to new members, creating a series of challenges such as how to ensure effective governance in a firm with multiple owners; how to sustain family peace when members have different levels of ownership, control and influence; how to manage conflicts between family owners with and without a management role in the firm; how to design dividend policy in the face of diverging family interests; and how to design ownership to provide the right incentives for those involved and allow passive members to exit. Only firms that design mechanisms to overcome these challenge will endure.

The growth dilemma arises when, in pursuit of expansion, families often have to raise capital in the form of debt or equity, which heightens the risk of them losing control. The challenge is to determine a capital structure to balance the needs of growth and control. A related question is whether to go public by allowing a fraction of the ownership to be publicly traded.

Further roadblocks come from the external environment, such as *inheritance laws* that force families to leave a significant amount of wealth to each of their children, potentially compromising the long-term stability of the business. We have seen how *inheritance taxes* affected Wang Yung-ching's succession. However, laws and regulation can also happen on a national scale as in the case of China's one child policy, where today's entrepreneurs often have only one or two heirs to succeed them and there is no guarantee of their ability or willingness to take over.

As we will see in Chapter 3, identifying roadblocks and designing a system of family and business governance to mitigate their effects is vital for protecting ownership. When roadblocks are severe, there is a tendency to dilute ownership (even if it is not desired). To be sustainable, families must use mechanisms to preserve ownership of key assets. We have seen how the Mulliez impose an in-house training program, strict career preparation for budding entrepreneurs, and a unique ownership structure. Wang Yung-ching used a specific ownership design to resolve the challenge of a complex and conflictual family structure by transferring ownership to a foundation and installing community leaders and hospital personnel as trustees.

Locating firms on the Family Business Map

Family assets and roadblocks are the critical components of what we call the *Family Business Map* – or the *FB Map* – which is illustrated in Figure 1.1. The importance of family assets will be a key determinant of the extent of family involvement, just as the severity of roadblocks will be a key driver of the ownership structure. By locating where a business lies on both axes, we

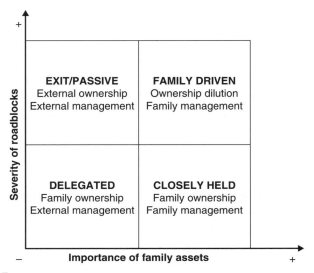

FIG 1.1 / The Family Business Map

arrive at different conclusions about how far ownership and management responsibilities are shared within the family and with outsiders.

Firms that have significant family assets and few roadblocks are represented by the lower right quadrant in Figure 1.1 and referred to as 'closely held'. Here the assets are embodied in the family's managerial contribution, which relies on key family member(s) being present on a day-to-day basis. Keeping ownership within the family does not constrain the firm either financially or in other ways. Hence our advice would be to continue as manager and owner. In a classic closely held firm, the family exploits its assets to develop the firm while circumventing the potential constraints of ownership.

Examples of such firms are not difficult to find. In 2012, Koch Industries had $112 billion in revenue and 70,000 employees around the world. Fred C. Koch founded the firm in 1940 and today 84 percent of the shares are owned by Charles de Ganahl Koch (CEO) and David H. Koch (Executive Vice President) who bought out their brothers. Similarly, Aldi (short for Albrecht Discounts), one of Europe largest discount food retailers with 6,100 stores worldwide, was co-founded by the brothers Theo and Karl Albrecht. It was split into two divisions (North and South) following a dispute over selling cigarettes in 1960. The family has been very private since Theo was kidnapped for 17 days in 1971. Karl Albrecht, who died July 16 2014 at the age of 93, lived four years longer than his little brother Theo. After the dead of Theo's youngest son in 2012, ownership has started to be transferred to the third generation. After the death of Berthold in 2012, ownership has started to be transferred to the third generation.

The opposite case – where the family does not significantly add value to the firm beyond what could be achieved by non-family managers, and faces insurmountable obstacles associated with family ownership – is depicted in the upper left quadrant of Figure 1.1. In this case there is a strong incentive for families to exit the business. Exit may take the form of an outright sale of the family corporation, where the family cuts all ties, but it can also be more gradual if the family becomes a passive minority owner without being involved in management. We observe this in many large US firms, where there is a gradual exit of the family as non-family managers are brought on board and the family's ownership is diluted to a symbolic level. In such firms, the importance of the family assets declines after the first or second generation. Non-family managers are progressively appointed and many of these firms develop into large corporations, requiring significant external capital to finance their expansion. As a result, the founding family has non-controlling minority ownership.

Delegated family firms are located in the lower left corner of Figure 1.1. The family delivers little enhanced management value beyond the level that non-family managers could achieve, but there are no major roadblocks threatening its ownership. In such instances there is an argument for professionalizing management (hiring top managers from outside), but no urgency for the family to exit on the ownership side.

The Swedish furniture company IKEA is an example of a corporation in this category. After the retirement of founder Ingmar Kampvad, the cost-and-value-oriented leadership that he had embodied for almost four decades was not apparent in the next generation. In the absence of enhanced value from the family once he stepped down, it was only natural for the family to stay out of top management. However, neither the company's expansion nor its finances are constrained in any significant way by family ownership, which has been retained thanks to a series of trusts and holding companies.

In many large European family companies the family is still the controlling owner but not involved in the day-to-day management, instead preferring to hire non-family CEOs to run their companies. Dutch brewery Heineken, founded in 1864 by Gerard Adriaan Heineken in Amsterdam, owns over 125 breweries in more than 70 countries and employs approximately 66,000 people (2007 figures). After the death of the charismatic family and company leader Freddie Heineken in 2002, external managers took over at the top, but his daughter, Charlene de Carvalho, remains the largest shareholder.

Finally, the upper right quadrant of Figure 1.1 depicts family driven firms where the founding family still delivers enhanced management value but ownership has been diluted, often as a consequence of growth. Here it makes sense for the family to continue to be involved in management, even if their ownership stake has been reduced to a minority. Typical of this are family firms that go public to finance ambitious growth plans. Samsung is an example. Founded by Lee Byung-chul in 1938 as a trading company; it has since grown to be the biggest multinational conglomerate in South Korea. His descendants own around 22 percent of the company. His third son, Lee Kun-hee, is the current chairman of Samsung Electronics.

Sometimes family businesses can grow so big that the family's ownership shrinks in comparison to other investors' stakes. Suzuki and Canon are examples of large businesses where the families hold top management positions but are not among the largest owners. In almost one out of six publicly traded Japanese firms we observe that the family manages the firm even if they are not among the biggest owners.

The *FB Map* as a planning tool

The *FB Map* is a powerful tool to help business families structure the ownership and management of their businesses and develop strategies to leverage their assets and minimize the roadblocks. Once the assets and roadblocks are identified, the ownership/management structure can be customized. The *FB Map* answers fundamental questions such as:

- Do we have the right ownership structure both between family and outside owners and among family members?
- Does the current ownership structure preserve the family assets? Does the current ownership structure mitigate the cost of roadblocks?
- Who shall manage the business today and tomorrow?
- Which succession model should the family choose to support the future of the family corporation beyond their lifetime?

These are once-in-a-lifetime questions for any business family. Succession is a particular challenge for many family businesses and often a source of suffering, not least in emerging economies. In fact, in our research we came across publicly traded family firms in Hong Kong, Taiwan and Singapore that lost more than half of their market value during succession.

By focusing on transferring family assets and reducing roadblocks, the *FB Map* helps reframe the challenge. It offers a palette of possible succession models, from letting ownership dilute, pruning the ownership tree, setting up family trusts and foundations, to relinquishing control through partial or full exit. Each of these involves opportunities and constraints depending on the specific family assets and roadblocks.

By identifying the right model of ownership and management design, the *FB Map* raises the key governance questions for family businesses. In a closely held business, these are how to transfer the strong family assets and how to anticipate future roadblocks. For example, how to maintain harmony between family members and other stakeholders after the death of the founder, and how to avoid interests diverging when family size and complexity increase over time?

In diffusely held corporations such as large publicly traded US firms, where the founding family is no longer in charge of management, the governance agenda focuses on incentive alignment and accountability: How to hire the best managers? How to compensate managers to ensure their decisions are in the best interests of the owners? How to structure the board such that it is accountable to the business and to the owners?

When families retain ownership but hire external managers – as is typical in many large European family businesses – the key issues are how to sidestep the roadblocks, how to finance corporate expansion and growth without diluting family ownership, how to hire and monitor the best managers, and how to differentiate the roles of family owners and external managers?

Finally, when families keep control of management but dilute their ownership stake, the key governance issues are how to leverage the family assets and how to maintain trust between family managers and external owners.

Different types of family firms

It is surprisingly difficult to define the family firm. Nobody would contest that the German precious metals and technology group Heraus, which has been owned and managed by the same family for more than 160 years, is a family firm. But what about a start-up owned by a single entrepreneur who hopes to sell the company in 20 years' time? Or a firm that's partly owned by the founder and partly by a private equity fund? Or one like Suzuki (Japan), where the family is not among the biggest owners but has continuously managed the company? To clear up the confusion, we focus on three characteristics: family ownership, family control, and family succession.

Family ownership.   One of the most basic elements of a family business is that the family behind the firm has a significant ownership stake. For most small and medium-sized family businesses this typically means a single member or a small group of members owns the entire firm or a majority stake. In some countries, majority ownership can be reduced to a minority stake over time as the firm grows in size. Large publicly traded companies where the family is the largest owner and owns a significant block (say more than 10 percent) of the shares are still referred to as family firms. Hutchison Whampoa, one of the largest publicly traded companies in Hong Kong is almost 44 percent owned by Cheung Kong Holding, which is in turn is 35 percent owned by the Li Ka-Shing family. We define both as family firms, since the Li family is the largest owner in both. Cargill, the largest private family business in the world, trades grain, poultry, beef, steel, seeds, salt and other commodities on six continents. The family owns 85 percent of the shares, the other 15 percent being distributed among key employees.

Family control.   A family exerts control over a firm by holding senior management positions and sitting on the board. For small and medium-sized family firms, this stems directly from being a majority owner. However, families behind larger (public or private) firms typically have controlling rights that exceed their nominal ownership. The separation of ownership and control is achieved through careful design, such as multiple classes of equity shares with different voting powers, a pyramid-like chain of corporate ownership, or shares held by passive block-holders.

Consider the following illustrations: In the US newspaper industry, nine of the twelve largest corporations have a dual-class share structure. By retaining the superior voting shares while issuing non-voting shares to investors, the family retains effective control. The dual-class share structure of the *New York Times* enables the Ochs Sulzberger family to control the company, though they own a minority of the outstanding stock. The majority of the shares in Tata Sons, the main holding company of the Tata Group, which has 28 listed companies and more than 80 subsidiaries, are held by charitable trusts. On 28 December 2012, Ratan Tata resigned as chairman of Tata Sons (and the key person in many of the larger subsidiaries), leaving the top management position to Cyrus Mistry, son of the largest minority owner in

Tata Sons. However, Ratan Tata and other family members keep control of the group through holding key positions in the charitable trusts.

Interestingly, a family may not have to use formal ownership mechanisms to achieve effective control of a business. A set of rules or specialized contributions as part of the legacy of the founder can perpetuate the natural authority of the family so that members hold key management and/or board positions generation after generation.

Kikkoman Corporation is an example of control beyond ownership. Founded in 1917 by eight families who produced soy sauce in the Edo region of Japan, it dates back to 1603, via the Mogi and Takanashi families. Through a foundation, the families currently own just over 3 percent of Kikkoman. Steel Partners, a New York-based hedge fund, is the largest owner with almost 5 percent. Despite their small ownership stake, family control is still possible not just because they hold the secret of making the soy sauce, but thanks to the rules established when it was founded: that the company must be managed by a family member, and that only one member of each of the eight families can work for Kikkoman. This was done to preserve family harmony.

Family succession.   The third element is the desire to see the firm prosper and grow in the hands of future generations. Successful handing down of ownership and control is the hallmark of many old family firms. It is more than 350 years since Jacob van Eeghen founded the Dutch van Eeghen Merchant Company. The company has changed its operational profile several times during its lifetime, but control has always been transferred from generation to generation. Van Eeghen is a proud member of the Henokiens, an association of 38 family firms that are more than 200 years old and still owned and managed by the founding family. These include the five Japanese companies: Akafuku Tea and Confection, Gekkakain Sake Company Ltd, the Hōshi Ryokan, Okaya Real Estate and Insurance, and Toraya Confectionary Co., which for centuries have retained management and ownership within the respective families while successfully implementing development plans.

Where family ownership is diluted over time to a level below a controlling stake although the family still exercises de facto control, it remains a *family-driven* company. If the family, despite its large ownership stake, hands over day-to-day control to professional managers, it is a *delegated* firm. If the family no longer holds a significant ownership stake or senior management positions, we refer to it as a *diffused* company. The most restrictive element of the above definitions is the requirement for a strong interest in transferring the ownership and control to the next generation. Many start-ups, small and medium-sized firms are sold (or liquidated) within 30 years without ever experiencing a succession.

From the above we can reasonably define a family firm as long as it has a subset of these characteristics, and the family behind the firm agrees that they exert a major influence.

Family firms as the dominant organizational form

We have often encountered a public belief that family firms are old fashioned, not very innovative, outdated and will most likely be competed out of business by more efficient business structures. Contrary to the notion that family firms are outdated and inefficient and will eventually disappear, new research confirms that:

- Family firms are the dominant type of business organization in most countries around the world. In all countries – except China and a few other socialist countries – freestanding small and medium-sized companies are almost always majority owned by individual entrepreneurs and their relatives, and often multiple family members work for these companies.
- The exact number of family firms within a given country will depend on the definition used: if we apply the ownership criteria, in most developed countries a large share of the biggest publicly traded firms can be classed as family firms.
- Even among the very largest corporations there is a significant number of family firms. One study found that families controlled slightly more than half of the publicly traded firms with an average firm market cap over $500 million in 27 countries. In the US, family ownership is present in around one-third of the 500 biggest firms.
- In Asia the prevalence of family firms is very high even among the biggest conglomerates. It is estimated that more than two-thirds of large business groups in countries like India, Taiwan, Hong Kong, Singapore, Indonesia, Malaysia and Thailand are family controlled.

• In Europe, family ownership is widespread. Almost half the public traded firms in Europe are family controlled, which is a higher fraction than in the US but still less than in Asia. Around half of family firms in Belgium, Denmark, France Ireland, Italy, Switzerland and the UK have a family member as CEO.

Longevity of family firms

The economic history of the world abounds with stories of boom and bust, but a few family businesses survive and stay competitive for centuries while generations after generations of family members take turns at the helm.

The Japanese construction company Kongō Gumi was founded in year 578 when Prince Shotoku brought carpenters from Baekje (now Korea) to Japan to build a Buddhist temple (Shitennö-ji). One of those carpenters stayed in Japan and started his own business. Over more than 1,400 years the Kongō family participated in the construction of many famous buildings, including the 16th century Osaka Castle, which played a major role in the unification of the country. At least 40 generations of Kongō family members have governed the firm, sometimes with sons-in-law that were adopted into the family. Kongō Gumi was the oldest firm in the world, in 2005 it had over 100 employees and annual revenue of ¥7.5 billion ($US70 million) and was still owned and managed by the Kongō family. However, the Asian crisis hit the company hard and ultimately it was liquidated in January 2006. Hence, the last president was Masakazu Kongō, the 40th Kongō to lead the firm. As of December 2006, Kongō Gumi continues to operate as a wholly owned subsidiary of Takamatsu and the Kongō family still continues to practice as carpenters.

This tragic cases illustrates that, despite their longevity, family firms do not go on forever. It is as much a challenge to prosper and grow for a family firm as it is for a non-family firm. Some of the world's oldest family firms are in Japan, reflecting the extent to which the country's culture was structured in the interests of family business long before the development of Western society. There are old European firms as well. The oldest wine company in France, Domaine de Coussergues, was founded in 1321. Two hundred years later – in 1526 – the arms manufacturer

Beretta was founded in Italy. The Dutch merchant company Van Eeghen was founded in 1662. A number of larger public traded firms in Europe have prospered for several centuries, including the Italian glassmaker, Pochet SA, which makes luxury perfume bottles for Christian Dior. Pochet has been owned and managed by the Colonna de Giovellina family since 1623 (for almost 400 years). The French publicly traded family business Wendel traces its origins to 1704, when Jean Martin Wendel acquired the Rodolphe forge in the Lorraine region and founded an iron and steel business that 250 years later would become one of Europe's largest steel companies.

Is size a guarantee of longevity? Is it only possible to survive for centuries if a firm reaches a critical mass that allows it to build the financial strength to survive a downturn (which is bound to happen if the firm lasts long enough)? The relationship between firm size and longevity has not been studied in depth, but we have come across a surprisingly large number of small firms that have survived for at least three generations without growing significantly. Whatever country you look at, there are plenty of family firms that stay small.

We believe that thriving old family businesses have much to teach younger families about how to overcome some of the constraints embodied in this particular organizational form. Hence, we will refer back to some of these examples throughout the book. One shared aspect of many of them is the emphasis on values. Satisfying mankind's basic needs is often a necessary condition of business longevity, and these are often spiritual rather than material. No wonder the most enduring businesses exemplify the importance of preserving values. Another shared aspect is that old family firms have developed efficient governance designs to cope with the many challenges they have faced over centuries. As we will see later in this book, younger families can study these firms to find inspiration for how to use family assets as strategic resources and how to design ownership and succession to cope with growing families.

Discover more

Bennedsen, Morten, Yann Cornil, and Robert J. Crawford. The Mulliez Family Venture. Case Pre-Release version, *INSEAD*, Spring 2013.

Bennedsen, Morten, Joseph P.H. Fan, Ming Jian, and Yin-Hua Yeh. The Family Business Map: Framework, Selective Survey, and Evidence from Chinese Family Firm Succession, Forthcoming in *Journal of Corporate Finance 2014.*

Bennedsen Morten, Francisco Pérez-González, and Daniel Wolfenzon. The Governance of Family Firms. *In Corporate Governance: A Synthesis of Theory, Research and Practice*, Baker, Kent H. and Ronald Anderson (eds), John Wiley and Sons, Inc., 2010.

Li Jin, Joseph P.H. Fan, and Winnie S.C. Leung. Formosa Plastics Group: Business Continuity Forever. Harvard Business School Case (N9-210-026), 2010.

Highlights

- The Mulliez family in France and the Wang family in Taiwan are examples of two families which have developed efficient long-term planning to exploit the potential of their family resources and to minimize the challenges arising from growing families.
- The Family Business Map (*FB Map*) is a long-term planning tool that helps families exploit the strategic value of their family assets and design governance mechanisms that reduce the cost of the challenges they face.
- Family firms are defined by three characteristics: family ownership, family control and family succession.
- The family firm is the most numerous business structure in almost every country around the world.

The next chapter discusses the concept of family assets. We present a number of cases that illustrate how family assets form the foundation of competitive business strategies. Family assets are the first pillar of our long-term planning framework.

chapter 2

Family Assets

Family firms have a strong sense of identity, which forms the foundation of their business strategies and sets them apart from non-family firms. It's tempting to assume that every family firm has its own unique culture, but in fact we find it more useful to generalize. Family contributions are surprisingly similar from one country to another – these family *assets* are the glue that holds the family and the firm together in a powerful collaboration. The assets that underpin family firms in Japan, India and Hong Kong resemble those in the US and Europe – regardless of the cultural or national setting, they are powerful generators of success. Much of the value is specific to the family, and without their ownership or management it would be lost. Family assets are different from other types of assets that are of comparable value for every business owner – whether they operate a standardized machine, make cars or own a patent.

In this chapter we seek to provide a basic understanding of family assets. In Chapter 4 we operationalize the concept using the Family Business Map (*FB Map*). Readers seeking a guide to measure family assets to use for hands-on long-term planning should skim through the next two chapters and focus on the *FB Map* in Chapter 4. We recount several family business stories in the hope that they will answer the following questions:

- What is it that a successful family brings to a firm?
- How can families develop business strategies based on family assets?
- Is it possible for an outsider (owner or manager) to imitate family assets-based business strategies, and if so for how long?
- How can families shape the firm's governance to enlarge the value of their family assets?

Later in this book we will show how family assets determine the broad long-term direction of the business, influencing decisions such as ownership design, corporate governance, the right time and form of exit, and so forth. Hence, identifying family assets is essential for family business owners engaged in long-term planning.

Of the many different family assets, we have chosen to focus on three (see Figure 2.1): (1) the family name and history, (2) the values underlying their leadership, and (3) their business and political networks. These, we believe, are universally powerful, being shared across companies, cultures and continents.

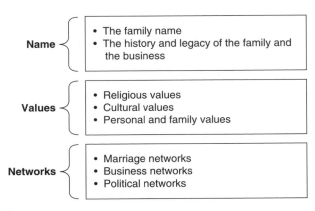

Name {
- The family name
- The history and legacy of the family and the business

Values {
- Religious values
- Cultural values
- Personal and family values

Networks {
- Marriage networks
- Business networks
- Political networks

FIG 2.1 Universal family assets

The family name and legacy

The family name is a unique asset for family businesses around the globe. It conveys the firm's reputation as well as ownership. Some families succeed in leveraging the name over centuries. As the following example shows, the value of the name and heritage cannot be overstated.

In the picturesque Awazu Onsen district off the north-west coast of Japan is a small inn that has arguably the most powerful family assets in the world. The Höshi Ryokan (see box below) was established in AD 717 and has been owned and managed by the Höshi family for almost 1,300 years. It is the oldest independent family firm in the world today (since the

THE HÖSHI RYOKAN

The Höshi Ryokan. Mr and Miss Zengoro Höshi in the tea room and the old garden. Photos by the authors.

The world's oldest independent family owned and managed firm is the Höshi Ryokan, in the Awazu Onsen area of Komatsu in Japan. According to legend, in AD 717 the Buddhist monk and teacher Taicho Daishi had a dream in which he was instructed by the deity who guarded Mount Hakusan to find an underground hot spring with curative powers in the village of Awazu. Taicho and his disciple, Garyo Höshi, went to the village and, with the help of the villagers, managed to locate the spring. Taicho told the sick to bathe in the waters and soon their health improved. He ordered his disciple to build an 'undefined' spa on the site and to manage it.

Since Garyo Hōshi, the first manager of the ryokan, the family has been in charge for 46 generations. The pattern of succession follows strict rules. In each generation, ownership and management responsibility is conferred on one person alone; other siblings leave the family through arranged marriages.

Today the Hōshi Ryokan is a modern inn with facilities to host up to 450 guests, but there is still a strong focus on tradition. The personal service that each guest receives starts with a traditional Japanese welcome: a tea ceremony. The hot spring feeds both indoor and outdoor bathing facilities. Over the centuries many important visitors have stayed in the ryokan including emperors, artists and prestigious families. Few foreigners find their way to the inn, even though it has featured in a number of international travel magazines.

liquidation of the 1,500-year-old construction company Kungo Gumi that we met in Chapter 1). It is the second-oldest independent firm, trailing by 12 years another Japanese hotel – Nishiyama Onsen Keiunkan – which has been transferred through 52 different owner families. The current owner-manager of the Hōshi Ryokan is Zengoro Hōshi, a member of the 46th generation. Following the death of his eldest son, Zengoro Hōshi is preparing his grandson to become the 47th owner-manager.

The first Hōshi was already doing business 700 years before Christopher Columbus embarked on his first voyage to the New World, and indeed even before the Vikings started to make trouble in Northern Europe. The name of the family and the inn are closely intertwined, and there is a sense of history in every corner of the property, from the beautiful garden to the famous tea room. Visitors come to appreciate that the family is the guardian of that history, and Zengoro Hōshi and his wife are very visible in the hotel, taking an active part in the day-to-day management. The family and its history are clearly central to the unique visitor experience it offers.

To what extent is this family asset transferable to future generations? As discussed in Chapter 6, the Hōshi family has developed a unique succession model whereby ownership and management of the inn are inherited by a single heir, typically the eldest son, although it can also be a younger son, a son-in-law or even an adopted son. While more radical than most succession models, it has allowed the family assets to be handed down from one generation to the next a record 46 times.

To what extent are those family assets transferable to an outside owner? Let's imagine that an international hotel chain bought the Höshi Ryokan. Not only would it lose its status as the oldest founder family owned and managed hotel in the world, but even if it retained the facilities, something would be lost – the magic of an unbroken line of Zengoro Höshi across 46 generations and the status of this old family in society. The hotel so embodies the history of the Höshi family that the brand and reputation would inevitably be undermined if sold to an outsider. This exclusiveness emphasizes our key point that family assets are relation-specific – a unique contribution by a particular family to a particular firm.

Modern marketing analysts might say that in the absence of a proactive marketing strategy, the Höshi is failing to exploit these assets. Indeed one may be tempted to think that Zengoro Höshi is not realizing its full market potential, especially given the premium that such a unique experience could command. Surely travellers would come from around the world – so why not open more Höshi inns?

It's clear the family does not seek to optimize the short term market value of their unique assets, perhaps because the yardstick by which they measure success is not size but endurance, or they feel that the Höshi style would be impossible to emulate in a different location. In any event, they must have found the secret of harmony long ago for their family business to have survived for 1,300 years.

The Höshi Ryokan is a perfect response to the four questions listed at the beginning of the chapter. First, the history and the legacy of 1,300 years of family involvement are a unique contribution to the inn. Second, they are what make the hotel unique and they are the foundation of the business. Third, the magic of the Höshi Ryokan would be seriously harmed if the new owners or managers were not part of the family. Fourth, the family has cultivated a very unique governance strategy focused on transferring family assets intact across every generation (as explained in Chapter 6).

Name and heritage are important for many types of family firms. There are numerous examples of very old family businesses that have used them to sustain a brand or a particular business model, such as the maker of fountain pens Faber Castell and the German car-maker Porsche. There are also first- and second-generation firms whose names are synonymous with the founder – like Versace and Georgio Armani. Indeed even very large firms can build a competitive business strategy on a name, as the following example illustrates.

H E R M È S

Born in Krefeld, Germany in 1801, Thierry Hermès opened a workshop in 1837 producing and selling hand-made saddles, bridles and other leather riding gear. In the early twentieth century, under the direction of his grandson, Emile-Maurice, the Hermès business expanded beyond the initial focus on riding gear into leather bags, luggage and other goods such as ready-to-wear clothes and silk scarves. The first Hermès travel bags in 1925 were a worldwide success, as were the signature Hermès *carré* silk squares launched in 1937. In time, Hermès became a worldwide brand with sales in South and North America, Russia and Asia. Today it is one of the largest, and arguably most admired, luxury-goods makers in the world, with roughly €1.7 billion in revenue, profits of €300 million, 300 exclusive stores and 8,000 employees.

Hermès' early growth and diversification were successful because the company remained faithful to the highest standards of quality. Even today its artisans are selected and trained in-house and across the world before they become involved in the production of Hermès goods. An artisan will spend between 18 and 24 hours hand-stitching one of the famed Kelly or Birkin bags in meticulous detail, often with just a handful of waxed threads, polishing the leather with agate to give it a matt or shiny velvet-like finish. New products often bear the personal touch of company leaders. For example, Robert Dumas-Hermès lent new life to the Kelly bag – a traditional Hermès product renamed after a photograph of Grace Kelly carrying one appeared in *Life* magazine – by introducing new colors and materials. His son, Jean-Louis Dumas, helped to invent the Birkin bag after a chance conversation on a flight with the actress Jane Birkin, who complained that she needed a medium-sized bag. When he delivered one to her door, he informed her: 'You and Grace Kelly are the only ones with Hermès bags named in your honour.' Another indication of the brand's prestige was the decision of Robert Dumas-Hermès to stop production for two weeks in the 1970s when virtually no orders came in. The proliferation of plastic and polyester had dampened demand for leather and silk items. Nevertheless, the family refused to develop products made of synthetic materials, even when critics accused it of hurting the bottom line by clinging to outdated practices and materials.

In the words of the recently retired CEO, Patrick Thomas, 'Unequivocally, Hermès' performance has been driven by strategic consistency since 1837, combining excellent creativity and craftsmanship, as well as a determination to never risk compromising the long term for a short term benefit.'

The Hermès name is a powerful family asset synonymous with enduring quality and luxury. The family has focused on making top-quality products for almost two centuries and the name has a unique status among the premier luxury brands in the world. The artisanal nature of the firm is maintained by extensive in-house production. For example, its silk scarves are handmade from silk produced on Hermès farms in Brazil. The family's unique contribution lies in keeping faith with a business model that prioritizes superior quality and never compromises on craftsmanship. This is the guarantor of its longevity – their continued involvement ensures that quality will be maintained in the future. In 2013, the long-serving non-family CEO Patrick Thomas was replaced with a family member in a continued effort to enlarge the value of the family assets, a clear illustration of the premise that family management is most valuable when those assets are strong.

Hermès is a 'north star' which lights the way for family owned luxury firms. Luxury firms are interesting because they tend to possess very strong family assets that are often embodied in the name and the heritage, as in this case. Luxury product categories include watches, pens,

fashion, cars, jets and boats. This huge market – estimates put sales at around US$170 billion in 2011 – has seen decades of tremendous growth, most recently in Asia and the Middle East. Since luxury goods offer utility as well as social status to customers, the name and legacy are powerful assets, bringing a human touch as well as authenticity. To safeguard the name, the family has understood the importance of favouring long-term quality at the expense of profitable opportunities in the short term.

Consistent with our predicted effects of family assets, the luxury industry is dominated by family firms. The largest among them, LVMH, belongs to the Arnault family, whose 50 brands include Louis Vuitton, Cartier, Faber-Castell, Tiffany, Rolex, BMW, Moët Hennessy and Chanel. The potential for developing business strategies based on name and heritage makes the industry a prime example of the advantages of family ownership and management.

So why have there been numerous cases where families have exited luxury companies and new conglomerates have evolved? Indeed, LVMH and Kering in France have bought out many families, while others have partly exited through public listings. As discussed in the next chapter, although the family assets may justify their involvement in businesses, owners often come up against roadblocks or obstacles to ownership. In an industry where multiple roadblocks exist, not least from changes in market structure, new ownership models have developed to overcome such challenges.

Name and legacy are powerful family assets for smaller entrepreneurial firms, especially in the luxury industry, but can they be an advantage for larger firms in a competitive market? The following examples confirm that they can.

Adolph Ochs's purchase of the *New York Times* (NYT) in 1896 saw the birth of a legendary family owned press corporation. The NYT had existed since 1851, but was burdened by rising costs. Ochs managed to cut costs in half and increase circulation from 9,000 to 76,000 in just three years. He separated news from editorial opinion and dropped the price of the newspaper. By the 1920s, daily circulation had risen to over 400,000.

Ochs's daughter Iphigene married Arthur Hays Sulzberger, who worked at the NYT and succeeded Ochs as publisher and president. Under his management from 1935 to 1961, the NYT diversified into radio, expanded to Europe and California, and increased circulation to 713,000. He was followed by relatives such as Orvil Dryfoos and the legendary Arthur Ochs 'Punch' Sulzberger, son of Arthur Hays.

The Ochs-Sulzbergers' 100-year reign at the NYT is a story of how a devoted family used their assets to build the most respected newspaper in the world, and how their control of it has given the family tremendous power. The NYT would not be the same without their influence, just as the Sulzberger family would not be the same without the paper. Over the last century they have enhanced its value beyond that of any other newspaper owner, even as they have encountered significant governance problems in keeping family control in the face of major market and industry challenges.

The Toyoda family made use of the family name in the aftermath of the safety-induced crisis that engulfed the auto-maker in 2009. It was Sakichi Toyoda who founded Toyoda Automatic Loom Works in Nagoya, Japan, and his enterprising son who developed 'Toyota Motors', which would one day become the largest car manufacturer in the world, as well as an inspiration to business with its innovative organizational systems. The Toyoda family has gradually ceded control of the corporation and is estimated to own less than 8 percent of the shares today.

From 1992 to 2009 there were no family members at the helm. But that year one of the biggest challenges the firm had ever faced erupted. In three separate but related announcements, Toyota recalled a total of 9 million cars worldwide after a series of safety problems: stickiness of pedals, floor mat placements, and anti-lock brake software. At the peak of these events, Toyota and institutions such as the National Highway Traffic Safety administration were involved in numerous investigations of real and potential safety issues, with court cases in several countries.

While it is beyond the scope of this study (and our knowledge) to analyze the technical aspects of the case, there was obviously tremendous pressure on Toyota to repair the damage to its corporate reputation. Its cars, while not the most fashionable in the world, were known for their reliability and safety. With all the recalls, investigations and court cases, the very identity of Toyota Motors was at stake.

In non-family businesses of this size, shareholders expect owners to react swiftly and to send a clear signal that the situation is being brought under control. Typically this involves dramatic changes in top management – existing managers being fired and replaced by others who are not associated with the crisis. Changes have to be visible to satisfy the demands of the shareholders, even if the top managers are not responsible for the mistakes made. But Toyota found another way out.

Of all stakeholders in Toyota, the Toyoda family probably had the most at stake since it was so closely identified with the image of the corporation. In January 2009, it was announced that later in the year Akio Toyoda would take over as President and CEO – the first family member to occupy the position in more than 17 years. Although he was in the process of being groomed for leadership of Toyota, his swift promotion was in response to the crisis. Beyond his leadership skills, it cleverly exploited the Toyoda name to send a powerful signal to the markets that with the family back in charge, the company was returning to its roots and would restore the values and reputation on which the business was founded. Only the family name could make such a powerful statement. Judging from the market reaction to the announcement, investors were convinced.

The German giant Siemens had a similar experience in the last decade, when internal and external governance issues, including accusations of bribery and other wrongdoing, hit the headlines. Normally the family kept a low profile, serving simply as an internal sparring partner with its trusted external managers, but in this instance they chose to become more visible to help convince investors and the business community that the company was committed to a new transparent governance structure.

From the smallest family business to the largest, be they in the East or the West, these stories reveal how powerful the family name can be when it comes to winning the trust of key stakeholders. It is a unique asset that is most easily preserved through new generations of family members being involved. Successful business families integrate the name and its legacy into their business strategies and develop governance structures that protect and enlarge its value.

Values-based leadership

One of the strongest and most universal assets in family firms is the set of values that extends throughout the firm. Values-based leadership is a popular concept in modern business and many great leaders inspire their organizations in this way. But family firms are special in that leadership is based on values that are core to the family and the business, and have held sway for generations – such that they are the DNA of the family and the firm.

leadership is based on values that are core to the family and the business

Values are essentially the principles upon which individuals base decisions in their private and professional lives, such as honesty, integrity and diligence in their relationships with others. Values-based leadership occurs when decision-making and governance in the firm mirror the values of the individual in charge. In family businesses, values will often be transferred from one generation to another.

Values-based leadership complements other forms such as experience-based decision-making. The latter can be very powerful in contexts which resemble previous situations that the firm (or leader) has encountered, but when the firm finds itself in a new situation, such as the first succession in a family firm or deciding how to exit a firm after years of being in charge, then such experience is lacking. We observed above how Hermès stayed true to its legacy in the 1970s in a period when synthetic materials became popular in the fashion industry, thereby exemplifying values-based leadership which had short term costs but proved hugely successful in the longer term.

Values-based leadership is practised in almost all the family firms we have observed. Values are shared by the existing members of the family, passed down by generations before them. They are transferred through the upbringing and education of the children in settings that are not directly related to the family business. The process is unique to families – transferring values in this way to external managers (with a relatively short tenure) is impossible.

Cadbury is an interesting example of a company driven by strong values for more than 180 years; values that through the work of Adrian Cadbury and the Cadbury Committee have had a lasting influence on modern corporate practice. The Cadbury Report with its guidelines on good corporate governance has been an inspiration for countries and international institutions alike.

At the peak, there were more than 200 Quaker firms in Britain. At a time when trust was in short supply, there were more than 75 Quaker banks in the country, including famous names like Barclays and Lloyds. The first steel bridge and the world's first passenger train line were developed by Quaker entrepreneurs.

Religious values can be a driving influence in business and many successful family firms are open about their religious anchoring. We saw in Chapter 1

CADBURY AND QUAKER VALUES

In the early 18th century, when the cocoa bean was first brought to England, it kindled a fantastic entrepreneurial spirit: by 1850 more than 30 hopeful chocolate entrepreneurs were competing to develop products fit for public consumption. In the beginning, shops sold tea and coffee while experimenting in the back room with all kinds of cocoa butter, which was later refined to make the cocoa drink. To achieve a liquid content, however, the oil could not be removed and different kinds of additives were used to thicken it such as potato flour, sago and even brick dust, iron filings and toxic substances like vermilion and red lead.

In 1824, 24-year-old John Cadbury set up shop on Bull Street in Birmingham. Not only did he sell tea and coffee but also a substance 'affording a most nutritious beverage for breakfast ... Cocoa Nibs prepared by himself'. The small firm struggled throughout his lifetime and it was only when his sons Richard and George took over that the business gradually began to grow into what would ultimately make them the biggest chocolate company in the world.

The Cadbury brothers and other Quaker entrepreneurs in the British chocolate industry (including their main competitors Rowntree and Fry) believed in a capitalism that improved life for all stakeholders, not least the workers in their companies. The business was never an end in itself; it was a road to fulfill a larger goal. For the early chocolate entrepreneurs their entire business strategy was motivated by providing tasty and healthy alterna-tives to alcohol. The Quaker founders were passionate advocates of temperance. They also engaged in the fight against child labor and air pollution. The Quakers were extremely hard working and subscribed to puritan ideas. Since their religion was prohibited in England, they ended up creating a religious and business net-work in which Quaker entrepreneurs could share contacts and experience at secret meetings around the country.

The business suffered for the first decade of the second genera-tion under Richard and George Cadbury. But even when times were hard they continued their father's commitment to doing good. They tripled the salaries of female workers, institutionalized a sick leave club, and took responsibility for providing education and church services for their workers. On principle Quakers were against using advertising to promote their products, insisting that good products sold because of their superior quality. But it was only when the Cadbury brothers gave in and started to advertise the nutritional advantages of their cocoa drink in the late 1860s and with the introduction of several chocolate bars that the business started to grow significantly. Ironically, a century later Cadbury were among the top British corporate spenders on advertising.

Possibly the boldest social experiment the Cadbury brothers undertook was the construction of 'Bourneville'. The vision was to move the factory out of Birmingham's slums and create 'a factory in a garden' to break the cycle of poverty among their workers. The Bourneville village became the Cadburys' headquarters for the next 130 years and a model of social capitalism. It subsequently inspired Milton Hershey in the US to build a similar project in Pennsylvania.

Being a philanthropic business family occasionally backfired for the Cadburys. For example, it came as a shock to learn that their cocoa beans were produced by slaves in the Portuguese colonies. For a family so socially engaged, the revelation that their basic source of wealth was based on slave labor was scandalous. After this episode, George Cadbury went into politics and, among other initiatives, bought two liberal newspapers.

Adrian Cadbury was born in 1929. An Olympic rower in his youth, he became the youngest chairman of the Cadbury company at the age of 36, soon after his father had taken the firm public. He remained in that post for 24 years until 1989, thereby becoming the longest-serving chairman. He also chaired the first ever committee for formulating principles of good corporate governance. The 'Cadbury Report' of 1992 incorporated a code of practice which has served as a basis for corporate governance reforms around the world.

In the early 2000s, when Cadbury was run by a non-family CEO, Todd Stitzer, the family's values continued to be reflected in business strategy. Stitzer set a target of 1 percent of pre-tax profits to be committed to programs that benefited the communities in which the business operated, a target that was almost always exceeded in reality. Cadbury also developed a plan for reducing carbon emissions across the company, joining forces with the United Nations, Anti-Slavery International, World Vision, Care, and VSO to create the Cadbury Cocoa Partnership. The company committed GBP 45 million over 10 years to improve the livelihood of cocoa farmers in Ghana, India, Indonesia and the Caribbean. It also cooperated with the Fairtrade movement to secure a decent income for cocoa farmers.

how the Mulliez family in France adhere to Catholic principles to guide both family and business development. In Asia, many successful family firms are driven by Confucian values. Hancock Chinawere, a successful South Korean ceramics manufacturer, has grown in 70 years from a small pottery factory to the world's fifth-largest tableware manufacturer. It holds to strong Confucian principles, with a focus on mutual respect and investing in workers similar to the Quakers that were the backbone of Britain's industrial revolution.

Cultural values can also be powerful family assets for business families, be they religious, political, social or economic. Sociologists have distilled these components into two dimensions by which most societies are ordered. The first is the importance of religion, which is closely linked with issues like parent–child ties, deference to authority, traditional family values, divorce, abortion and even suicide. The second is the importance of survival and focus on material resources.

By asking individuals around the world about their values, it is possible to classify nations into seven cultural groups including Catholic Europe, Confucian Asian culture, South Asia, Latin America and Africa. Family assets continue to be very powerful in cases where their cultural values are the foundation of business ventures in a foreign setting. For example, there are commercially successful Chinese communities in most countries around the world, as evidenced by the vibrant 'Chinatowns' that have proliferated in New York, London, Melbourne, Singapore and elsewhere.

Chinese families are not alone in exploiting cultural values to do business outside China. Forever21 is a Korean family business with origins in the Los Angeles textile industry. Koreans dominate much of the cheap clothing industry in LA, exploiting Korean traditions such as working in textiles, strict discipline and investing in family and cultural networks. It has grown into a billion-dollar global chain, controlled and managed by the founder, his wife and two daughters.

Many conservative German families have successfully grown business ventures in Latin America, where their traditional values of discipline, trust and regularity have proved valuable in the more casual Latin American business culture. Italian families have been successful in the construction industry in Canada and to some extent in the US.

Many values-driven family firms are relatively old; the values have been preserved across several generations. However, in societies that have experienced dramatic upheaval – be it cultural, political or economic – this is unlikely. In modern China, for example, few private businesses are more than 30 years old. But despite the challenge of developing values-based family assets over generations, China's entrepreneurs have sought to re-establish their cultural values, sometimes in innovative ways.

In the following story of a knife-maker in southern China, the 'fast-track' approach to culture-building may sound artificial, but is perhaps understandable given the disruption to China's culture and commercial activities by war and political upheaval in the past 100 years. Many entrepreneurs seek to harness history and culture to boost productivity and efficiency.

YANGJIANG SHI-BA-ZI 阳江十八子

Yangjiang Shi-ba-zi is a knife-making company in Yangjiang, a tourist city in Canton Province famous for its knife industry. Its earliest records of knife production date back more than 1400 years to 557 A.D., when a famous warlord, Madam Xiang (冼) and her army, stationed in Yangjiang, ordered the locals to make steel knives and swords. Today, the city's 1,200 knife factories are responsible for almost 60 percent of kitchen knives produced in

China, and the Shi-ba-zi company is the largest of them. Shi-ba-zi is the family name (李) composed of three words (十八子) meaning '18 sons'.

The owner, Mr. Li, was determined to revive the knife culture and to associate his family name with it. Inspired by the martial arts, he built a knife museum at corporate headquarters to display not only the knives made by his company but also weaponry used in Chinese traditional martial arts. He has even ventured into the hotel and tourism business hoping to attract visitors to the city and the museum to experience the culture. He imbues his employees with the spirit of martial arts and they follow a code of conduct inspired by the latter. Like his ancestors, his factories also make swords, and his retail outlets carry not only kitchen knives but also ancient weaponry. Mr. Li is clearly attempting to build his company and products on Yangjiang's history and culture.

Whereas religious and cultural values can be a powerful aid to business within a culture/country of adoption, personal and family values can be influential within a family business.

The founder of Formosa Plastics Group, Wang Yung-ching, is a good example of how personal values translated into corporate strategy. The hardship he experienced throughout his childhood created a business leader with very strong values to which the success of the group can be attributed. Hard work, frugality and rigour made Wang Yung-ching something of a management guru, but his philosophy was simple: 'Get to the root of the issue'. Only by understanding the fundamentals, he believed, could problems be solved efficiently. He liked to work out every detail of a specific process (even brick-laying had a standard operating procedure) and he firmly believed in giving back to the community. These values carried over with the transition to new ownership after his death.

There are many such examples of how the values of founders become the governing principles of family firms. A key source of inspiration for the famous IKEA business model was founder Ingvar Kamprad's upbringing in rural Sweden. Like many of his neighbours, his values were forged from the hardship of his childhood and applied to a business model that focused on cutting costs in the production, transportation and sales processes.

Another example of the power of family values is the Italian luxury fashion group Versace, whose founder, Gianni Versace, was assassinated in 1997. His elder brother, Santo Versace, is the current chairman and co-CEO. His younger sister, Donatella, is the artistic director and the public face of the group. Both were closely involved from the outset in the late 1970s: Donatella started out heading the young company's public relations, and Santo oversaw the managerial aspects of the business. The three worked closely together. After Gianni's untimely death, the siblings continued his legacy. Donatella's daughter, Allegra, as Gianni's only heir, received his (50 percent) share in the company. Much of the design philosophy and interest came from their parents, who provided services to the Italian aristocracy – their father was a personal financier and their mother a seamstress.

The company has to a large degree internalized the family culture. Because the family owns a large share and oversees all major functions (design and management), the culture has stayed the same over the years. This consistency shows in the design output and customers remain loyal to Versace because of its distinct style and the legacy it represents.

It is important to emphasize that values are more easily shared within families because they provide a stable structure and relationships, allowing the continuous transmission of cultural, religious and personal values that take time to establish. Family business owners can search for external managers with similar values, but it is harder to anchor these values in the firm if the family is no longer managing it. Even if outsiders seem to share the family's values, it is not clear how deep they run, particularly if a trade-off has to be made in the interests of short term profit.

Going back to our checklist, we can see that values fit the definition of *family assets* very well: they strongly influence the way family businesses are organized; they are easily transferred within the family but harder to transfer outside; and they can be the foundation for very successful business strategies.

Are the above examples exceptional or applicable to most family businesses? To answer this question we surveyed 3,000 small and medium-sized private family firms in Denmark. We asked the controlling owners questions that covered several dimensions of personal and cultural values, particularly how important relationships were in their personal life, including family, friends, leisure time, politics and religion. For example, if a family owner was religious, would that affect the way he or she governed the family firm? Would right-wing business owners be tougher than their left-wing counterparts?

To complement personal and cultural values, we asked them what accounted for the success of a marriage, (fidelity, income, being from the same social class). They were asked to identify the single most important factor for a happy marriage. We also questioned them about their trust in different institutions in society, from political institutions and the police force, to trade unions and humanitarian organizations.

Our survey found that the values of family business owners were different from the population at large. Perhaps not surprisingly, they were more right-wing. Two-thirds of them agreed or strongly agreed with the statement 'Politics today is too little concerned about creating better opportunities for small and medium-sized companies.' Less than one-third subscribed to the view that politics should be more concerned about social and egalitarian issues. Although they were on the whole right-wing, they were not particularly interested in politics.

The survey helped us answer the question about whether values-driven family business leaders do things differently, in particular whether religious values affect decisions. On average, our family business owners were no more religious than the rest of the population. We identified the 10 percent most religious among our sample of controlling owners and examined to what extent their business policies were different from the rest of the sample business owners. When asked how important different motives were for their business efforts, one-third said that securing resources for future generations was an important driver. But among the religious business owners this fraction was 20 percent higher – over 40 percent of them cited family motives as an important incentive. When asked who they would prefer to succeed them in a management position, 11 percent of non-religious owners wanted to be succeeded by a family member, while the fraction was twice as large (22 percent) among the religious owners.

Values not only affect the organization of the family around the firm, but also the way individuals interact with each other, notably the way interests are debated and views exchanged. We found that religious owners were twice as likely to have experienced serious conflict with other owners, and almost 50 percent more likely to have experienced conflict with other family members (compared with non-religious owners).

We also asked religious and non-religious entrepreneurs whether they knew the true financial value of the company. Only one in four of our business owners had a clear idea of its value, but close to half of the religious business owners gave an affirmative answer.

Then we asked if the family firm had an ambitious climate strategy, with the aim of determining whether the owner's business strategy was affected by non-profit-driven values. Only one in four family businesses claimed to have an ambitious climate strategy. However, more than one in three religious business owners affirmed that they had an ambitious climate strategy. Then we asked those entrepreneurs with a climate strategy if it would increase profits in the future. In general, few of the business owners believed it would, but the religious business owners were almost 40 percent more likely to believe their values-driven strategies would boost profits than non-religious owners.

Overall these results suggest that religious entrepreneurs are people whose strong values influence almost every business decision.

Networks

In business, networks of friends and relatives are vitally important. They facilitate the exchange of resources and information among stakeholders by providing trust and security. Trust derives from past investment in relationship-building as well as the threat of losing one's reputation and the relationship when trust is violated.

All business leaders rely on their personal networks, but leaders of family firms are even more dependent on them. Successful business families use their standing in the local or national business and political community. Family networks are based on relationships nurtured over many years, sometimes over generations of family stewardship. Like other family assets, they tend to be unique and difficult to transfer across individuals or organizational boundaries.

Family networks can be powerful strategic assets for young entrepreneurs. Large business families often have a hidden strength in promoting and nurturing entrepreneurship. We have seen how the Mulliez family has developed the family network into a powerful business model from which new entrepreneurial activities are constantly evolving. We also mentioned how the children of Wang Yong-ching's family have been successful in their own business ventures. The internal family network gives young ambitious entrepreneurs access to advice, coaching and experience from some of the most successful business people around.

Family networks can also be institutionalized. All across Asia, business families have powerful networks that help them in good and bad times. The networks can be purely business networks but they are often strengthened by bonds between families through marriages. Historically, families in many different cultures have used marriage as a powerful way of improving business. Marriage is not just about love; it has a major impact on the success and sustainability of a family business. This is not simply because the descendants have children who may later become part of the workforce or even heirs to the family business, but because the families behind the couple bring additional resources. Entrepreneurs are therefore very careful about their children's choice of partner.

In Korea family networks in business played a major part in history: 'Tae-jo Wang-gun' (877) – who unified Korea – married no less than 29 times to build ties with many local dynasties. In present history, Korean Chaebols (conglomerates) use marriages to build powerful business networks. Samsung, for example, has marriage networks with Dongbang corp., Life corp., Dong-ah corp., Meewon corp., and LG. LG created a huge business network via marriage with Daelim corp., Pyeunksan corp., Kukdong corp., Doosan corp., Hyundai, Hanjin, Kumho corp. Both Samsung and LG are also connected by family to many politicians and other influential people in Korean society.

In Singapore, via the marriage of their offspring, the Didwania clan, owner of a worldwide steel supply chain, is connected to a Calcutta-based family of tycoons, the Gabodia. In South Asia, the heir to the Chaudhary Group, whose worldwide industrial empire has its headquarters in Nepal, is married to a daughter of the Mittal Group, which dominates the world steel industry.

This practice is not limited to Asia. In Russia, Oleg Deripaska, one of the country's wealthiest oligarchs and owner of the world's biggest producer of aluminium, is married to a granddaughter of former Soviet president Boris Yeltsin. In Ukraine, the country's second wealthiest oligarch, Viktor

Pinchuk, is married to the daughter of former president Leonid Kuchma. In Mexico, the heiress of one of the biggest business group owners, Maria Asuncion Aramburuzabala, is married to Tony Garza, US Ambassador to Mexico.

A diagram of an extended family tree connecting clans could provide an accurate representation of many emerging economies. But business marriages are common in developed countries too. In Japan, elite families are known to arrange their children's marriages to members of other top business families and politicians to further their economic interests. Perhaps the most well-crafted network is that of the Toyoda family that controls the Toyota group. It is connected via marriage ties to two former prime ministers (Nakasone and Hatoyama) and seven top business families, namely Mitsui (the biggest pre-war *zaibatsu*), Shimizu (a worldwide general construction corp), Kajima (a worldwide general construction group), Ishibashi (Bridgestone), Uehara (Taisho Pharmaceutical Co), Saito (Daishowa Paper Manufacturing Co), and Iida (Takashimaya Department Store).

The Desmarais family in Canada owns Power Corporation and is connected to former Prime Minister Jean Chrétien by marriage (André Desmarais and France Chrétien). Examples abound in continental Europe. One of the richest shipping tycoons of the 20th century, Aristotle Onassis, was married to Athina Livanos, daughter of another shipping magnate, Stavros Livanos. In Spain, billionaire Esther Koplowitz is married to Fernando Falco, the Marques de Cubas, scion of a prominent Spanish family. Crystal heiress Fiona Swarovski is married to Austria's finance minister. More recently, Jessica Sebaoun-Darty, heiress to French electronic appliance empire Darty, wed Jean Sarkozy, son of former President Nicolas Sarkozy.

To convince those who believe that the above are exceptions rather than the rule, we conducted a study of marriage decisions of the offspring of business people in the past 20 years in Thailand. We identified 200 marriages where at least one side was associated with the top 150 family businesses in the country. These families were almost all Chinese who migrated to Thailand in the 19th and the early 20th centuries.

Among the 200 individuals with a family business background, almost 9 percent married members of the Thai royal family; almost 25 percent married offspring of politicians, bureaucrats and military leaders; about 21 percent married a member of another big family business; almost

26 percent married members of small to medium family businesses; 6 percent married foreigners, and 15 percent married 'other' categories, such as university professors. Political and business network marriages thus accounted for approximately four out of five marriages. Only one in five marriages had no obvious commercial aspect.

We also investigated the market reaction to these marriages. For a typical 'network' marriage, the family firm's net-of-market stock return increased by 4 percent around 40 days after the wedding date. By contrast, if a family business owner's daughter married a non-network individual (such as a university professor) the cumulative net stock return was neutral after the wedding.

So, having sons and daughters (or even business founders themselves) marry into a network is clearly good for business. Interestingly, we found that family businesses which depended on government contracts and concessions, such as telecommunications and real estate, were more likely to have family members engaged in network marriages. If two family businesses had a potential customer–supplier relation, respective members were more likely to marry – somewhat akin to Thai-style vertical integration. Not surprisingly, if two families were in the same business, they were more likely to inter-marry – thereby turning a competitor into a friend.

Of course, the marriage of business family members may have other benefits. Japanese family firms traditionally encourage daughters to marry promising 'salary men' who are employed by their fathers' companies. Furthermore, sons-in-law are often formally adopted by the bride's family, particularly when double-bonding through marriage and adoption bypasses a lack of family successors. Another potential benefit of marriage is to discipline a potential successor. Where a son of a wealthy family may have more interest in spending money than growing the business, pushing him into marriage may help to check his extravagant lifestyle and to refocus him on family affairs.

Another powerful strategy is networking with politicians and regulators. Numerous family firms through the ages have had ties to local or national politicians; a pattern repeated the world over. One study suggests that politically connected firms account for as much as seven percent of the global capital markets (which is likely to be an underestimation because information about political ties is difficult to trace). Even in the US, many senators and members of Congress serve on the boards of large and small companies.

Evidently, politicians need financial support from business owners; and by supporting politicians, business owners may enjoy various benefits including tax breaks, subsidies, access to credit and to the government's development plans, and even protection from hostility. These are substantial advantages in emerging markets where institutional protection of private property rights is weaker.

Political connections can take many forms: institutional, where a politician is a shareholder or an officer of the family business; network, where the CEO or a board member is linked to politics through previous work experience; family, where family members close to owner-managers are actively involved in politics; and, financial, where firms make monetary contributions.

As far as we know, the earliest political leader turned businessman was Liu Hong （刘宏）, the penultimate Emperor of the East Han Dynasty (AD 156–189), and the first ruler in China's history to sell official positions to those willing to pay. Each position had a price tag, although there was room for negotiation. Today in China, almost 30 percent of the CEOs of publicly traded companies are former government bureaucrats. We might anticipate this figure to fall as China's capital market develops, but a recent study of 1,300 of the largest Chinese firms found that the percentage had actually increased over time. However, given that bureaucrats are in charge of allocating key commercial resources such as land, electricity, finance, and raw materials, such venality is perhaps less surprising.

Which family businesses have gained most from political connection in modern times? We cannot be sure, but the family businesses of ex-President Shuarto in Indonesia might be a good guess.

During the Suharto regime, a number of the largest Indonesian business groups were controlled by his family, among them the Bimantara and Citra Lamtore Groups which were controlled by his children. Others such as Nusamba Group, Salim Group and Barito Pacific Group were controlled by his long-time allies. These business groups benefitted tremendously from the Suharto connection, growing from almost nothing to among the biggest in Indonesia. Indeed their stock prices in the later years of the

EX-PRESIDENT SUHARTO OF INDONESIA

Suharto was born poor in a small village near Yogyakarta. After his parents divorced he was brought up by foster parents. During the Japanese occupation of Indonesia, Suharto served in the Japanese-organised Indonesian security forces and later the Indonesian army. Following independence, he rose to the rank of Major General. An attempted coup on 30 September 1965, countered by Suharto-led troops, was blamed on the Indonesian Communist Party. The army carried out an anti-communist purge, killing over half a million people, and Suharto wrested power from Indonesia's founding president, Sukarno, and was appointed president in 1967. Over 30 years later, he was forced to resign in 1998 in the aftermath of the Asian financial crisis.

In May 1999, *Time Asia* estimated Suharto's family fortune at US$73 billion in total in cash, shares, corporate assets, real estate, jewellery and fine art. Of this, US$9 billion is reported to have been deposited in an Austrian bank. The family is said to control about 36,000km² of real estate in Indonesia, including 100,000m² of prime office space in Jakarta and nearly 40 per-cent of the land in East Timor. Suharto topped Transparency International's list of corrupt leaders, and was alleged to have misappropriated between US$15 and 35 billion during his 31-year presidency. Both his son and half-brother were convicted of corruption, but even though charges were filed, Suharto himself was never convicted before his death in 2008.

regime were visibly sensitive to the state of the president's health. When his condition was rumoured to have deteriorated, the share prices were hit hard – much harder than other Indonesian business groups.

On 6 January 2001, a group of business tycoons won the general election in Thailand and formed an administration led by Thaksin Shinawatra. In total, 13 business tycoons ran for election to the Thai parliament and all were elected. Nine of them were supported by Thaksin and were referred to as 'Thaksin Connected' (TC) firms. Thaksin and his supporters' business interests were broad ranging but focused particularly on new technology such as telecommunications and IT. The regime implemented a number of reforms that benefited the TC firms, including erecting entry barriers to foreigners in the telecommunications sector, modifying existing concession contracts, and giving tax exemptions to Shin Satellite, a TC firm owned by Thaksin. Not surprisingly, the TC firms did extremely well during the period when he was in power.

Political and regulatory networks are valuable in all countries and all business cultures. In China, political patronage is critical for businessmen to gain access to resources controlled by bureaucrats at various levels. As in most emerging markets, it is difficult for Chinese businessmen to obtain loans from banks unless they have connections with local government officers or officers of the state banks. The same is true for family businesses in India, Africa, and other countries where weak institutions and corruption prevail.

In China, the imposition of anti-corruption laws on high-level bureaucrats is primarily politically motivated and has little to do with the business sector. We collected information from over twenty anti-corruption legal cases involving leaders of China's various provinces. We then examined managers and directors of all publicly traded companies in each of the corrupt bureaucrats' jurisdictions, to identify whether any of them had been reported as bribing the bureaucrat, or whether they were connected with the bureaucrat through prior job affiliation. We found a host of such connections. For example, in Beijing, the Party Secretary (the top bureaucratic position of Beijing City) Chen Xitong was arrested and sentenced to 16 years in prison in 1995 for corruption. Among the 11 publicly traded companies headquartered in Beijing at that time, we were able to identify (using public information) five companies whose managers had bribed Chen and his family, and three whose managers were connected with Chen. Only three companies in Beijing were free from bribery or connections.

Our experiment was designed to compare the ability of these three groups of companies to obtain loans (particularly long-term loans) from banks whose lending policies were heavily influenced by bureaucrats. If political connections (or even outright bribery) were instrumental to the companies' access to finance, we expected to observe a significant drop in their debt capacity – particularly long-term debt capacity – subsequent to the arrest of the corrupt bureaucrats. This was indeed the case: their debt capacity was half that of companies which were not implicated in bribery.

The stories of Chinese firms connected to local bureaucrats and of family firms connected to Suharto in Indonesia and to Thaksin in Thailand are far from unique. Business tycoons the world over regularly run for office, including Tung Chee Hwa in Hong Kong, Ferenc Gyurcsàny in Hungary, Yulia Tymoshenko in Ukraine, Rafic Hariri in Lebanon, Silvio Berlusconi in Italy and Paul Martin in Canada. It should come as no surprise that family firms benefit from connections with tycoon politicians, but are these simply extreme cases or can we generalize from such examples? Is there any context in which political connections are not valuable?

To investigate this question we went to the least corrupt country in the world according to the international corruption watchdog Transparency International – Denmark – where we estimated the value of being connected to local municipalities (to avoid focusing on more powerful national politicians). Surprisingly, we found that local political connections for small and medium-sized firms were indeed very valuable. Well-connected firms performed much better than non-connected firms, and local government contracts contributed significantly to their profit generation.

Being politically connected help businesses in all countries around the globe. Even in those countries free from corruption, where democratic institutions are well established, being politically connected is a strong family asset for large and small firms alike. It can help family firms increase their market share, win more and bigger contracts from the public sector, and get access to finance; and in some countries it can offer protection from competition or assist firms in times of financial trouble.

However, it is worth emphasizing that relying on political connections comes at a cost. Using political networks exposes a family business to political risks. When political leaders fall from power or are removed from office, and their successors are connected to competing firms, then preferential treatment may give way to discrimination. If the revenue generated through the political connection constitutes a large fraction of the firm's total, then a reversal of political fortune may be catastrophic for a politically connected family firm.

Being politically connected may oblige the firm to engage in activities that are non-profit-maximizing to further the politician's agenda. For example, it has been documented that politically connected firms in France enjoy an increase in market share and volume but not necessarily in profits. The reason for this is that politicians pressure such firms to hire more labour to achieve the political goal of reducing unemployment. So while political connections can boost revenues, they may at the same time eat into profits.

We do not claim that all business owners engage in politics for their own benefit. On the contrary, we believe that many – if not most – business people go into politics because they want to make a difference. A majority firmly believe that their experience in the private sector will make a positive difference in the public sphere. One such example is Fok Ying Tung in Hong Kong.

FOK YING TUNG HONG KONG

An outstanding example of a visionary family business tycoon turned politician is the late Henry Fok Ying Tung, a Hong Kong businessman whose fortune was ranked eighth in Hong Kong and 181st worldwide. His business interests included restaurants, real estate, casinos and petroleum. He died in 2006, in Beijing, at the age of 83.

A defining characteristic of Fok's family enterprise was its ties with China's central government and its involvement in, as well as influence on, Hong Kong politics. This dated from the Korean War, during which he smuggled weapons and other military materials into mainland China despite a United Nations arms embargo. When China initiated its economic reform and open-door policy in 1978, Fok was among the first to invest in the mainland. His continued commitment won him the trust and appreciation of the Chinese government. Ultimately, he was no longer simply a businessman but a national figure in his own right, and was appointed vice-chairman of the National Committee of the Chinese People's Political Consultative Conference in March 1993.

His role in central government gave him great influence in Hong Kong. The media reported that it was Henry Fok who introduced Tung Chee Hwa to Jiang Zemin (the former president of PRC) as a possible candidate for office as the first Chief Executive of Hong Kong. It is said that in the early phase after the handover of Hong Kong, Tung was nominally Chief Executive but it was Fok who advised him.

Another interesting example of a business tycoon who made a huge difference to his country is the late Chung Ju-yung – founder of South Korea's Hyundai Group. Born and raised in a small village in North Korea, he moved to South Korea when he was 22 and went on to become one of the country's most prominent businessmen until his death in 2001. Throughout his career he invested in North Korea, even when there was considerable political risk and little economic incentive to do so. Among many other deeds, Chung Ju-yung is famous for having managed to slip 1,001 head of cattle across the demilitarized zone to help feed the starving North Korean population.

Discover more

Amore, Mario Daniele, and Morten Bennedsen. The Value of Local Political Connections in a Low-Corruption Environment. *Journal of Financial Economics* 110(2), 387–402, 2013.

Bennedsen, Morten, Robert J. Crawford, and Rolf Hoefer. Hermes. Case Pre-Release version, *INSEAD*, Fall 2013.

Bertrand, Marianne, Francis Kramarz, Antoinette Schoar, and David Thesmar. Politicians, Firms and the Political Business Cycle: Evidence from France. Working Paper, 2007.

Bunkanwanicha, Pramuan, Joseph P.H. Fan, and Yupana Wiwattanakantang. The Value of Marriage to Family Firms. *Journal of Financial & Quantitative Analysis* 48(2), 611–636, 2013.

Bunkanwanicha, Pramuan, and Yupana Wiwattanakantang. Big Business Owners in Politics. *Review of Financial Studies* 22(6), 2133–2168, 2009.

Cadbury, Deborah, and Morten Bennedsen. Cadbury – The Chocolate Factory: Principled Capitalism (Part 1) and Sold for 20p. (Part 2). Case Pre-Release version, *INSEAD*, Spring 2013.

Faccio, Mara. Politically Connected Firms. *American Economic Review* 96(1), 369–386, 2006.

Fan, Joseph P.H., T.J. Wong, and Tianyu Zhang, 'Politically Connected CEOs, Corporate Governance, and Post-IPO Performance of China's Newly Partially Privatized Firms'. *Journal of Financial Economics* 84(2), 2007, 330–357.

Fisman, Raymond. Estimating the Value of Political Connections. *American Economic Review*, 91(4), 1095–1102, 2001.

Highlights

- Family assets are the unique relationship-specific contributions that families deliver to their firms. Values-driven leadership, names and legacy are essential in most family firms, as are family, business and political connections in every society we have studied.
- Prestige, status and influence are common to family firms across cultures. In short, family assets are global – regardless of firm size, industry or country.
- It is easier to transfer family assets within the family than to outside owners or external managers. Children inherit the family name at birth and absorb cultural, religious and family values from a very early stage.
- A network may depend on individuals, but family entrepreneurs can 'transfer' their network to their children through social activities and family events.
- Identifying these family assets is the key to understanding the enhanced value that is delivered by the family to the firm. Thus the first step in long-term planning for any family business is to evaluate the presence and strength of existing family assets.

In the next chapter we discuss the many constraints related to being a family firm. These roadblocks to the prosperity of the family and the business constitute the second pillar of our long-term planning framework.

3
Roadblocks

Roadblocks are any type of obstacle that entrepreneurs encounter in the business. In this chapter we introduce the most common that are specific to family firms and show how removing them can consume much time and energy. Roadblocks are often bigger and tougher for family firms than for other types of business. Some are common to all family businesses world-wide, others are specific to a particular business environment, culture or even country. For the business to be sustainable, families need to anticipate future roadblocks and understand how to bypass them.

Figure 3.1 groups the most common roadblocks that affect family businesses into three categories: family, institutional and market roadblocks. Some roadblocks are persistent; others emerge in response to changes in the fundamentals – the family, the market or the institutional environment. Left unattended, each roadblock has the potential to destroy an successful business and the family behind it. Only by anticipating them can they be overcome and the family's ownership and control be preserved.

each roadblock has the potential to destroy an successful business

FIG 3.1 / **Common roadblocks**

Family roadblocks

Around the world, spouses and children experience the satisfaction of mixing work and family life on a daily basis, meeting the challenge of running a business together. In the previous chapter we argued that the family's assets – their unique input to the enterprise – are the building blocks of a competitive business strategy. However, the satisfaction of working together can soon turn to frustration if the family creates roadblocks to the firm's development, or if personal conflicts spill over into the professional sphere.

Ultimately the success of the business depends on the quality and drive of the entrepreneur and his/her family. A shared sense of discipline and incentive is essential to the firm's early success. Unlike salaried employees, family members are not bound by contractual arrangements but by informal constraints such as norms, traditions and codes of conduct. These underpin the family hierarchy as well as the system of reward and punishment. But the quality of their input and drive cannot be taken for granted. Just as the family can propel the business to success, so it can throw up roadblocks if circumstances change, such as a decline in someone's health or changes in marital status, the size of the family or distribution of wealth. A significant change in any of the above dimensions can affect business continuity and break the implicit contract between family members when it comes up for renegotiation, for example as a result of a succession.

Family development – the power of numbers

In its most basic form, the family is a blend of biological and social components, all of which can turn into roadblocks. An obvious biological aspect is that a family tends to grow over time, subjecting the business to what we refer to as 'the power of numbers', generation after generation.

In most cultures, parents are keen to divide wealth equally among their offspring. When the family fortune is tied up in the firm, this implies a dilution of ownership to a widening circle of members. The tendency to dilute is often compounded by inheritance laws that oblige parents to divide inheritance equally among the heirs.

Let's begin by illustrating some of the roadblocks associated with the power of numbers through the 100-year history of a lumber yard in Denmark, which represents a situation typical for small and medium-sized businesses around the world.

VORDINGBORG LUMBER YARD

Vordingborg Lumber Yard was founded more than 100 years ago by local tradesmen in what was at the time an important town in Denmark. The story begins in 1912, when Phillip Brorsen, a former customs officer, bought the lumber yard. After the First World War, the lumber industry boomed. Financial statements from the 1920s record that profits exceeded the equivalent of USD 9,000 for a business where labor costs were below USD 300. As sole owner, Brorsen became a wealthy man, and his family pillars of society.

But from 1930, Brorsen, who had three sons and two daughters, had health problems. He re-called Hans Christian, his first son, , home from France. His second son, Kaj, meanwhile had worked in the family business; but it was Hans who was made general manager, while Kaj was given the responsibility of managing the sawmill. Hans had been educated in the lumber business in Finland and had worked as a "wood expert" in France, but he had no wish to manage the firm; his dream was to be an engineer and to expand his horizons beyond provincial Denmark. This was in sharp contrast to his brother Kaj, who dreamed of bearing the family torch after his father. Both frustrated in their designated roles, their relationship soured.

Despite their father's attempts to resolve the conflict, the two fought for control of the company in the early 1930s, their respective orders and counter-orders causing endless problems for the workers. When Philip Brorsen recovered from his illness, he stepped in and bought a forest on the island of Funen for his younger son, leaving Hans in charge of the lumber yard.

As is common for many family enterprises, the ownership of Vordingborg Lumber Yard was diluted over the 100 years that it remained within the Brorsen family. In the second generation it was jointly owned by four of the founder's children. In the 1960s and 70s it was further diluted when the third generation received shares. By 2005, a few years before the family exited the business, there were 21 family owners, the largest with around 13 percent. Ultimately, many of the fourth generation family members had less than 2 percent ownership.

As the above story shows, the ownership dilution arising from the expansion of the Brorsen family created a number of roadblocks. First, sibling rivalry took its toll. Despite the founder's intervention, the two sons could not work together. Henceforth, the family agreed that only one member should manage the lumber yard, although friction remained for decades as the respective branches continued to push different agendas.

Secondly, the ratio of involved and non-involved family members inverted, starting in the second generation when one of the founder's daughters threatened to 'sell her shares to the milkman' if the family would not let her take cash out (to support an extravagant lifestyle). Over time, there was increasing pressure from a majority of the owners to increase the dividend, and ultimately to sell the firm, while the minority of 'insiders' involved in the day-to-day business wanted to limit pay-outs to consolidate the firm's finances for future operations and investments.

The third roadblock was about family involvement in management and board. After the initial succession dispute, it was decided that there could be only one captain on the ship. In addition to selecting future managers, the family tried to ensure that the board reflected the different branches of the family.

The Vordingborg Lumber Yard case highlights how the power of numbers can pull apart family, ownership and management – the three crucial dimensions of any family firm. In a founder-led firm, the three are closely linked, but in succeeding generations they begin to unravel as the family 'subdivides'. Ownership may be split among family members or even opened up to outside investors, just as management may include a mixture of both. As the separation becomes more apparent, at some point – typically around the second succession – those with ownership but no management involvement will start to outnumber the owner-managers. The proportion of non-family minority owners will increase, as will non-family managers.

The four most common roadblocks arising from the power of numbers can be classified as (1) dividend versus growth, (2) ownership design, (3) effective corporate governance, and (4) career opportunities.

1. The dividend versus growth challenge.   In the early years of the business, resources are scarce and nobody expects a dividend. The main focus is on funding future investment for the stability and growth of the company. There is little chance for interests to diverge. But this can change dramatically once the ratio of family members involved in the firm falls. For those involved in management, the priority will be expansion and consolidation; profits should be reinvested rather than paid as dividends. Meanwhile, the 'outsiders', realizing that neither they themselves nor their offspring will share the pecuniary and non-pecuniary benefits, start to question the absence of a dividend and advocate for any profits be spent this way rather than reinvested.

If the firm is cash-rich it may experiment with paying a dividend after a successful year, although as one family manager told us, 'This is when the trouble begins!' Why? Because before the first dividend family members neither expect nor assume that a dividend will be paid. But after the first pay-out they realize that a steady flow is possible and they come to expect it, especially if it's large enough to raise the individuals' living standards.

2. Ownership design in growing families.   Dilution of ownership is a natural consequence of a growing family. If it threatens to dilute his/her authority, or even to attract corporate raiders, the founder (or steward) will need to consider whether and how to concentrate ownership within the family, for example by transferring a controlling block of shares to active members, and only a symbolic stake to non-participating family. However, the perceived unfairness of this may create resentment and be a potential source of conflict. Indeed the design of the ownership structure in response to the power of numbers is among the major roadblocks faced by family enterprises (see Chapter 5).

3. Effective corporate governance in firms with diluted family ownership. After two or three generations, maintaining the balance between dispersed ownership and efficient operational and strategic decision-making in the firm becomes more tricky. For example, how does the family make its influence felt when the firm and the family start to separate? How can the management be structured in a way that enables efficient strategy implementation? What is the optimal structure and composition of the corporate board, and should the family form its own board in parallel to the corporate board?

4. Rules for career opportunities in the family firm.   The involvement and career development of family members requires planning and communication. We often come across young people who have been 'left in the dark' about the hopes and expectations of parents (particularly strong-willed fathers). They don't know when they are supposed to get involved, what they are expected to do, or how their career in the firm will work out. In larger families there is a risk that members may compete with each other, or be seen as a 'glass ceiling' blocking the career opportunities of outsiders. In the absence of fair and transparent rules for involvement and clear career paths, this can create significant challenges.

How large can a family become without compromising the interests of the firm? In fact, it can be surprisingly large and still be hugely successful. Remember that there are over 780 descendants of the founder of the Mulliez family, who we met in Chapter 1, including almost 600 with ownership in the family investment company – and the business is only 100 years old. To our knowledge, the largest entrepreneurial family in the world are the Janssens in Belgium, one of the founding families of chemical giant Solvay. It is thought that between 2,000 and 2,500 members share the family fortune which flows in large part from their stake in the industrial conglomerate.

For young family businesses in emerging markets, it will be reassuring to know that families like these have managed to stay united despite the firm having several hundred owners. A leading member of a very large French dynasty told us: 'The challenge is to become a hundred; after that there are more things that unite the family than divide them. At that point most or all family members have other careers, and the family becomes a source of additional strength.'

Family conflicts

Just as families can make a unique contribution to a successful firm, they can also be a source of conflict that spills over to the business. Most parents want to give their children a good start in life, and since the firm occupies a central place in their own lives, they dream of seeing their children happily working together in the business. They typically try to find positions for those children interested in the firm, ideally giving each child an equal opportunity to satisfy their ambitions. For siblings who love and care for each other, this can be rewarding both personally and professionally, but in many cases reconciling their personalities and ambitions puts the working relationship under strain.

Striving for recognition from parents who have devoted their lives to the business, it's only natural for children to compete to succeed in the firm. And if several children are competing for recognition using the business as the battlefield, conflicts are bound to arise. This can be costly for both the family and firm.

One of the main challenges in maintaining family harmony is how to allow each child to 'live their dreams' without affecting the prosperity of the business. There are many cases of families who have failed to balance the dreams of individual members with the wellbeing of the firm, including the Pritzker family in the US, the Porche/Piëch family in Germany, Reliance's Ambani brothers in India, and the Ho gambling dynasty in Macau.

It is common for founders of firms to impose their authority on the family. They often have strong personalities which go unchallenged in the firm as well as at home, and children who question the founder's judgment (in either sphere) put themselves at risk. Indeed deference towards the founder and his/her legacy often continues to influence the members of the second and third generations.

In the story of the Vordingborg Lumber Yard, Tim Brorsen, who was for many years the third-generation CEO, told us that until the fourth generation the family had always found a way to reconcile their diverging interests, even if debates were sometimes heated. In his opinion, respect for the founder was key to individuals being willing to compromise and resolve their personal and business issues. All third-generation family members had childhood memories of the founder Philip Brorsen, hence their appreciation for his work and achievement. The fourth generation never knew him in person; for them he was a picture on a wall, someone who featured only in family stories. Once respect for the founder was gone, with it went the willingness to compromise. For Tim, this was a key factor in the family's decision to sell the lumber yard in 2007.

Importance of key individuals

Founders and family stewards make a huge difference to their companies and are harder to replace than key people in diversely held businesses, simply because they master the family assets in a way that non-family managers will have difficulty reproducing. But they can be vulnerable in two respects: whether they have the health and strength to keep going, or the sense to understand when to let others take over.

Health

In 2005, Li Ka-shing, the 77-year-old founder and chairman of Cheung Kong Group in Hong Kong and the wealthiest man in Asia, was unexpectedly hospitalized. The stock return on his publicly traded flagship company declined sharply at the time of his hospitalization. Clearly, investors were uncertain what would happen to the group if he died and he was still perceived as a crucial asset. Fortunately, he recovered and so did the business. Now 85 years of age he still heads the vast business empire.

Despite the many examples of talented individuals who built a business out of nothing and played a key role in making it a national (even international) champion, the importance of their health is often underestimated. While diversely held corporations tend to 'manage' this risk and keep the subject on the board agenda, family firms expend surprisingly few resources on it. Ignoring simple questions like the following can be a costly oversight.

- How dependent is the firm on key individuals?
- Could it cope with a serious illness or the death of those key individuals?
- What could be done to reduce the impact of such a crisis on the firm?

There are many examples of how heads of major business empires die unexpectedly: In Argentina Francisco Norberto Soldati Láinez, the head of the second largest construction group died from a polo accident at the age of 51. In Peru Carlos Rodriguez-Pastor Mendoza, bank owner and financial entrepreneur, died from a heart attack at the age of 60. In Libanon Rafic Baha El Deen Al-Hariri – the country's prime minister and richest business man – was assassinated at the age of 61. Nasser Al-Kharafi, CEO and Chairman of the biggest business group in Kuwait, died of a heart attack in his hotel room at the age of 67. In Germany Stefan Schörghuber CEO and Chairman of the eponymous real estate company died unexpectedly at the age of 47. In Hong Kong Kwok Tak-Seng CEO and Chairman of Sun Hung Kai properties – the largest real estate group in Hong Kong – died from a heart attack. These unexpected deaths delivered a severe punch to the affected business groups who in most cases were unprepared for the exit of the business owners.

Researchers have examined large samples of family businesses to measure their vulnerability to the personal well-being of key individuals and 'health shocks' among family members. Using data on the deaths of more than 5,000 CEOs and their close family members (children, spouses, parents and parents-in-law), they found that the shockwaves from such traumas in the family sphere had serious repercussions on the firm.

When the CEO died, firms saw a performance drop of close to 30 percent – enough to wipe out the surplus of a typical small or medium-sized company. Although there were signs that performance had begun to bounce back four years later, the loss of the CEO was extremely costly, not least the cost of finding a replacement. The study also found that a death among the immediate family of the CEO – particularly a child or a spouse – also had a sharp impact: firm performance declined by around 10 percent for several years thereafter.

The death of an owner-manager is naturally a huge shock to the family and the firm. Thus it is interesting to understand if smaller health 'scares' also impact the performance of a family firm. The analysis of thousands of hospitalization records for CEOs in small and medium-sized firms revealed that even relatively short hospital stays had negative impacts on firms. While a one- or two-day hospitalization had little impact, when a hospital stay exceeded five days there was a measurable drop in firm performance that year and the following year: a 10-day hospitalization of the CEO reduced operating performance by 4 percent the first year and 2 percent the second year.

Despite the strong evidence that the absence of the key individual is a real challenge, most family firms simply take them as they come, ignoring the reality that health shocks can create a significant roadblock and may put the survival of the firm at risk.

Entrenchment or 'knowing when to let go'

THE WORLD'S OLDEST BOSS

Born in 1907, the late Sir Run Run Shaw was the oldest boss in the world. He eventually announced his retirement in 2010, at the age of 103, indicating that his 79-year-old wife would suc-ceed him as chairman of Television Broadcasting Limited (TVB), a publicly traded company in Hong Kong.

In the 1950s, Shaw and one of his siblings founded Shaw Brothers, a production company that became a pioneer of the post-war Chinese movie industry. His success was due to a mixture of luck, hard work and innovation: luck because his main rival died in a plane crash early in his career; hard work as he was actively involved until an advanced age; and innovation because he pioneered the use of 'Huang-mei Diao', a traditional singing style in central China, and Kung Fu in the movies.

His movie empire was hugely successful during the 1960s and 1970s, when it had a virtual monopoly on the Chinese movie market. But when the market declined in the 1980s, so did his empire. Since the younger generation did not appreciate traditional style movies as much as its predecessors, the Shaw Brothers ceased new movie production in the late 1980s. Run Shaw redirected his energy and resources to television. He was the controlling owner of TVB in Hong Kong from 1980. Again, TVB had a local monopoly on TV programs.

Shaw was highly respected within the Chinese community in Hong Kong and China, and was renowned for his donations to education and disaster relief. Shaw donated billions of Hong Kong dollars to educational institutions in Hong Kong and mainland China. More than 5,000 buildings on Chinese college campuses bear his name, as does Shaw College of the Chinese University of Hong Kong. He also established the Shaw Prize, often referred to as the Nobel Prize Asia.

He married twice. He had two sons and two daughters with his first wife, but none worked for Shaw Brothers or TVB, hence there was no obvious successor to the business. His second wife had no children. In the absence of a succession plan, rumors circulated that TVB would be sold to a property tycoon on the mainland, but this never materialized. When it was finally sold in 2011, Shaw was 104. Shaw died aged 106 years on 7 January 2014.

Sir Run Run Shaw is one of the most influential and admired business leaders in Asia in the last 100 years. He made a great contribution to the entertainment and movie industry and he was one of the biggest philanthropists but he failed to find a successor, family or non-family, to take over his media and entertainment legacy. Ironically, when, in 2006 at the age of 98, he was admitted to hospital with pneumonia, TVB's stock price went up by almost 20 percent. Rather than reacting negatively, investors in TVB seemed to view the founder's illness as the first hope of change.

Power of numbers	Harmony and psychology	Importance of key individuals
• Growth versus dividend • Ownership design • Corporate governance • Career development	• Conflict management and family governance	• Human resource management • Entrenchment

FIG 3.2 / Key challenges of family roadblocks

His case is by no means unique. The retirement roadblock is frequently observed in many successful family businesses around the globe. When 97-year-old Arnold Maersk McKinney Moeller died in April 2012, the share price of the world's largest shipping company – Maersk – went up 7 percent. Yet he had dedicated his whole life to adding value to his father's shipping company and under his leadership it had become a leading player in the global shipping industry. Although he had stepped down as CEO of Maersk years before, he remained chairman of the family foundation, the biggest shareholder in the public traded company. Judging by the stock price reaction to his death, shareholders must have perceived that it would be an opportunity to implement value-enhancing changes.

Figure 3.2 sums up the key challenges related to the different family roadblocks. Families are a key resource for the business, but they also bring added risk. Thus a key objective of long-term planning should be to reduce the cost of roadblocks by designing mechanisms to minimize potential conflict and optimize their input, present and future.

Institutional roadblocks

Entrepreneurs constantly battle with the institutional environment in which their firms operate. Broadly speaking, institutions set the rules for all human interaction, and therefore shape the challenges businesses face. The institutional context refers to the legal and regulatory codes in a given country, and thus influences how individuals interact with each other. It can be defined by specific laws and regulations, or have a broader sense, such as the level of protection given to investors or the level of corruption that prevails – in other words the culture that shapes the business environment. For example, if corruption is widespread, it will be difficult for a private business to thrive, and if corporate taxes are heavy, it will be hard to attract new investment.

We focus on how institutional settings affect incentives for family businesses. Inheritance laws, for example, shape the way that businesses are transferred through generations. In countries where protection of private property is weak, family firms have an advantage because the members of the family foster trust with each other and with stakeholders, so the cost of doing business is reduced. In some instances, institutional arrangements impact family businesses even when this was not the original intention.

Before we discuss how institutional roadblocks affect family businesses more generally, let's take a look at the Wendel iron and steel dynasty, and their 300-year history of overcoming dramatic institutional challenges in a changing world.

300 YEARS OF ROADBLOCKS: THE HISTORY OF WENDEL IRON AND STEEL

In 1704, Jean-Martin Wendel, the son of an army officer, acquired the de la Rodolphe forge in Hayange, a small town in the Lorraine region of eastern France. Exploiting local supplies of iron and wood, Wendel and his son Charles built Hayange into the largest iron enterprise in Lorraine in the 18th century. In the 1780s, Charles's son Ignace built France's most technologically advanced forge at Le Creusot.

During the French revolution, which overturned the nation's established institutions, one member of the family was sentenced to death and most fled the country, with the exception of Charles's widow, who kept the company until the new regime confiscated Hayange in 1795. That same year, Ignace died of an opium overdose in Vienna.

In 1803, Napoleon offered an amnesty to émigrés, and Francois de Wendel, Ignace's son, returned from exile and rebuilt the furnaces. On his death in 1825, Wendel et Cie was the third largest iron-producing enterprise in France. It became the largest in 1870, employing some 7,000 workers and producing 134,500 tons of pig iron and 112,500 tons of iron a year.

After the defeat of France by Prussia in 1870, Lorraine was annexed by Germany; the region remained part of Germany for almost 50 years. Most of the family and workers stayed in France. During the First World War, the production plant was confiscated by the Germans. Things improved with the peace treaty in 1919, by which Lorraine was restored to France.

Following the German occupation of France in 1940, the Wendels were expelled from Lorraine by the Germans, the plant was taken over and some of it was dismantled and moved to Bohemia.

After the end of the war, the number of employees was one third of the pre-war level and the industrial outlook was bleak. In 1946, France's coal mines were nationalized. The last forge-master, François II de Wendel, died in 1949. The company, still under family control, fell into decline.

In 1978, in the turmoil that weakened Europe's steel-making industry, the entire de Wendel empire was nationalized without compensation.

Few family firms have survived such dramatic institutional roadblocks as the Wendel steel empire. When the Revolutionaries put a price on the head of one of their ancestors, most of the family fled the country. Henceforth they were based in Germany and elsewhere, while the enterprise remained across the border in Lorraine, on France's eastern border. However, when the business climate improved during the Napoleonic era, the family managed to repossess the forge and build up a thriving enterprise. Then, when Lorraine was ceded to Germany following the FrancoPrussian war of 1870–1871, the roles were reversed: the company was now part of Germany while much of the family and workforce stayed in France. Only after the First World War were family and firm reunited in France, when Lorraine was restored to France in 1919. The tables were turned once more with the outbreak of the Second World War and the Nazi occupation of France in 1940, when the company was again seized by the Germans, and only reclaimed by the Wendels in 1945.

It is extraordinary how the Wendel family bounced back – again and again. Few companies face such overwhelming roadblocks and survive, both as a family and as a firm. Of course, war and revolution affect businesses regardless of the type of ownership, but the Wendels were unique in the way the family was severed from the company and yet managed not only to get it back but to continue.

In 1978, led by the young Ernest-Antoine Seillière, the 300-member family decided to continue the venture without the steel operation and with drastically reduced wealth. With the creation of *Wendel Investissement* suddenly they were investing in steel plants rather than managing forges. By the mid-2000s the now publicly traded investment company was worth more than a billion euros.

In the meantime the Wendels had become one of the largest business families in the world. Today there are more than 1,000 family members in Wendel Participation, the holding company that owns around 38 percent of the publicly traded Wendel Investissement.

War and revolution are dramatic roadblocks for any business, but the ability to survive them may be greater in family firms. In Japan, the Höshi Ryokan suffered during the Second World War. Owner-manager Zengoro Höshi told us how his father and mother survived when there were no customers for five years. Out of a sense of responsibility to their employees, they simply closed the door on the magic world within and spent those five years feeding their employees and taking care of each other. While this might be judged farsighted, for a family with a 1,300 year history of running the ryokan, five years was a relatively short downturn.

The Wendel family at the forge in Lorraine where it all started.

Institutional roadblocks sometimes arise from rules and laws implemented with little thought to their business implications. Possibly the most far-reaching example of this is China's one-child policy, which restricts family size in order to control population growth. It officially limits married couples to one child, although exemptions are granted to people in rural areas, ethnic minorities, and parents who have no siblings themselves. The policy was introduced in 1978 and applied to first-born children as of 1979. According to official statistics, 35.9 percent of China's population is subject to the one-child restriction.

While the policy was established to alleviate social, economic and environmental problems, the government failed to foresee its implications for business – perhaps understandably as there were hardly any private businesses in China before the 1980s. According to official estimates, the policy prevented 400 million births from 1979 to 2011. Controversial both within and outside China for the manner in which it was implemented, it is often cited as responsible for China's gender imbalance.

The corporate landscape of China is in many ways very different from other Asian countries. Over the last decade, a new generation of entrepreneurs has created millions of family firms, and many of those entrepreneurs are now approaching retirement. Due to the one-child policy, China's entrepreneurial families have far fewer children than business families elsewhere in Asia. (Recall that Wang Yung-ching, founder of the Taiwanese conglomerate Formosa Plastics, had over a dozen legitimate and illegitimate children). In mainland China, one or two children is typical. This creates a challenge for business succession, particularly if the only child is not interested in or capable of running the business. Not surprisingly, this lack of heirs is a major roadblock for China's family firms today.

Inheritance taxes, cultures and laws

No entrepreneur likes to pay tax. Corporate taxes are essentially a roadblock to growth, which is why firms invest so many resources in tax planning. Family businesses are no different in this respect, particularly as some taxes put a larger burden on family businesses than on other business types.

Inheritance tax, paid by those who inherit the estate (monetary wealth and property) on the death of a relative, has been around for a long time. Perhaps the earliest recorded inheritance tax was that instituted by Augustus, Roman Emperor between 27 BC and AD 14, whereby a 5 percent tax applied only to inheritance bequeathed in a will, and the deceased's grandparents, parents, children, grandchildren and siblings were exempt.

Inheritance tax varies significantly from country to country. It is imposed in Belgium, Finland, France, Germany, Ireland, Italy, Denmark, Norway, and the Netherlands. Countries that have recently abolished estate tax altogether include Australia, Austria, Canada, Hong Kong, India, Israel, New Zealand, Russia, Singapore and Sweden, as have states in the US such as Utah, New Hampshire and Louisiana.

Inheritance tax influences the transfer of wealth and is a particular burden on entrepreneurs. Wealthy families generally pay tax from their cash resources and distribute the remaining wealth between their dependents. But the fortune of many business families is often tied up in the business. Thus if they are liable to pay, say, 10 to 20 percent on the estate, part of the business may have to be liquidated and all available cash removed. No wonder they consider it a roadblock.

In many countries, legal loopholes can be found for business transfers. A typical provision is to give preferential treatment to firms transferred within the family with the aim of making it easier to pass them on to the next generation. In 1994, the European Commission issued a recommendation to its member states to support the transfer of small and medium-size companies from one generation to the next, as follows: 'The Commission requests the Member States to ensure that family law, succession law and the payment of financial compensation cannot jeopardize the survival of business and to reduce taxation on assets in the event of transfer by succession or by gift,' and warned that 'inheritance taxes extract liquidity and assets from businesses'.

The many options open to business owners to reduce inheritance tax have spawned an entire industry of tax lawyers and consultants. While it is not our aim is to provide a handbook on the topic, we address the issue of how taxes affect ownership design in the next chapter. For now, let's see how inheritance tax acts as a roadblock and the outcome it has on family businesses, starting with a country that recently removed inheritance tax on businesses transfers: Greece.

The Greek government abolished the high tax on business transfers within the family in 2002. According to Professor Margarita Tsoutsoura, Chicago Booth School, under the previous tax regime, investments by firms undergoing an intra-family transfer of ownership had dropped more than 40 percent around the time of succession. High inheritance tax has also been blamed for a lower propensity for intra-family succession, slow growth in total assets, and the depletion of cash reserves (presumably used to pay taxes). It was argued that the effect on investment was due to the families' financial constraints – the money needed for investment and growth of the businesses had gone to the state.

In addition to taxes, laws of succession can be an even bigger roadblock, although it varies across countries and continents. In certain cultures it is still the case that only sons can inherit a business or are entitled to a disproportionately large share. In others, all children receive the same ownership stake independently of their contribution to the firm. In some countries, the law prevents wealth being transferred unequally. In Italy, for instance, the minimum share that may be given to one child is much higher than in the US. Such laws constrain the way ownership is transferred to future generations – and can represent a roadblock. Researchers have shown that legal limits on the transfer of wealth to heirs affect the performance and investment patterns of family firms.

Labor regulations

Labor issues can be a significant constraint for family firms when their business model depends on local networks and culture. LEGO, the famous toy bricks company, was founded almost 100 years ago in Billund, a small town in Denmark. As the company expanded internationally from the 1970s onwards, it faced a cost-related challenge. LEGO bricks are made of cheap plastic. The key inputs are plastic, precision molding, and creativity in design. Most industrial companies would have shifted production to countries with lower labor costs, such as in Asia, but being a family company with strong social ties to Billund, LEGO resisted pressure to move the production outside Denmark. Indeed, it went through a very tough period and the company was struggling to survive, but the emotional connection with its roots made it very difficult to shift production elsewhere.

Ultimately, LEGO bounced back and has seen a strong increase in market share around the world. There are still manufacturing plants in Billund, Denmark, but the molding is now also done in Hungary and Mexico. Brick decoration and packaging is carried out at plants in Denmark, Hungary, Mexico and the Czech Republic. The LEGO Group estimates that in the course of five decades it has produced some 400 billion LEGO blocks. Annual production averages approximately 36 billion bricks, equivalent to 15 bricks per year for every child on the planet.

Labor issues can arise as a result of regulation which affects how difficult and costly it is to hire and fire workers. While this varies significantly from country to country, we have investigated to what extent family firms are affected by labor market regulation. Firing costs make it costly to down-size the workforce, and therefore difficult for a firm to adapt to changes in the business environment. On the positive side, the protection of workers can increase their willingness to invest in a company that will hold on to them. Tough labor market regulation can also be a barrier to entry for new firms and thus a source of monopoly rent for incumbent firms (in many cases these are family firms).

Our research has shown that family firms have a relative performance advantage in countries with weak regulation of the labor market, notably because they are better at managing stakeholders and have a more loyal workforce. Their superior relationship with their workers may help family businesses to keep costs down thanks to less frequent turnover than in less regulated labor markets.

Let's end this discussion with an example of a completely different way in which regulation can be a roadblock for family businesses.

Labor and business regulations can take many forms and be driven by different motivations. When the apartheid regime was ousted in South Africa, the African National Congress (ANC) wanted to provide all ethnic groups with equal economic opportunities. To overcome years of racial discrimination, the government had to give (white) businesses a stronger incentive to recruit non-whites and to promote economic and social development. The solution created by the ANC government was the Black

BLACK ECONOMIC EMPOWERMENT IN SOUTH AFRICA

The Black Economic Empowerment Programme (BEEP) was launched by the South African government to redress the inequalities of apartheid by giving disadvantaged groups of citizens (blacks, coloreds, Indians and some Chinese) economic opportunities previously not available to them. It included measures such as employment equity, skills development, ownership, management, socioeconomic development, and preferential procurement.

In the transition from apartheid after 1994, the new government (dominated by the African National Congress) decided that direct intervention in the distribution of assets and opportunities was needed to resolve the economic disparity created by apartheid policies that had favored white business owners. According to the BEEP, each business was evaluated on seven dimensions:

Element	Weighting
Ownership	20 points
Management Control	10 points
Employment Equity	15 points
Skills Development	15 points
Preferential Procurement	20 points
Enterprise Development	15 points
Socio-Economic Development	5 points

Economic Empowerment Programme (BEEP). This evaluated businesses via a scorecard reflecting the degree of non-white representation in the management, ownership and development of the business, as well as the company's commitment to developing economic and social opportunities for a broader cross-section of South Africans. Companies that scored well were in a better position to win government tenders since procurement contracts were awarded accordingly.

Many businesses in the apartheid era were owned and managed by white families, and the BEEP programme therefore represented up a roadblock as most were reluctant to give up control or give away a significant ownership stake. Yet if they failed to show that ownership was distributed among a wider group of citizens, they would have limited opportunities for doing business. In response to the dilemma, many white businesses redesigned ownership, for example by listing the company on an exchange or introducing a limited form of employee ownership.

Property rights

The upholding of property rights relies on more than simply what the law stipulates. Private businesses are better protected in some countries than others. In the US and UK, owners enjoy strong legal protection. In Kenya, property rights are protected in principle, but due to poor law enforcement and a high level of corruption it is harder for entrepreneurs who are not well connected to protect their businesses.

Simply put, where law enforcement is poor, it is harder to do business. A firm's existence depends on its contracts with workers, suppliers, management, customers, governments and others, so if contracts can be breached with impunity, they become less binding, creating a major obstacle to doing business.

Family firms may do better (or at least fare less badly) in such settings if they are primarily staffed by family members since there is less need for contracts; they rely less on the courts and more on trust. So when weak property rights are a constraint on business, family management makes sense.

The following is an example of how risky it can be to trust outsiders in a country where property rights are poorly protected. It involves the brewing company Huang He (Yellow River), named after the second-longest river in China, a leading private company in Gansu, a remote inland province. When the founder decided to appoint an outside manager for the first time, it turned out to be a disaster. The professional manager, abusing the founder's trust, embezzled large amounts of cash and ownership shares to external companies under her control.

Another example is Gome Group, the largest electronic retailer in China. While Gome's chairman Huang Guangyu was in jail for corruption in 2011, the (non-family) CEO attempted to take control by diluting his ownership

HUANG HE （黄 河） GROUP （CHINA）

Huang He Group is one of the largest business groups in Ganshu Province, a remote area of north-western China which is the center of its beer-brewing industry. The group was founded in 1985 by Yang Jiqiang as a township and village enterprise, an early form of private company in communist China. Huang He operated as a family business: Yang Jiqiang was chairman and CEO and his four sons worked for the company.

When Yang Jiqiang decided to take the group to the next level – bringing in professional managers – he thought of hiring Wang Yanyuan, a local newspaper reporter who had helped to organize a publicity event that was quite successful in promoting the company. He was so impressed by Wang's performance that he appointed her as vice-CEO. Wang Yanyuan quickly won the trust of her boss. The Group's flagship company, Lanzhou Huang, went public in 1999 and the details of the IPO, such as assembling the board of directors, were handled by Wang. The IPO brought in RMB 300 million in cash. Wang became vice-chairman and CEO of the new publicly traded company.

Wang Yanyuan and members of her family set up a string of companies shortly after she joined Huang He. Through a series of transactions between 1997 and 1999, Wang siphoned off assets and cash of Huang He into these companies, notably a controlling block of shares (almost 20 million) sold to a company in Beijing controlled by her parents, at RMB 1.2 per share, substantially below Huang He's per share net asset value of RMB 5.05.

It was obvious that Yang Jiqiang had trusted the wrong person. Before he had a chance to fire her, Wang Yanyuan sought to start a 'mutiny' within the company and went to Beijing. In November 1999, Yang and Wang held separate board meetings in Lanzhou and Beijing, both claiming authority over the same company. The police arrested Wang in the middle of the Beijing board meeting.

and voting power on the board. Fortunately, Huang was able to deal with the situation from jail with the help of his family.

In these cases it proved premature to trust non-family managers, especially in a context where the protection of property rights is weak. In such environments, loyalty carries more weight than ability.

Expropriation by outsiders is not always as flagrant as in the Huang He and Gome cases. Hired managers can exploit their employers in many different ways: taking excessive risk, underinvestment, shirking, overpaying themselves, and so on. These kinds of 'agency' problems happen all over the world, but the extent of the damage caused by hired managers is undoubtedly larger where property rights are weaker because they are less constrained by the law.

Researchers have documented that countries with better protection of property rights tend to have more diffused ownership, while weak protection of property rights is associated with more concentrated ownership. By concentrating ownership, that is, keeping the costs and benefits of running a business within the family, the family has a strong incentive to protect their property regardless of how far the state is willing to help.

Corruption

Political institutions are those agencies and organizations that create and enforce the law, mediate conflicts, make policies and provide representation. Where strong political institutions prevail, the system is more transparent and consistent; elected politicians are held to account and tend to allocate resources for the well-being of society. In a system with weak political institutions, where politicians' self-interests prevail, institutions are prone to corruption and manipulation by special interest groups.

In this way the state becomes an important determinant of business success. Regulations and policies influence how and to whom critical resources are allocated, including land, energy, raw materials, financing, and so on. In China, for example, the state has had a long history of suppressing entrepreneurship. People in business were traditionally in a lower class than bureaucrats, farmers, and even laborers, and criticized for any form of profit-seeking such as stockpiling (buying low/selling high). Businesses could only succeed with the government's blessing and protection.

When it comes to allocating resources, bureaucrats and politicians may choose to award a contract to a business because it is productive and wins the bid by beating out its competitors. But they might just as easily decide to award it to a rival business on criteria such as loyalty, ideology, political correctness, or as a result of bribery. Entrepreneurs who seek access to resources therefore need to understand the rules of the game and play accordingly.

Corruption has a profound impact on business activity – allocation rules often go against legal/social norms and corrupt politicians typically encourage opacity and special relationships. Competitive advantage is not derived from productivity but from the ability to deal with a bureaucracy that is hostile and unjust. While weak institutions tend to create roadblocks for all private businesses, they may provide scope for family businesses to exploit their strong networks, particularly their political connections, as discussed in Chapter 2.

Figure 3.3 summarizes the major challenges associated with some of the most important institutional roadblocks that we have discussed.

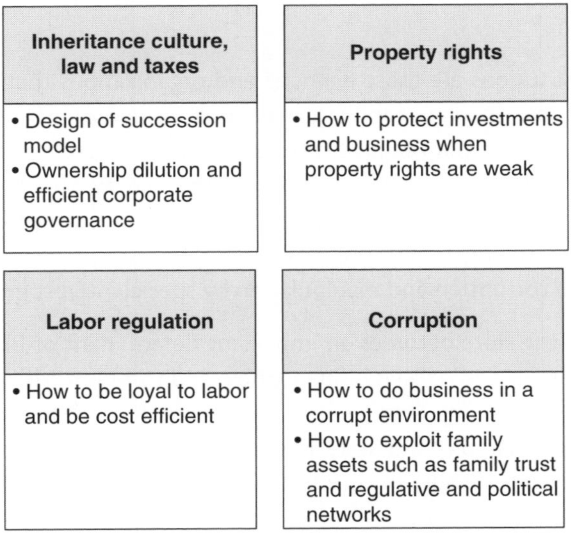

Inheritance culture, law and taxes	Property rights
• Design of succession model • Ownership dilution and efficient corporate governance	• How to protect investments and business when property rights are weak

Labor regulation	Corruption
• How to be loyal to labor and be cost efficient	• How to do business in a corrupt environment • How to exploit family assets such as family trust and regulative and political networks

FIG 3.3   **Key challenges of institutional roadblocks**

Market roadblocks

Changes in the market create new opportunities as well as new challenges. They can be a source of growth for firms that exploit them, while those that don't may be wiped out. Again, changes in the market affect all firms, but they may have a bigger impact on family businesses.

We have already seen how the Wendel family overcame the roadblocks of revolution and war to build the biggest iron and steel company in Europe. Even then they were still confronted with two significant market roadblocks that had a severe impact on the business. The first was the change in the steel market during the late 1960s and early 1970s – notably competition from countries with lower labor costs. Like the rest of the European steel industry, the Wendels had no answer to this challenge, and, like other steel factories, they were nationalized in 1978. A second market-induced roadblock arrived with the advent of the global financial crisis in 2008. The Wendels had just completed their first leveraged investment in a large French company when the cost of borrowing skyrocketed. Within a short time the share price plummeted, wiping out almost 80 percent of the value of the company.

Market roadblocks can have a devastating impact on family businesses that resist change. Our next example shows how family banks in Hong Kong suffered when institutional protection was removed and they were exposed to competitive market forces.

THE RISE AND FALL OF FAMILY-OWNED BANKS IN HONG KONG

Most of the Chinese-owned banks in Hong Kong were started in the period 1946–1949. With the rise of the Chinese Communist Party, a number of wealthy Chinese families and business tycoons fled to Hong Kong with their capital. By the Banking Act of 1948, the Hong Kong government issued 143 banking licenses, and a large number of Chinese-owned banks came into existence.

In 1978, the government began to license foreign banks. As international banks entered Hong Kong, the competition intensified, posing unanticipated challenges for the Chinese family banks. To remain competitive they needed capital to expand, hence many of them went public. But a side effect of raising equity capital was dilution of family ownership, and many eventually lost control of their banks to outsiders. Today, less than a handful of banks in Hong Kong remain family controlled.

As the banking market was deregulated, traditional relationship banking lost its competitive edge, while professional services and image became more important. The remaining Chinese family banks had to adapt or be acquired. For example, in 2006, Liu Chonghing Bank removed the family name (Liu), and became Chonghing Bank in a move by the controlling family to retain its image of a family run bank catering to local customers, while creating a young and trendy image in order to move into new markets in China.

The Chinese banks made the transition from relationship-based banking to market-based competition as the value of family input declined while demand rose for professional management. If families could not make the transition, someone else would. Not surprisingly, as family ownership diluted, family banks became takeover targets. Examples include Yuenlong Bank, which was taken over by the Commercial Bank of China (招商银行) in 2009; Bank of East Asia which was subjected to a hostile takeover threat from a Malaysian-based family business group, and Winghang Bank, rumored to be in discussions with Industrial Bank of China.

Before the Second World War, there were thousands of small, local newspapers in the industry in the US. As late as the 1950s, of the almost 1,800 newspapers in the US, more than two-thirds were family owned. Fifty years later, there were just 12 and media groups accounted for approximately half of the newspaper market.

The media industry has seen dramatic changes in industry composition due to changes in technology, in readership, and the globalization of news. Revolutions in printing technology and reading habits were huge challenges for most small and medium-sized family businesses. They wanted to keep control but needed capital for expansion, while investors wanted a say in running the business in exchange for their investment.

A few families that managed to finance expansion without sacrificing control are left in the industry, including such famous names as the Ochs Sulzbergers of the New York Times, alongside newcomers such as Rupert Murdoch.

Growth is often a major roadblock for small and medium-sized family businesses. In our experience, too many founder-run or second-generation firms never get beyond being small because the growth process stops. Three closely related challenges exist for such firms. The first is the founder's lack of ambition to take the firm to an even higher level. We know of many family firms that have reached a level of development beyond which the founder (or heirs) never want to go – they are simply content to stay true to the founding vision and not grow beyond this level.

The second challenge is the fear of change – although change is bound to happen with continued growth. To expand, firms have to conquer new markets, possibly in other parts of the world, or to move production away from the birthplace of the business to low-cost producers like China, Vietnam or Cambodia, and perhaps to replace old hands with younger workers with a different set of skills.

The third challenge is the organization of the owner-manager's time. Too many family firms have a highly centralized operating mode in which the owner-manager is involved in every part of day-to-day operations. Being successful and liking the control, the owner-manager never creates an organizational structure in the formal sense. Everything depends on him or her, with the result that he or she spends 100 percent of the time managing day-to-day business. He or she then has no time to plan long term, or to see the need for a change in strategy or in the way the business is run. Again, growth remains stagnant.

Let us end this discussion with a final example of how market changes affect the presence of family firms in the luxury industry. We have already seen how the industry was dominated by individual families which for centuries had produced high-quality items. Until the last decade of the

Competition and growth	Industry concentration and globalization
• Growth and control • Ambition, changes and organization	• Cope with globalization • Cope with industry changes

FIG 3.4 / **Key challenges of market roadblocks**

18th century, the luxury market was almost entirely in Europe; it was easy for leather-goods maker Hermès or graph-instrument maker Farber Von Castell to manufacture products in the suburbs of Paris or Switzerland and reach wealthy customers in Switzerland, Germany, France or England. With the new century, however, wealth was accumulated on a new scale in America, and the many relatively small European luxury companies had to find ways to satisfy the newly rich American's unbounded taste for elegance. Fifty years later, the market changed again. Now massive wealth started to be accumulated in Asia, and, with the oil crisis, in the Arab world.

It has been a real challenge for the old family companies in the luxury industry to set up marketing and sales structures so far from their traditional markets. Even if there is an unprecedented desire for luxury goods in these new markets, this challenge has had – as shown in the next chapter – a profound impact on the structure of the luxury industry today.

Figure 3.4 summarizes the challenges associated with the two most important market roadblocks that we discussed above.

We end this chapter by summarizing the challenges associated with the most common roadblocks we have observed in family firms across the world (Figure 3.5):

We have highlighted several examples of roadblocks to family businesses in East and West, each generating a particular challenge for managers and owners. Many of them threaten the ownership structure of the family firm. If there are too many family members, ownership may be over-diluted. If growth requires outside investment, the family's control can be

Family roadblocks

Power of numbers
- Growth versus dividends
- Ownership design
- Corporate governance
- Career development

Harmony and psychology
- Conflict management and family governance

Importance of key individuals
- Human resource management
- Entrenchment

Institutional roadblocks

Inheritance culture, laws and taxes
- Design of succession model
- Ownership dilution and efficient corporate governance

Property rights
- How to protect investments and business when property rights are weak

Labor regulation
- How to be loyal to labor and cost efficient

Corruption
- How to do business in a corrupt environment
- How to exploit family assets such as family trust and political and regulatory networks in a corrupt environment

Market roadblocks

Competition and growth
- Growth and control
- Ambition, changes and organization

Industry consolidation and globalization
- Cope with globalization
- Cope with industry changes

FIG 3.5 Summary challenges of roadblocks

contested in the future. If inheritance taxes are too burdensome, it may result in the exit of the family through sale of the company. Thus significant roadblocks for a business-owning family often have implications for the design of future ownership structure.

Discover more

Bennedsen, Morten, Hannes F. Wagner, Sterling Huang, and Stefan Zeume. Family Firms and Labor Market Regulation. Working Paper, 2013.

Bennedsen, Morten, Francisco Pérez-González, and Daniel Wolfenzon. Do CEOs matter? Working Paper, 2013.

Bennedsen, Morten, Francisco Pérez-González, and Daniel Wolfenzon. Evaluating the Impact of The Boss: Evidence from CEO Hospitalization Events. Working Paper, 2014.

Tsoutsoura, Margarita. The Effect of Succession Taxes on Family Firm Investment: Evidence from a Natural Experiment. Forthcoming in the *Journal of Finance*.

Highlights

- Family firms face obstacles – roadblocks – many of which are common to families, firms, industries and countries.
- Family roadblocks arise from the family's growth, as well as a misalignment of interests, between either individuals or branches of the family.
- Institutional roadblocks arise from the cultural and legal settings in which the family and the firm operate. These include the specific regulative and administrative context as well as the broader religious and cultural environments that affect how families and businesses are organized.
- Market roadblocks arise from changes in product, capital and labor markets.
- The objective of designing corporate and family governance is to reduce the challenges associated with a particular set of roadblocks.

Roadblocks are the second pillar of the Family Business Map. In the next chapter we show how the map can be used to generate efficient long-term planning based on the identification of family assets and roadblocks.

4

The Family Business Map

We cannot overemphasize the importance of long-term planning. Entrepreneurial owner-managers are extremely busy people – they start early and work late, often seven days a week. They are never relieved of the pressures of day-to-day management and its ability to steal every available hour in the day. No wonder, then, that they find little time to plan 20 years ahead.

The fact is, however, that family businesses will not achieve the goals and vision they aspire to without long-term planning. Close your eyes and imagine where your family and business will be 20 years from now. If you want to be eating apples 20 years hence, you have to plant the trees *now*. And if you plant orange trees today, don't expect to get apples in the future – you must do the right thing from the beginning.

In later chapters we will encounter many examples of business families who did not plan for succession. But even those who do plan for succession often discover too late that the chosen model has shortcomings – to return to our metaphor, they realize that the orange trees planted by previous generations should have been apple trees. What is clear is that the chosen ownership and/or succession models have lasting consequences for both business and family, especially if they turn out to be the wrong ones.

In this chapter we show how a family business can map out the next 20 years and establish customized forms of governance to achieve its goals. We call it the Family Business Map or *FB Map*. It provides guidelines for future ownership and management structures that allow the family to exploit the potential of its assets and mitigate the cost of roadblocks. To revert to our earlier metaphor, it recommends the right tree to plant and how to cultivate it so that it bears healthy fruit in the future.

The *FB Map* proposes a three-step process: Identify, Plan, Cultivate. In step 1, the entrepreneur *identifies* the current status of the family business, akin to the crucial preparation before planting a tree. This means evaluating current and future family assets and roadblocks – to what extent family assets contribute to current and future business strategies and how transferable they are to the next generation, as well as the family, market and institutional obstacles that exist now and in the future.

In step 2, he or she *plans* the path to succession and associated governance structure. The *FB Map* helps the entrepreneur to think about the overall succession structure, and to make future ownership and management choices based on what has been identified in step 1. The *FB Map* helps the entrepreneur to understand the opportunities and the challenges embodied in various configurations of ownership and management structures – given the unique contributions the family delivers and the set of family, market and institutional roadblocks it faces. Metaphorically, the *FB Map* helps the entrepreneur to plant the right tree, minimizing the chance of lemons growing where there should have been apples.

In step 3, the entrepreneur *cultivates* the right form of governance given the choice of succession model. The *FB Map* highlights the questions to focus on after the specific plan has been chosen. To facilitate a harmonious implementation, all dimensions of corporate and family governance must be mutually supportive. This requires that the entrepreneur understand the interactions between the different aspects of governing business and family so that ownership design, family governance and corporate governance can all be aligned to ensure smooth progress towards the goal. This is where he/she waters and cares for the planted fruit tree in order to maximize growth.

Step 1: identify

In previous chapters we have seen many examples of key family assets and roadblocks. The existence of strong family assets increases the benefit of having family members in top management, just as the existence of major roadblocks makes it harder to keep business ownership concentrated in the family. Thus any long-term planning should begin with a rational assessment of asset/roadblock conditions and how these might change over the next 20 years, notwithstanding the family's best efforts to preserve their assets and bypass the obstacles.

strong family assets increases the benefit of having family members in top management

At this stage our aim is to conduct a health check on the opportunities and the constraints of a family business:

- Which family assets are important for operating the businesses today and in the future?
- What constraints exist or are likely to arise in 10 or 20 years?
- What is the current ownership and management structure?

In Figure 4.1, a family business is located in the bottom right corner. Ownership is concentrated in the family, and they are running the firm on a day-to-day basis. This structure is consistent with few roadblocks. The firm's development will not constrain family ownership, and the strong family assets means that they are the best managers of the firm.

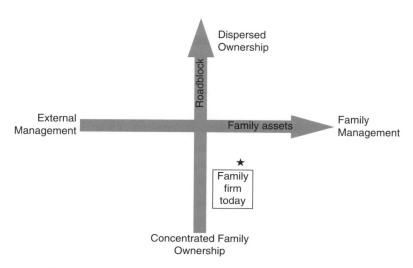

FIG 4.1 The *FB Map*: identify

The set of questions listed below is designed to help families to identify key family assets and roadblocks. Note that these will vary from one culture to another; no single set of questions can account for them all. Depending on whether they are being applied to China, the United States, Africa etc., they will need to be adapted. However, since we have seen many similarities across nations and cultures, they are a good starting point.

The questions for self-checking the presence, strength and transferability of family assets for a given family enterprise are presented in Table 4.1. They should be answered by the owner or one or more well-informed family member, using a scale from 0 to 5, where 0 = least relevant, and 5 = most relevant to the family and/or business.

The first seven questions seek to identify the strategic importance of values-based leadership. First, we ask about the current owner-manager's personal values and how important they are for the organization and business strategy. Where these constitute a cornerstone of the family business both internally and externally, score 5; where they play little part in the way the business is run, score 0. Q2 asks to what extent the owner-manager's values are shared by the family. The next three questions aim at identifying different types of values-based leadership. Q3 relates to the influence of religion – in Chapter 2 we saw how driven religious owner-managers can be. In our research, we found that religion as a family asset depends more on being religious *per se*, that is on serving a higher goal, rather than on the specific religion such as Christianity, Islam, Buddhism, etc. Q4 asks about cultural values. We have seen how Chinese, Korean and German cultures provide powerful business platforms within the home country and exported to other cultural settings. Q5 identifies the presence and strength of family oriented values, since they influence the ability to work as a team, as well as the willingness of individual members to sacrifice self-interest for the sake of the venture. Q6 asks how values support business organization and dealing with employees and customers.

Q7 addresses the transferability of values-based leadership to future generations. We have already probed whether the owner's values are shared by the family members, but here the focus is on their transferability to the pool from which future business stewards will be drawn. While values can permeate an entire generation, in many cases they die out or are lost. For example, traditions that are essential for the way business is conducted

Table 4.1 Identifying family assets (to be filled in by owner-manager or involved family member)

Family assets	**Values**	1	Are the current (owner-)manager's personal values an important part of how the firm's business strategy is implemented?	0—1—2—3—4—5
		2	Does the family have shared values and are these aligned with the current (owner-) manager's values?	0—1—2—3—4—5
		3	Is the family religious?	0—1—2—3—4—5
		4	Are cultural values an important part of the firm's business strategy?	0—1—2—3—4—5
		5	Does the family share strong family values, emphasizing family cohesion and unity?	0—1—2—3—4—5
		6	Is the business operation based on strong moral values (e.g. keeping one's word, treating employees, customers and suppliers well, etc.)?	0—1—2—3—4—5
		7	Are the identified values already present in – or easy to transfer to – the next generation of family members?	0—1—2—3—4—5
	Heritage	8	Is there a unique and enduring competitive advantage, such as a secret formula or specialized skills?	0—1—2—3—4—5
		9	Is the company strategy built on the heritage of the firm and its product(s)?	0—1—2—3—4—5
		10	Does the business strategy rely on long-term relationships with customers and suppliers?	0—1—2—3—4—5
		11	To what extent is the family name used as part of the business strategy?	0—1—2—3—4—5
		12	Has the firm and/or family history been written or published in a form that can reach a wide audience?	0—1—2—3—4—5
		13	Can the legacy and name of the family business be sustained as a competitive advantage for the next generation?	0—1—2—3—4—5
	Connec-tions	14	Does the founding family have a strong network in the political or regulatory sphere?	0—1—2—3—4—5
		15	Does the founding family have a strong business related network?	0—1—2—3—4—5

(continued)

Table 4.1 Continued

Family assets	Connec-tions	16	Is the family closely linked (e.g., by marriage or social ties) to important business or political families?	0—1—2—3—4—5
		17	Are connections an important part of the general business environment in the country/countries where the firm operates?	0—1—2—3—4—5
		18	Is the business in an industry where regulative and political connections are particular useful, e.g. because licensees are needed?	0—1—2—3—4—5
		19	Does the family invest in their network?	0—1—2—3—4—5
		20	Can the identified networks easy be transferred to the next generation?	0—1—2—3—4—5

in China are passed on to children brought up 'at home', but successful entrepreneurs often send their children to Europe or the US to get an international education, with the result that these traditional values die out with the passing of the older generation.

Q8 through Q13 assess the importance of name and heritage as a family asset. Q8 asks to what extent the business has a competitive advantage, which we have found to be a prerequisite for using the name and heritage as a strategic tool. Q9 seeks to identify if the competitive strategy today is based on the firm's heritage. In previous chapters we heard about the Henokiens – companies who are more than 200 years old and whose history is at the core of their business strategy. They are selling not just a history but a level of experience and quality far beyond that delivered by younger firms.

Q9 pinpoints the role of customer and supplier relationships as another legacy-based business strategy. Ascott, a high-end Hong Kong-based global tailoring business, has created its own heritage-based competitive strategy thanks to a worldwide customer base whose loyalty is second to none. With outlets in Hong Kong, New York, London and other capitals, Ascott has organized its business to serve its customers around the globe.

Q10 asks about the use of eponyms – companies that are named after the families that own and manage them. This powerful strategy is used by large and small firms alike, including carmaker icons Ford, Toyota and Peugeot, tire manufacturer Michelin, as well as centuries-old companies such as Thiercelin, a seven-generation French business that sells high-end spices. The name is a guarantee of quality in a market where quality is easily compromised and fraud is difficult to detect. Obviously, firms can successfully exploit family assets even without reference to the name. The Mulliez name, for example, is unknown to the hundreds of thousands of customers who frequent Auchan supermarkets or Decathlon sports outlets.

One way to exploit the family name and heritage as a business strategy is to make the history of the family and the venture widely known, which is why Q11 asks if a history has been published. Some families have a very public story. The Scottish-born Keswick family behind the centuries-old East Asian trading company Jardine Matheson, for example, has been portrayed in several global bestsellers and at least one Hollywood movie ('Taipan').

Q12 asks to what extent the name and heritage can be used as a business strategy by future generations. Among various types of family assets, this is one of the easiest to transfer. For example, Zengoro Hōshi is grooming his grandson to be the 48th generation managing the Hōshi Ryokan. Being a Hōshi ensures that the history and magic of this little hot spring hotel will live on when he eventually takes over.

The final set of questions covers the importance of connections. Q13 asks to what extent the business is helped by connections with politicians and regulators. These are crucial irrespective of the country. For example, whether for a supermarket chain in Kazakstan or Kenya, local council officials may hold valuable information about which locations will be available in the future to build new stores. Advance notice of urban planning proposals can give a head start relative to competitors who have fewer political connections. Whereas Q14 identifies general business connections, Q15 asks about social ties to business and political families. As we have seen, it is common for top business families around the world to marry into each other, thereby fostering trust on which to build long-term business relations.

Q16 measures the power of connections for conducting business in a specific environment. Connections-based business strategies are useful in Western Europe, but they are absolutely essential in less developed countries such as those in Africa, and in political settings like that in China. Q17 asks to what extent the family prioritize connections in their business strategies, and Q18 asks to what extent they are transferable to the next generation. Unlike name and heritage, political and business connections are rarely transferred without loss from owner-managers to their heirs, even when they invest in transferring as much as possible.

Filling out the above questions will provide the business family with a foundation for answering the structural questions posed in Chapter 2:

- What is the unique contribution of the family to the firm?
- To what extent is this contribution transferable to future generations?
- To what degree is current (and potentially future) business strategy founded on these family assets?
- How can the firm be organized to increase the business value of the family assets?

Answering these questions will be an important step towards planning for the future. To make the *FB Map* even more effective we suggest that the scores from the three sections be added separately and aggregated into a total family asset score. While it is possible to use equal weighting for each question and each section, in our experience the application is stronger when weights are assessed according to the specific cultural setting. The higher the total score, the more important family assets are as a strategic tool. As a rule, while 90 is the maximum score, more than 45 points signals that family assets constitute a solid foundation for the current business strategy and the way the firm is run.

Once the strategic importance of key family assets is understood, it is time to identify the roadblocks facing the family and the firm. Table 4.2 is a checklist of 20 questions for assessing the present and future roadblocks, again on a scale from 0 to 5 (0 = not a constraint, 5 = a major constraint on the business either now or in the future).

We have divided the roadblocks into three groups depending on whether they originate at the family level, the market/industry level, or the institutional level. The first seven questions identify roadblocks at the family level. Q1 and Q2 ask if succession planning is problematic or delayed, and how easy it is to find and groom a successor. Q3 asks about the level of communication around succession and other business activities. It may

Table 4.2 Identifying roadblocks (to be filled in by owner-manager or involved family member)

Family	1	Has succession become a pressing issue?	0—1—2—3—4—5
	2	Does the family lack human resources or is it difficult to nurture a suitable successor?	0—1—2—3—4—5
	3	Is open and constructive communication lacking?	0—1—2—3—4—5
	4	Are there diverging branches and/or diverging agendas between different branches or individuals?	0—1—2—3—4—5
	5	Is there a lack of governance to resolve differences and reach decisions among family members?	0—1—2—3—4—5
	6	Do family members or branches have diverging interests around the design of the future ownership structure?	0—1—2—3—4—5
	7	Do family members or branches disagree on dividends, investment, and/or employment policies?	0—1—2—3—4—5
Market and industry	8	Is the firm's core market characterized by limited growth opportunities?	0—1—2—3—4—5
	9	Is the firm capital-intensive, or does future development depend heavily on external financing such as share issues, bank loans or even private lending?	0—1—2—3—4—5
	10	Is the firm in an industry with increasing competition or in transition?	0—1—2—3—4—5
	11	Are operating costs deteriorating?	0—1—2—3—4—5
	12	Does the firm lack innovation and transition ability?	0—1—2—3—4—5
	13	Can the firm retain high-end talent?	0—1—2—3—4—5
	14	Is the local labor market thin, heavily regulated, and/or characterized by labor disputes?	0—1—2—3—4—5
Institutional	15	Is the firm's development influenced by macro-policy changes?	0—1—2—3—4—5
	16	Are there specific laws or regulations that constrain family businesses?	0—1—2—3—4—5
	17	Are inheritance tax/laws a constraint on succession planning?	0—1—2—3—4—5
	18	Do corruption and lack of enforcement of property rights constrain business activities?	0—1—2—3—4—5
	19	Is local government intervention intensifying?	0—1—2—3—4—5
	20	Is the firm's development confined by government-controlled factors and the market?	0—1—2—3—4—5

be open and inclusive, non-existent, or confined to a few key family members. Q4 identifies opposing interests and potential conflicts. Q5 asks if there is a governance mechanism, such as family meetings or arbitration procedures to guide the family through potential conflicts, and Q6 explores conflicts about ownership design, which can be a potential source of both incentives and disagreements. Q7 relates to disagreements over investment, dividend payouts and employment policies, which tend to intensify when the ratio between those who work in the firm and those who do not shifts in favor of the latter.

The next seven questions identify the presence of market and industry roadblocks. Since many family enterprises remain loyal to the products and markets on which the firm was founded, they are more affected by a general contraction in their core markets (Q8). Q9 asks how capital-intensive the industry is, since for many family firms raising capital implies losing control to banks or public equity markets. Q10 is directed towards industry trends such as consolidation. The media industry worldwide, for example, has seen a dramatic decline in numbers, with many family businesses being bought up by larger players. Q11 and Q12 identify the family firm's ability to stay competitive – can it control costs and keep on innovating? The last two questions address labor market issues – the firm's attractiveness to talented workers and whether the available talent pool is deep enough to meet its recruitment needs. A thin labor market is a serious roadblock because family firms tend to be loyal to the locality and less quick to move production to low-cost locations.

The final set of questions concern institutional roadblocks such as the macro economic environment (Q15). How sensitive is the firm to macro economic changes? Are there threats to the country's political and economic stability? Q16 asks about laws and regulations that impact family firms' abilities to operate. We saw in Chapter 3 how China's one-child policy and the Black Economic Empowerment Programme in South Africa have had serious consequences for family enterprises, albeit implemented for different social reasons. Q17 probes the influence of inheritance laws and taxes on the ability to transfer family firms to future generations. Q18 asks about corruption and legal enforcement. These are some of the biggest institutional roadblocks for the growth of business, notably in mainland China. Q19 asks if government intervention/regulation of business is intensifying and thus a barriers to growth. Finally, Q20 identifies to what extent the growth of the family business is restricted by government and market roadblocks.

The responses elicited to the above checklist will provide the owner-manager with a clear picture of the challenges they face today and in the future. In later chapters we provide many examples of how this information can be used to identify and implement governance mechanisms that safeguard both the business and the family. Beyond the detailed information embodied in the individual answers, we find it useful to aggregate the scores to a measure of the severity of roadblocks for the family enterprise under scrutiny. As a starting point questions can be given equal weight, but later it may be valuable to assign different weights according to the particular business culture in which a firm is located.

The family asset and roadblock checklists provide the basic input to the planning and cultivation steps of the *FB Map*. From the aggregated number of points for family assets and roadblocks we define the 'Family Sustainability Score' (or FS-score) by dividing the total family assets score by the total roadblock score. This provides a scale on which to measure the relative strength of the family assets and the constraints, and thus an indication of how challenging it will be to sustain the family business in the future. This simple number can be a powerful planning tool, in particular when benchmarked against other family businesses in the same cultural context. We provide an example of such benchmarking below.

Step 2: plan

In step 2, the *FB Map* provides guidelines for long-term planning of ownership and management by answering the all-important planning question: *Given the current and future set of family assets and roadblocks, what is the best ownership and management structure to sustain the long-term growth of the family business?*

We begin with the owner-managed firm, where ownership is concentrated within the family and the founder or heir is the top manager. This is the most typical form of family business across the globe and is depicted in the lower right quadrant of Figure 4.2. The *FB Map* shows which direction the owner-manager should take to maximize the long-term success of the

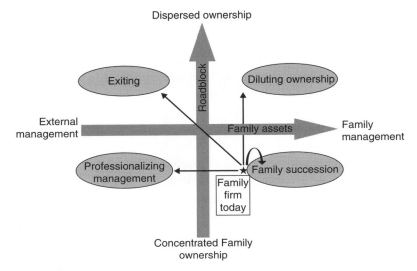

Dispersed ownership

Roadblock

Exiting

Diluting ownership

External management

Family assets

Family management

Professionalizing management

Family firm today

Family succession

Concentrated Family ownership

FIG 4.2   The *FB Map*: plan

business. Sustaining the close family business model through a succession of ownership and management will require the family to preserve and transfer critical family assets across generations. Since powerful family assets are often the foundation of a successful business strategy, the transfer of these assets to future generations of family stewards becomes crucial. Furthermore, the owner/manager should also think about how to design ownership and governance such that the roadblocks are reduced. The 40 members of the Henokiens – the association for family firms that have been owner managed for more than 200 years – are proud examples of families that successfully have remained in the bottom right corner of the *FB Map* for generations.

When family assets are disappearing it is time for the family to relinquish control on the management side through replacing family managers with external managers. If the family does not deliver any special contribution to the business, the firm will benefit from access to the external market, where the quality of managers is often higher than the caliber that arises from within the family. In this case, the business will move from the closed owner-managed model (lower right quadrant) to the separating-owner-ship-and-management model (lower left quadrant). The world-famous furniture chain IKEA is an example of a family business where the family has kept very concentrated ownership but where non-family members have taken over the top management positions.

For many family businesses, family assets continue to provide the foundation for a successful business strategy but the roadblocks are so challenging that the family chooses to dilute ownership by bringing in new investors. Such firms will move from owner-manager-model (lower right quadrant) towards the diluted-ownership model (upper right quadrant). The Hong Kong-based publicly traded East-Asian trading house Jardine Matheson is an example of an old family business where every new generation of the Keswick family continues to be involved in top management while ownership has been diluted through the use of public share markets.

Sometimes families can end up with a very small ownership stake but still contribute significantly on the management side. The Toyoda family owns less than 8 percent of Toyota Motors. Faced with heavy inheritance tax and capital needs, the family relinquished its controlling stake over time, but because of its unique contribution to building consumer trust in the quality of its cars, it still manages the company. Toyota is not unique in this respect. Other Japanese families such as those behind Kikkoman, Suzuki or Canon effectively control their companies without significant ownership.

Finally, in cases where family assets are non-existent or will die out with the current generation, and insurmountable roadblocks related to the continuation of close family ownership are foreseen, owner-managers should consider partial or full exit of the businesses. If the family delivers no unique contribution, and/or its ownership is characterized by family conflicts, or the business is too small to continue as an independent firm, there are good reasons to focus on an exit process. This may take the form of an outright sale of the company, but may be less dramatic, with the family staying on as a minority owner. Such firms move from the lower right corner towards the upper left corner in Figure 4.2. In recent years many families behind well-known luxury brands such as Donna Karan, Bulgari and TAG Heuer have sold their companies to the conglomerate LVMH.

Generally, we find it beneficial to use the aggregate scores above to advise on which pattern to take in Figure 4.2. If the aggregated Family Asset score is low, families should rely more on external management (move left); if it is high, they should continue being involved in top management (move right). If the Roadblock score is high, firms should search for new investors (move up); if the Roadblock score is low, we would advise the family to keep the firm closely held (move down).

The FS score defined in step 1 is a simple measure that reflects the ability to sustain the legacy of the family business. The higher the score, the greater the propensity for a within-family succession. The lower the score, the greater the propensity for an exit from the family business. An exit can take three forms: exiting from ownership, exiting from management, or both. Families with a very low FS score should carefully evaluate their asset and roadblock conditions and gauge the optimal exit path. A general rule of thumb is: An FS score significantly above 1 is high. One significantly below 1 is low.

The long-term planning process is fraught with uncertainty not least unforeseen changes in asset/roadblock conditions. Owner-managers should regularly evaluate whether any change in conditions will have long-term effects or is simply a temporary deviation from the predicted pattern. In the former case, the family should adjust its reading of the *FB Map* to meet the new conditions. Otherwise it should implement strategies to navigate through the short-term situation without altering the long-term path. In both cases, the approach to succession should be gradual and flexible but robust enough to cope with any immediate obstacles.

While we illustrated the power of the *FB Map* starting with the owner-managed firm, it is an equally powerful planning tool for family enterprises located in other quadrants. For example, Hermès was located in the lower left corner, since for more than a decade it has had Patrick Thomas as a non-family CEO. However, having decided that the family assets are crucial to sustaining the quality/history focused business model, they have chosen to appoint a new family member to take over at the top (moving to the lower right quadrant). Similarly, Toyota was in the upper left corner, with minority ownership and external management. But in response to the crisis in 2009 over safety issues, Akio Toyoda was appointed CEO (moving to the upper right corner).

It is also entirely possible for a family to buy back the family firm after a full exit. In the small Norwegian fishing town of Ålesund, the Kleven family had fully exited the shipyard their grandfather had founded between the two world wars. However, the family – led by a group of female cousins – recently managed to buy back the shipyard, and is now both controlling owner and deeply involved in management. Figure 4.2 can thus be replicated for family businesses initially located at any point on the diagram.

Step 3: cultivate

Having, in steps 1 and 2, chosen the tree and planted it in the ground, the foundation has been laid for harvesting the fruit in 20 years time. However, there is no guarantee of a good crop; the tree has to be taken care of until the fruit is forthcoming. The same is true of a family business. Once the path to succession has been decided, there is a need to plan and execute specific tasks that help the family achieve its long-term goals.

In Figure 4.3, each of the four planning paths generates specific tasks to cultivate the right form of governance.

For a *within-family succession* (staying in the lower right quadrant), the task is to cultivate a family successor and enhance family governance to share and transfer family assets. In Chapter 6 we discuss the four major challenges involved in a close family succession: (1) nurturing a culture of succession, (2) transferring the assets, (3) being competent, (4) planning,

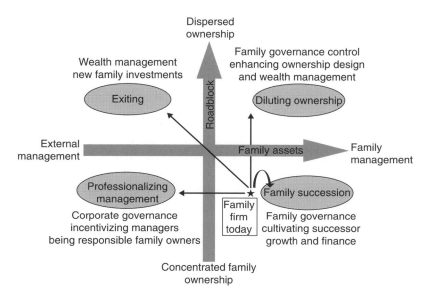

FIG 4.3 The *FB Map*: cultivation

and how the family can overcome them to maximize the chances of long-term sustainability. Since the family fortune is typically tied up in the firm, wealth management is not the most important issue here. Similarly, given its concentrated ownership, concerns about corporate governance, external investors and outside managers will not top the agenda.

A family that chooses to *delegate business decisions to non-family managers* (moving to the lower left quadrant) should focus on enhancing corporate governance by incentivizing and monitoring managers, and cultivating responsible family owners to work with them. The organization and composition of the corporate board is essential, as is the structure of the managers' remuneration and incentive programs. Here again, most families will have their wealth tied up to the business and wealth management is not necessarily top of the agenda. However, families on either side of the lower quadrants should cultivate ownership and control structures within the family to avoid future roadblocks

A family that chooses to *manage the business while substantially diffusing its ownership* (moving to the upper right quadrant) should focus on strengthening family governance and nurturing capable family successors in preparation for future succession. Ownership design is essential for such families who will be focused on how to keep control when new investors enter the firm and the following chapter aims at helping families in the search for suitable ownership models. Developing control-enhancing and control-preserving mechanisms that allow the family to feel secure while diluting their ownership stake will be high on the agenda. Wealth management will also be important, in particular when the introduction of new investors allows individual family members to accumulate wealth outside the firm.

A family that decides to *sell off the family business* (moving to the upper left quadrant) should seek to professionalize the business, arrange for family members to exit from their positions smoothly, and recruit non-family managers with appropriate skills. It should strive to improve corporate governance by setting up a board of directors, and to enhance the transparency of reporting. Once it establishes a fair price for the business, it should gradually offload the family shares and ultimately find a buyer. The family may introduce strategic investors such as a private equity fund to facilitate the transition. We discuss several models of exit in Chapter 7.

Of course, there will still be a need to manage their wealth after the exit. The family should therefore devise a wealth management plan to channel the family fortune towards the best possible use. Establishing a family office to deal with wealth management, tax issues and education programs for younger family members is recommended for rich families. Structuring corporate governance and nurturing succession candidates will be less important for families after exit.

Identify, plan and cultivate are the three steps that form the essence of the *FB Map*. They help to guide long-term planning and enable the family to choose the right path. But even when the right path is chosen, there is a lot of cultivation to do. The following chapters are dedicated to providing an 'idea bank' and tools for the planning process by focusing on ownership design, succession and exit.

How to apply the *FB Map* from outside

The *FB Map* is not only useful for families that run businesses; it is a powerful analytical tool for any individual, firm or institution with an interest in analyzing the future of a given family business.

For example, imagine a cash-rich enterprise analyzing the opportunities for acquiring a family business. In this instance, the *FB Map* can make two major contributions. First, it provides an indication of which target firms may come up for sale in the future by looking at their FS scores. Firms with low scores may be easier to acquire than those with high scores. Second, it provides valuable input to the negotiation process. For example, the buyer should take into account the fact that the value of family assets is, by definition, difficult or impossible to transfer to new owners. Third, understanding the roadblocks to continued family ownership and/ or management puts the buyer in a stronger negotiating position from which to obtain a lower price or more favorable conditions.

Now imagine a private equity firm investing in private family businesses. In this case, the FS score can be used as a screening device for potential targets. The identification of strong family assets and roadblocks can be part of the process of negotiation and structuring the investment, including pricing the equity stake. Thereafter, it can also provide useful input to foster future collaboration between remaining family members and the PE firm. If there are strong family assets, it will be important for the PE firm to keep the founder or other key family members active in management and to structure incentives accordingly. In many instances, PE firms are expert in implementing governance mechanisms that reduce roadblocks, be it structuring the finance side of investment, easing personal tensions within the board of directors, or providing input to aid market expansion.

Where the *FB Map* is used as an analytical tool for investing in publicly traded family firms, analysts can use the FS score as a rough measure of the long-term sustainability of a publicly traded family business and integrate this notion into their trading recommendations. The *FB Map* provides a structured approach to analyze strategic opportunities and key governance challenges relevant for private and institutional investors.

Similarly, the FS score can be used as an input to governments and regulatory agencies seeking to carry out a 'health check' on the family business sector in a given country, or for a multi-country analysis, for example by the European Union, the OECD or the World Bank. FS scores make it possible to compare the long-term sustainability of family firms both within and across national borders. They can be applied as input to recommendations for institutional changes in laws and regulations, and as input for developing national plans for improving the business environment for small and medium-sized enterprises.

The most critical factor for outsiders to be able to use the *FB Map* is effectiveness in gathering information about family assets and roadblocks from publicly available sources. To answer all the questions in Tables 4.1 and 4.2 it is necessary to be a family member who also holds a key position in the enterprise. Thus, we need to develop an alternative set of questions that can be answered by an analyst who do not have access to the family behind the enterprise being scrutinized. Again, this will depend on the cultural and political environment in which the firm is operating. In our experience there is significant variation in what counts as 'public information', as well as what information is most relevant as input to the *FB Map*. Rather than a universal checklist, it is important to adapt to individual countries or to different groups of similar countries.

To illustrate the power of the *FB Map* as a planning and analytical tool we applied it to a set of 15 publicly traded firms in China. We chose Chinese firms for two reasons. First, family businesses in China are young; the majority have not yet been through their first succession. Given the 'one-child' policy and the location of many family businesses in remote parts of the country, there is great uncertainty about which succession path is feasible or desirable. Second, as one of the most vibrant economies for future acquisitions, many private equity and other investment funds are looking carefully at opportunities in China. Our analysis thus serves as a blueprint for how to analyze Chinese family businesses, given the fact that relatively little information about firms is available.

Table 4.3 provides background information for our 15 selected family businesses. Note that there is significant variation in location, products and size. To analyze the firms, we first construct a set of questions to identify family assets and roadblocks for each firm in a way that does not require 'inside information'. Table 4.4 lists the questions, each with an explanation. Whereas the list clearly identifies family assets and roadblocks, it is different from the lists in Tables 4.1 and 4.2. This is partly because it is based on verifiable information but also because we have fitted it to a Chinese cultural and institutional framework.

Since the analysis is based on non-qualitative information, the questionnaire should be filled out using a 'yes or no' instead of the 0–5 scale suggested for family members. The analyst should give 'yes' answers a numerical score of 1 (and 'no' answers a score of 0), adding up the scores separately for assets and roadblocks to obtain the respective totals.

When we filled out the questionnaire for each of the 15 firms, in the 'Culture and Core Values' section under 'Family Assets', the average score was 0.45 per question, 'Leadership Characteristics' scored 0.53, and 'Political and Business Connections' scored 0.58. Clearly, connections are more important than either leadership or culture/values.

Under 'Roadblocks' the average scores for the three subgroups are Family 0.44, Market/industry 0.4, and Institutional 0.53. The political system would seem to be the biggest constraint for these 15 Chinese firms, but neither can family roadblocks be overlooked. As the founder ages, family clashes may start to surface, which can be just as destructive as institutional roadblocks.

Table 4.3 Company name, location, business and revenue of 15 Chinese family businesses

Company name (in English)	Company name (abbreviation)	Company name (in Chinese)	Headquarter location	Main business	Revenue in 2010 (¥ Billion)
Midea Group	Midea	美的集团	Guangdong	Home appliances	74.559
New Hope Group	New Hope	新希望集团	Sichuan	Fodder, finance, dairy, real estate, energy	7.785
Hailiang Group	Hailiang	海亮集团	Zhejiang	Copper products processing	9.053
Guilin Sanjin Pharmaceutical Co., Ltd.	Sanjin	桂林三金集团股份有限公司	Guangxi	Proprietary Chinese medicines	0.985
SANY Heavy Industry CO., LTD.	SANY	三一重工股份有限公司	Hunan	Construction and lifting machinery	33.955
Guangsha Construction Group	Guangsha	广厦建设集团有限责任公司	Zhejiang	Real estate, construction	2.273
Zhejiang Longsheng Group Co., Ltd.	Longsheng	浙江龙盛集团股份有限公司	Zhejiang	Chemical raw materials	6.677
Jiangsu Hongdou Industry Co., Ltd.	Hongdou	江苏红豆实业股份有限公司	Jiangsu	Textile	2.139
Lifan Industry (Group) Co., Ltd	Lifan	力帆实业（集团）股份有限公司	Chongqing	Motorcycle, automobile	6.771
GOME Electrical Appliances Holding Ltd.	GOME	国美电器控股有限公司	Beijing	Home appliances chain store	50.91
Chaoda Modern Agriculture (Holdings) Ltd.	Chaoda	超大现代农业集团	Fujian	Agriculture	6.964
BYD Company Limited	BYD	比亚迪股份有限公司	Guangdong	Rechargeable batteries, automobile	46.685
Li Ning Company Limited	Li Ning	李宁有限公司	Beijing	Sportswear	9.479
Nine Dragons Paper (Holdings) Limited	Nine Dragons	玖龙纸业(控股)有限公司	Guangdong	Paper products	17.746
Baidu, Inc.	Baidu	百度公司	Beijing	Search engine	7.915

Table 4.4 Outside check of family asset and roadblock in 15 Chinese family businesses

			Questions	Purpose of the question	Score (1 if yes; 0 if no)
Family assets	Culture and core values	1	Does the family or the firm have values related to the product characteristics?	Testing whether the family has injected its core values in the firm.	
		2	Do the explicit values of the family or the firm originate from Chinese culture or Confucianism or Taoism?	Whether the family values are of religious origin.	
		3	Is the main business driven by assets such as history, culture, craft and commercial traditions?	Whether the family links its family asset to a historical or cultural tradition.	
		4	Does the main business of the firm have more than 15 years of operating history?	Measuring the history of firm. Normally, the longer the history, the more likely it is to form a unique culture.	
		5	Does the success of the main business rely on a unique craft or secret recipe?	Determining whether the firm has a unique competitive advantage that can be protected by the family.	
		6	Does the founder or the firm have non profit-oriented goals and specific investments in energy saving, carbon reduction, environmental protection and charity?	Investigating whether the founder has strong values, whose influence can make a difference in corporate strategy and performance compared to other firms.	
		7	Does executive management or the board of directors include family members who are not the founder, the spouse or direct heirs?	Testing whether the family values are important beyond the immediate family.	
			Average		
	Leadership characteristics	8	Is the founder's level of education lower than a bachelor degree?	Testing whether the founder relies on experience leadership, which is relatively special compared with leadership based on academic knowledge.	
		9	Are there more than 100 search results related to the founder's ideas, speeches and conduct?	To see whether the founder has an open and visionary mindset.	
		10	On average, do non-family executives serve more than five years in office?	Testing the executives' cohesion and stability.	
		11	Do independent directors consist solely of university professors and bureaucrats?	Determining whether the firm leans towards family control by studying outside members of board. If the independent board lacks actual independence, it shows the board of directors is controlled by the family without an external balancing force.	

(continued)

Table 4.4 Continued

		Questions	Purpose of the question	Score (1 if yes; 0 if no)
Family assets	**Leadership characteristics**	12	Did the founder start the business with his sons or daughters; has the next generation been working more than ten years in the firm?	Inspecting whether the family has a potential future leader.	
			Average		
	Political and business connections	13	Among the family members that hold positions in the firm, are there any NPC deputies and CPPCC members, or industry association leaders?		
		14	Is the founder or his/her parents a former bureaucrat, or is any family member married to other business family or political figures?	Evaluating the family's political and commercial networks.	
		15	Are there any photos on the internet of the founder with political leaders at the provincial, ministerial or higher level?		
		16	Was the founder or any family member the recipient of an individual government-granted award such as 'Model Worker'?		
			Total Family Asset Score		
Road-blocks	**Family roadblock**	17	Is the founder over 60?	The age of the founder indicates how urgent the issue of family succession is.	
		18	Does the founder have only one child; are children under 18; or do none of them work in the firm?	Measuring the family's human resources. Generally, the more children, the better chance that there will be a capable successor.	
		19	Second generation family members have NOT worked in an outside firm for more than three years; and do not have a foreign master's degree or above	Investigating the competence of the second generation family members.	
		20	Does the founder or his/her family have less than 50 percent ownership; or does the firm have multiple founders?	Determining the potential challenge that family ownership may face. If the firm was started by multiple persons and the shares were divided equally, there is a greater chance of infighting in the future.	

Category	No.	Question	Notes
	21	Are there any reports on family member disagreements, or media scandals such as affairs with entertainment stars or spending extravaganzas?	Determining whether the family governance is to be improved. Those with a history of scandal and extravagance are probably not ideal successors.
		Average	
Market and industry roadblocks	22	Apart from the founder, are there any executives or directors who are current or former bureaucrats?	Testing whether the firm is overly reliant on government. Political connections can be a double-edged sword. Over-reliance may cause the firm to lose vitality.
	23	In the past three years, have there been published negative reports about the firm's product, management, public security, corporate governance, or was the company investigated?	Investigating the firm's public image.
	24	In the past three years, has the debt ratio increased, or cash flow/revenue decreased?	Investigating the strength of the capital chain and the severity of the competition the company faces.
	25	In the past three years, did the rate of revenue growth decrease, or is there no well-known brand?	Investigating the market situation of the firm.
	26	In the industry or the territory to which the firm belongs, is there increasing government control such as environmental, labor and security standards?	If yes, then the operating cost of the firm is increasing.
	27	Does the firm have constant and large-scale investment in R&D?	Measuring the firm's innovation and transition ability.
		Average	
Institutional roadblocks	28	Will macro-policy changes such as tax or currency adjustment, or international exchange rate fluctuations affect the company greatly?	Examining the influence of macro-policies on the firm
	29	Is there a serious social gap between the wealthy and the poor (the Gini coefficient > 0.45)?	Evaluating social stability
	30	In the past three years, was local GDP growth rate greater than the national average?	Local government's intervention in firms can be inferred from GDP growth rate. Those higher than the national average may be the result of boosting the political achievement, which calls for local firms' cooperation.
	31	Do the firm's operations rely on government resources such as land, minerals, other natural resources, utility, bank loans or government orders?	Investigating whether the company's resources and market are manipulated by the government.
		Total roadblock score	

The average across the 15 firms for 'Family Assets' is 7.8, and for 'Roadblocks' is 6.87. The lower roadblock score may be related to the sample chosen, since most companies selected are successful listed firms (even if some problems have been exposed), hence they face fewer market and industry constraints. Or it may be because these firms have developed since China's economic take-off and have not yet faced a serious recession.

We are now ready to answer the following question: *Given the identified family assets and roadblocks, which succession model should these firms follow?* To answer it we place each firm according to its score on family assets and roadblocks on the *FB Map*. According to the total in the two dimensions, we can then estimate the optimal ownership and management structure (which may deviate from the actual structure).

Of the 15 sample firms, 6 of them fall in the lower right quadrant in Figure 4.4, which means they have sufficient family assets and not too many roadblocks for the second generation to continue as owners and managers, thus becoming a real family firm.

Notably, although the model suggests that Midea Group has the conditions for a family succession, in fact the founder's son Jianfeng started

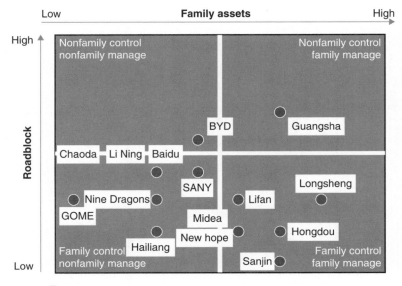

FIG 4.4 / The *FB Map* for a sample of 15 publicly traded Chinese companies

another firm without ever holding positions in his father's company. Midea is now run by professional managers, but we cannot rule out the possibility of Jianfeng taking over the holding company and becoming the successor in the future.

Another seven firms fall into the lower left quadrant in Figure 4.4, indicating that future ownership and management may be divided, becoming a family controlled, professionally run enterprises. The last two fall into the upper right and upper left quadrant, but very close to the 8-point boundary. Although we cannot be sure of their succession model, compared to the other 13 firms, these face more roadblocks, meaning there is a higher chance of family ownership dilution in the future.

Investigating a succession model from the family sustainability score

Investors, potential partners, governments and families want to know how sustainable the current ownership and management structures are, and which structures are most promising for the future. To this end we constructed the FS score for our 15 Chinese companies. As before, the FS score is equal to the ratio of family assets score to roadblocks score (Figure 4.5).

The higher the ratio, the more promising a family succession will be for both ownership and management. Remember, the FS score only reflects

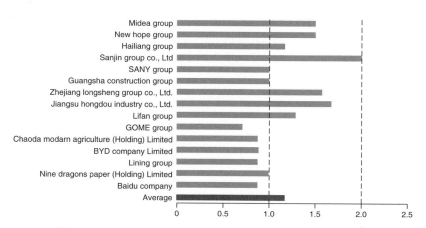

FIG 4.5 / The family sustainability score for 15 publicly traded Chinese companies

the current situation. For example, the successors to the founders of Baidu and GOME are still too young for a family succession to occur in the near future. But this does not mean the founders cannot plan for family governance in the long term to cultivate a suitable family successor. Generally speaking, with an FS score greater than 1 it is relatively safe to plan for family succession in the near future. Hence, an outside investor that wants to buy into companies in order to have a controlling interest should think about targeting firms with the lowest FS scores, which have fewer alternatives and may be more interested in outside investment or an outright sale.

Highlights

- The Family Business Map – *FB Map* - is a powerful structured tool for long-term planning in family firms.
- The *FB Map* is a three step procedure:
    - Step 1 identifies family assets and roadblocks.
    - Step 2 plans the overall governance strategies that leverage the value of family assets and reduce the cost of roadblocks.
    - Step 3 cultivates the chosen governance models by setting up key focus areas for the future development of the family and the firm.
- The *FB Map* can be used to analyze the sustainability of family firms for analysts and potential investors.

In the next chapter we discuss how the *FB Map* can be applied to design the best possible ownership structure to sustain the future of the family firm.

5

Ownership Design

Designing an optimal ownership structure is one of the most important – and challenging – tasks any family business can engage in. The ownership structure affects the incentives, behavior and ultimately the performance of family members, family managers and other stakeholders in the firm. It determines the distribution of power between individuals within the family and with non-family owners. It is particularly crucial where family members disagree about how to take the firm forward, not least because it determines the allocation of voting rights, the transferability of owner-ship rights, and how profits and losses are shared.

One of the most striking features of family firms is the variety of own-ership arrangements. We begin with examples of old European family firms whose ownership shares have been diluted and compare this to an interesting case of active ownership design in Asia. This leads us to a brief discussion of how ownership design is related to changes in roadblocks. Next we identify the four principal challenges in designing an ideal own-ership structure: (1) to raise capital to expand without giving up family control, (2) to counteract ownership dilution as a result of the power of numbers, (3) to go public, listing the businesses either as a whole or in part, (4) to integrate institutional ownership such as trusts and foun-dations. Given the current popularity of trusts, we reveal some of the pitfalls that can be encountered when using trusts to hold complex assets. We end with four mini-case studies of how ownership can be structured to resolve specific challenges, in the hope that these will inspire families facing such situations.

Variety of ownership structures

In many family firms, ownership is diluted with every new generation that comes along. In Europe there are numerous examples of families where hundreds – even thousands – of members hold shares. More than 200 family members own the German industrial conglomerate Thyssen. Around 600 members of the Mulliez family own shares in the holding company that controls the giant supermarket chain Auchan, the sports retail chain Decathlon, and many other successful retail brands. Almost 1,000 members of the Wendel family own the private holding company Wendel Participation, that owns around 38 percent of the publicly traded Wendel Investissement. In Belgium, the Janssen family counts close to 2,500 family members, who together have a controlling stake in the 150-year-old Solvay petrochemical group.

One typical method that large European firms have implemented to fight the power of numbers is to entrust the ownership of the family firm. Maersk – the biggest shipping company in the world and founded in 1904 – is a publicly traded family firm where the family controls the company through three foundations where two have charitable purposes and one is a family foundation. These foundations control the majority of the voting rights in Maersk and almost half of the outstanding shares.

While these old and successful European families have designed ownership and governance to overcome the issues that arise when individual ownership stakes shrink, not every family is so fortunate. Ownership dilution can eliminate all sense of incentive or individual responsibility, and ultimately end in deadlock between different branches of the family – hurting the family as well as the business. We have seen many examples from all over the world of deadlocks in family firms arising because of opposing interests between family branches. Redesign of ownership structures can be a powerful way of solving such deadlocks, – as the following example shows:

Li & Fung

Li & Fung Limited is a global trading group supplying high-volume, time-sensitive consumer goods. Garments make up a large part of the Li & Fung business, as does the sourcing of fashion accessories, furnishings, gifts, handicrafts, home products, promotional merchandise, toys, sporting and travel goods.

Founded in Guangzhou (Canton) in 1906, Li & Fung is headquartered in Hong Kong, from where it co-ordinates the manufacturing of goods through a network of 70 offices in over 40 countries. While cost considerations have resulted in the concentration of manufacturing activities in Asia, recent years have seen an expansion of Li & Fung's quick-response capabilities in the Mediterranean, Eastern Europe and Central America, areas that are closer to its customers in Europe and the US. Li & Fung is the controlling owner of a number of other public and private firms that together form the Li & Fung Group. Li & Fung Ltd has an annual turnover of USD 12 billion and employs 15,000 people worldwide.

The experience of Li & Fung exemplifies the seriousness of the control issue of ownership dilution, although the Fung family was ultimately able to find a solution. One of few companies in Hong Kong with more than 100 years of history, Li & Fung was listed on the Hong Kong Stock Exchange in 1974. The founder had 11 children, all of whom inherited shares in the business, as did members of the third generation. Before Victor and William Fung took over the leadership in the 1980s, no single member of that third generation had a controlling stake.

Victor had a Masters degree in engineering from MIT and a PhD in business economics from Harvard Business School, where he later joined the faculty. His younger brother William was a Harvard MBA. When summoned home by their father, the brothers quit their jobs in the US and returned to Hong Kong, sensing that the family business had problems. Family members were fighting, branches were divided and it was impossible to restructure the governance of the firm. Thus Li and Fung was in a deadlock when the two brothers returned and their combined ownership stake were not big enough to impose their view on the family.

When China and Britain began discussing the future of Hong Kong in the mid-1980s, some members of the family felt that the impending return of the territory to China would mark the end of Hong Kong; Victor and William saw it as an opportunity. They borrowed billions of Hong Kong dollars from a consortium of banks, used part of the loan to buy out the publicly traded shares in 1989, and the remaining funds to buy back shares from other family members at an 80 percent premium on the share price. After this family version of a management buyout, they re-listed the company on the Stock Exchange in 1992.

To reorganize the ownership of Li & Fung Ltd, they set up a holding company (of which they each held 50 percent) as the sole owner of the original company, which in turn was the controlling owner of the publicly traded retail part of the Li & Fung empire. An interesting feature was the establishment of a family trust, the J.P. Morgan Trust Company (Jersey) Limited, for the family of Victor Fung. Its existence ensured that the future involvement of Victor's branch of the family could not dilute ownership to the extent that he had experienced in his own generation.

The brothers thereby secured a controlling stake to make the necessary changes to the family business. Although reforming the ownership was a painful process, without it they would not have taken the business to the next level, nor would Li & Fung be the successful and respected company it is today. We believe that Li and Fung is a prime example of how visionary family members can design new ownership structures to reinvent the family business.

Roadblocks that shape family ownership

Ownership can be active or passive – passive if it is diluted over generations as more family members receive shares. Active ownership can take many forms such as listing the company, introducing trust and/or foundational ownership, or concentrating ownership by buying out other family members. We emphasize that sound ownership design is

sound ownership design is the key to good governance

the key to good governance and the most effective way to minimize the impact of roadblocks, whether they arise in the family or the market, or in the institutional environment. Figure 5.1 illustrates how active ownership design aims at minimizing the cost of the current and future roadblocks that can be identified in the family business.

Family structures and family development is one of the most common drivers for families to redesign ownership structures. As we have seen, ownership diffuses over time as the family extends. Larger families divide into branches and diverging interests often arise. The path towards smaller ownership shares and increasing confrontation emphasize the need to change ownership. There are many objectives that a revised ownership structure aims at fulfilling. Some of the most common include: securing the family's ability to control the firm in the future, allocating control power to the most talented and interested individuals, allowing individual family members to sell shares at will, allowing non-managing family members to sustain a certain standard of living and avoiding future family conflicts.

The family's extension will be influenced by long-term demographic trends – the birthrate, social and cultural values – which have an influence on family size. In China, for example, the one-child policy means that ownership diffusion is less of an issue for family firms. Indeed the main issue they have to contend with is often a shortage of family talent or interest to sustain the business. It has to be assumed that many family firms either hire non-family managers (relinquishing control) or sell the business (relinquishing both ownership and control) sooner than elsewhere in Asia.

In Chapter 3 we discussed how inheritance law and taxes may affect how ownership can be redesigned around succession. In some countries the law

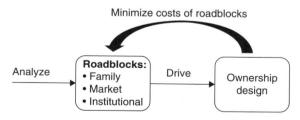

FIG 5.1 Active ownership design aims at minimizing the cost of current and future roadblocks

imposes an even distribution of ownership among family members; in others it is more flexible, that is, allowing greater concentration. In North America and Europe, family members receive relatively equal shares of ownership, although those more involved in the business tend to get a bigger share. In countries with high inheritance tax, owners may be obliged to sell off or divest businesses before retirement. Some may choose to transfer ownership to a trust, foundation, or foreign entity which is subject to lower tax rates.

Customs and norms can have a strong say in how ownership is distributed. In Asian countries where the Confucian influence is still strong, sons inherit the lion's share of ownership, while daughters must be content with a minority share – or even no share at all and compensation in the form of a dowry upon marriage. In the Middle East, most family members are included in the business in accordance with custom and Sharia law, where sons get ownership but also have an obligation to take care of female family members. While allowing only male heirs to inherit clearly discriminates against daughters, it serves to slow the diffusion of ownership as well as the family fortune.

Successful family businesses often face the dilemma of how to finance new investment: when new business opportunities come along they lack the internal funds and human resources to pursue them. The option of borrowing or selling shares to raise finance jeopardizes family control. Indeed, many enduring family businesses have resisted the temptation to venture out of their comfort zone (the stable local environment) for this reason. In capital-intensive, cyclical and fast-changing industries or markets, however, families often have to make significant investments to stay competitive. The moment they sell equity to outsiders, they start to lose control of the business. While borrowing from the bank may be preferable to equity financing, it is not necessarily a better option because the bank can abruptly cut off funding if the loan/interest is not paid on time. In extreme cases a family may have to file for bankruptcy and lose the business to the bank.

The four most common challenges in ownership design

As discussed above, the urge for redesigning ownership is often driven by the presence of current or future roadblocks threatening the stability of the firm and the family. In the following chapter we will provide a detailed discussion of the four most common challenges. Retaining control while growing; dealing with ownership diffusion due to the power of numbers; using trusts and foundations; and going public. Each of these challenges can potentially change the involvement of the family, the future of the business, and the relationship between individual family members. For each challenge we will provide examples and discuss advantages and disadvantages of specific ways of redesigning ownership to mitigate the cost.

Challenge 1: retaining control while growing

Control and ownership go hand in hand in the early life of a family firm. The entrepreneur sets up a firm and keeps ownership in the family. Even if outsiders are invited to invest, the family typically retains a majority share, giving them absolute control over decision making. The need for external capital to finance new business activities can threaten that control, particularly when markets increase in both size and geographical spread.

At the beginning of the 20th century, there were around 1,500 primarily family owned newspapers in the USA. As the media industry developed on the product front (from individual newspapers to media .), the market front (from local to national to global media markets) and the technology front (from physical typesetting and printing to electronically delivered newspapers, radio and TV), most of those 1,500 families exited the business. Only a handful managed to find a way to raise enough capital to be able to stay in business without losing control to new investors, being bought by a competitor, or simply going out of business.

In the luxury industry, many family businesses faced a similar challenge in the latter part of the 20th century. In 1977, Henry Racamier took over the management of his mother-in-law's family firm, Louis Vuitton, a manufacturer of luxury luggage and accessories. Like many luxury firms, Louis Vuitton went through hard times in the 1960s and 1970s, when demand for traditional luxury items fell dramatically as the baby boomers came of age. To remain in operation many family owned companies resorted to short-term solutions. While they continued to control design (though not always production), they delegated retailing to specialists in the field, often merely for a license fee. When Racamier discovered to his astonishment that it was the retailers who were making the biggest profits, he resolved to transform Louis Vuitton into a vertically integrated operation.

Racamier's plan required that Louis Vuitton open its own retail stores, cutting out the middleman. His timing was good. In the West, the 'Reagan Revolution' was reviving the taste for luxury after the hippie era of indifference to appearances. Moreover, markets in Asia and the Middle East were taking on a growing importance. In 1978, Racamier opened five outlets in Tokyo, offering Louis Vuitton products at prices comparable to those in Europe.

By 1984 global sales at Louis Vuitton had increased 15-fold, to USD 143 million, with profits of USD 22 million, and a profit margin of 40 percent, nearly double that of its competitors. To finance further expansion Racamier sold stock in the company both on the Paris Bourse and on the New York Stock Exchange. He merged with Moët Hennessey to form a luxury conglomerate, LVMH, which immediately began to acquire other luxury brands.

Since the profit potential of his strategy was clearly going to last into the foreseeable future, Racamier's innovations forced all family run luxury firms to ask themselves the same questions.: Did they wish to remain small family businesses with an elite customer base in Europe, or were they ready to risk entering the global marketplace? And if they chose to do so, how should they design ownership and finance investment to avoid losing control of the business?

From then on, new ownership structures developed in the luxury industry in response to what were essentially market roadblocks. Old companies like Hermès, TAG Heuer and Bulgari, as well as first- and second-generation companies like Donna Karan and Polo Ralph Lauren, went public. Other families sold up or affiliated with powerful luxury conglomerates such as LVMH or Kering (former PPR). Thus the conglomerate luxury business group evolved as a response to changing market roadblocks.

Careful ownership design allows families to balance the need for growth and control in fast-growing business ventures by creating control-enhancing mechanisms and severing the direct link between investment and control. In rethinking the relationship between the right to a return (income) and the right to a say (votes), they manage to concentrate control in the hands of the family while sharing the returns with a broader group of investors. There are many ways families can disentangle the right to a return from the right to a say, keeping the latter in the family's hands.

Pyramids.   A pyramidal structure is used to preserve control in the family, even when ownership is diluted. The pyramid represents a chain of corporate control, typically with a private family controlled investment company at the top that has a controlling stake in the next level intermediate corporation, that has a controlling stake in a second-level company, that has a controlling stake in a third-level company, and so on. By maintaining a controlling stake down through the pyramid, the family has de facto control over all the corporations in it, even though it is not entitled to a large share of the cash flows from the lower layers.

To see the power of a pyramid to preserve control, imagine a family with an investment company that owns 51 percent of the shares of Firm A. Assume that the remaining 49 percent of the shares are held by other investors, none of them having more than 10 percent. Firm A controls Firm B through an ownership stake of 51 percent, and the rest of Firm B's shares are held by smaller investors. Who receives the returns from Firm B and who controls it?

If Firm B decides to pay a 1 dollar dividend, Firm A receives 51 cents. If Firm A decides to pass this on to its owners, then the family will receive 25 cents, that is, 25 percent of the return generated by Firm B. Almost three quarters of the returns are distributed to the smaller investors in both B and A. Looking at the control side, the family has absolute control of Firm A, since it has 51 percent of the voting rights and there are no other significant shareholders. Furthermore, by controlling the board in Firm A, the family has de facto control of Firm B, since Firm A is the controlling shareholder. Hence the pyramid structure secures absolute control of the firms for the family but financial returns are shared with other investors.

Why would an outside investor invest in either Firm A or Firm B if the family has de facto control? Many investors prefer passive investing because they do not have the resources to engage in actively governing the business they are investing in. This is particularly true of institutional investors. They trust the reputation of the family and delegate control accordingly.

Many family business groups around the world use pyramidal structures to concentrate control. Toyota Motor, Samsung Electronics, Levi Strauss, Du Pont, and so on, are all controlled via pyramidal structures, as are a number of major Canadian family firms such as Bombardier, Bronfman, Desmarais, Irving, McCain, Molson and Péladeau. The Agnelli family in Italy controls its many businesses through a highly elaborate pyramidal structure involving many layers. So does the Korean Shin family that created the Korean/Japanese Lotte conglomerate. The pyramidal structure first evolved as a way to control their business activities in both Japan and Korea but was later used as an efficient way of expanding their global activities.

Dual-class shares.   Larry Page and Sergey Brin founded Google in 1998 and took it through an IPO a mere six years later. Google floated in 2004 with two share classes: the superior voting shares carry 10 times as many votes per share as the limited shares. Today the founders are estimated to hold around 30 percent of the outstanding stock but have absolute control over the corporation since they own most of the voting shares. While it is too early to say if Google will ever develop into a fully fledged family firm, dual-class shares are a common vehicle for families that want to float the shares without giving up control, as seen in a number of family based media companies in the United States.

The essence of dual-class shares is simply the different voting rights they carry. Those with superior voting rights are held by the family, while those with limited voting rights are sold to outside investors. This way the family keeps absolute control over the business but shares the returns with the other investors.

What proportion of voting rights do the two classes have each? In practice, this will be partly determined by corporate law, which varies from one country to another. In Northern European countries, for example, where dual-class shares are particularly popular, superior voting shares typically carry ten times as many votes as the limited voting shares. In many countries it is also possible to issue preference shares which have no voting rights but give preference to dividends in compensation.

The Wallenberg family in Sweden controls a large number of listed and private Swedish corporations through a combination of dual-class shares and a pyramidal ownership structure. Dual-class shares are used to keep control over their investment company, Investor AB. The A shares constitute around 40 percent of the capital but control around 87 percent of the votes; the B shares constitute around 60 percent of the capital but control only 13 percent of the votes. Through a family foundation the Wallenbergs own a large portion of both classes of shares. Thanks to its voting shares the family is entitled to almost half of the votes even though it owns only a fifth of the capital.

Cross shareholding.   This is an ownership structure whereby companies hold stakes in each other (e.g., two family corporations have a 10 or 20 percent share in each other). Cross shareholdings are popular among Japanese business networks and include a large number of firms in the *keiretsu* system. One of the most well-known examples is the Mitsubishi network of corporations, set up by the family with the family controlled Mitsubishi Bank in the centre (known as the Bank of Tokyo-Mitsubishi UFJ after a series of mergers). Its close cross-ownership structure includes big names such as Mitsubishi Corporation, Kirin Brewery, Mitsubishi Electric, Mitsubishi Motors, Nikon, Nippon Oil and others. Another prominent example is the Mitsui family's controlling interest in a web of corporations centered around Mitsui Bank (now Sumitomo Mitsui Bank). Firms in this cross-ownership structure include Fuji Photo Film, Mitsui Real Estate, Mitsukoshii, Suntory and Toshiba.

Cross ownership is not exclusive to Japan. The Shin family use cross ownership in their ownership design of the Lotte group. The Agnelli family has cross ownership between firms in their business group. The late Wang Yung-ching used cross ownership between the four key companies in Formosa Plastics Group to reinforce his control of the group.

Besides pyramidal structures, dual-class shares and cross ownership, other mechanisms include voting caps (no shareholder regardless of size can hold more than a certain fraction of the votes), golden shares (shares with specific rights that, for example, can block the sale of the company), and staggered boards (boards cannot instantly be replaced when majority ownership is traded). One of the most popular is to set up a trust or a foundation, which we return to below.

Challenge 2: dealing with ownership diffusion due to the power of numbers

We have seen several examples of how the power of numbers dilutes ownership. In the typical scenario, the founder divides the ownership of the business among his children, and they do likewise, until after several generations ownership is diffused. Although the business remains family managed, there is no single dominant owner. As the ownership circles widens, communication costs increase, along with the problems of 'free riders' and lack of consensus. Shoring up control becomes a matter of urgency. So, what are the options?

Dual planning (early phase remedy).   A family board or committee can be set up to elect managers and handle various governance issues. If the business has no board of directors, a family board can take on this function. If it does have a corporate board, the family committee will serve as an additional layer of communication where the members discuss family and corporate issues and reach consensus, thereby facilitating the corporate board's job. It may also bolster the corporate board by freeing up seats to bring in non-family members with outside expertise and unbiased opinions. A family board should include representatives from all branches of the family (typically five to seven people), and meet two to four times a year.

A family board is an early phase remedy, but if the family grows rapidly or there is a lack of communication between members it may be less effective in defending their interests. Problems associated with family boards include conflicts of interest, domination by one branch, and failing to provide unbiased advice. Good communication is a prerequisite for a well-functioning family board, just as conflict and poor communication in a family will undermine it.

Pruning the tree.   When ownership dilutes and family governance fails to resolve issues of incentives or conflicts of interest, it is time to rearrange things. Many old families resort to mechanisms of ownership redistribution that allow them to prune the tree either gradually over time or through major readjustment once every generation. The most typical forms of redesigning ownership include unequal transfer of ownership to future generations, the creation of an internal market for trading shares and buying out individual or group of family members.

We saw how the third-generation Fung brothers re-concentrated family ownership of Li & Fung through a family buy-out, but such moves are extreme as well as rare. A modified approach is to set up a family share buyback program to acquire shares held by family members with only a remote interest in the business. In Europe, the Wendel and Mulliez dynasties have established an internal market for buying and selling family shares, which they open for a short time, typically around the annual family assembly. One family we know of has developed an electronic stock exchange where family members can submit, sell and buy offers at any time.

In a smaller owner-managed corporation, the family will often prune the tree once every generation. Remember the Henokiens, whose member companies are at least 200 years old and include the Hōshi Ryokan in Japan? Other members, such as the Dutch trading company van Eeghen, the Dutch alchohol producer de Koyper, the Italian confetti company Peligrino, the Italian music company de Mouzini, the French spice company Thiercelin and the Japanese confectionary company Gekkonen – have all found ways to prune the ownership tree, either by conferring ownership on one child in every generation, by buying out less active family members, or by dividing business activities between family members.

One important issue when families establish an internal market for shares or engage in share buybacks is how to price them. If the business is publicly traded, the buyback price can be set at the market price plus a predetermined premium. If it is privately held, then a predetermined method of valuation should be performed to establish the buyback price. We advise family members to take this step very seriously and engage trusted outside advisors. Too often, conflicts over valuation can tear families apart or be a catalyst for future conflict.

An alternative to reducing the number of family owners is to transfer ownership to a trust. A family trust is an efficient way to solve the governance constraints related to the burgeoning family tree and to bind the family's interests together for the foreseeable future, which leads us to the next challenge.

Challenge 3: using trusts and foundations

Trusts play a significant role in societies where common law prevails. There are an estimated 400,000 to 500,000 family trusts in New Zealand. A significant part of the ownership of many large family businesses in the United States, including Wal-Mart, Ford Motors, the New York Times and Cargill, are placed in trusts. In a sample of 216 publicly listed companies in Hong Kong, we found that almost one third were controlled by family trusts, including flagship companies such as Sun Hung Kai Properties, Cheung Kong Holdings, and Henderson Land.

All around the world, trusts are commonly advocated by banks and corporate finance institutions as the standard solution to questions related to ownership design. While we affirm that trusts can be a powerful mechanism to protect ownership, in particular for tax planning, families should be aware of the challenges that can arise.

A trust is a legal entity governed by a charter. The rules of trust ownership are regulated by national laws which vary significantly across countries and even regions. Trusts can be perpetual or they can last for a fixed number of years, and may be costly to dissolve before the stipulated date. Trustees are appointed to govern a trust and to protect its interests. They tend to include capable and interested family members, and/or outsiders with special capacities in the management of trusts and firms. Thus, for a trust that owns a controlling share of a family business, the trustees act as the link between the family and the board and management of the firm. Beneficiaries – those who receive the benefits (payouts) from the trust – are typically family members, but they can include a broader group of recipients. Charitable trusts distribute funds with a social or charitable objective.

Foundations are created to administer a large ownership stake in a particular company, often donated by the founder. In most countries it is impossible to reverse the transfer and there will often be restrictions, such as that the foundation cannot sell the company or dilute its ownership stake beyond a certain limit. Thus it serves as a vehicle for the founder to extend family control after his/her death. The foundation itself is a non-profit entity which has no owners or members. Its board members are often self-elected, constrained only by law and the foundation's charter, which frequently stipulates a broadly defined social purpose – for example, to act in the company's 'best interest' and use excess revenue for charitable purposes. Often, but not always, the founder's family continues to play a role in the management of the company.

Foundations are popular in Northern Europe, where a number of well-known companies have set up such structures, including Bertelsmann, Heineken, Robert Bosch and Carlsberg. Similar structures were not uncommon in the US until 1969, when a law effectively prevented foundations from owning more than 20 percent of business companies.

THE NEW YORK TIMES

When Adolph Ochs purchased *The New York Times* in 1896, it was the beginning of a legendary newspaper as well as a family owned corporation. *The New York Times* had existed since 1851, but was suffering from rising costs. Ochs managed to cut costs in half and increased daily circulation from 9,000 to 76,000 in only in three years. Ochs, originally a typesetter, was also the controlling owner and publisher of a local newspaper in Tennessee, *The Chattanooga Times*. Through a combination of trustworthiness and integrity, Ochs managed to become a respected and successful publisher, unlike his competitors who did not hesitate to distort the truth and invent scandal.

Ochs incorporated his personal principles in the *New York Times*. He separated news from editorial and political opinion and dropped the price of the newspaper. By the 1920s daily circulation had risen to 400,000. Ochs's daughter Iphigene had married Arthur Hays Sulzberger, who began working in the company and succeeded Ochs when he died in 1935 as publisher and president.

Under the management of Arthur Hays Sulzberger from 1935 to 1961, *The New York Times* diversified into radio, expanded across the entire USA and to Europe, and saw circulation increase to 713,000. As publisher he continued the principles of his father-in-law and was a strong advocate of press freedom and democracy. In addition to its financial success in the period,

> the *New York Times* won the prestigious Pulitzer Prize for outstanding journalism in the USA several times. Today it is the newspaper that has won the most Pulitzer prizes and is regarded by many as the finest newspaper in the world.

The New York Times is, in our view, one of the most inspiring cases of trust ownership. To mitigate the consequences of the power of numbers, Adolph Ochs established a family trust owning 50.1 percent of the common shares before his death (1935), the remaining shares being owned by his spouse and children. The charter stipulated that the trust would hold the controlling stake until the death of Adolph's daughter Iphigene, after which the shares should be evenly distributed among her four children. The trustees were Iphigene, Arthur (Punch) Sulzberger, and Julius Ochs Adler, his nephew.

For Adolph Ochs, the trust was a commitment to continuing family ownership and family management at least for the next generation. By concentrating control in the trust and allocating the shares to his grandchildren after it ended, he ensured that de facto control of the firm would remain in the hands of the Ochs-Sulzbergers for at least 50 years. The trust was also a commitment to give the four grandchildren (and their future offspring) an equal opportunity to be involved in the *New York Times*, since no individual could take over the corporation.

In the 1960s, new roadblocks arose as a result of developments in the newspaper industry, and new capital was required to fund its expansion. Once again, a re-design of the ownership structure was the key to raise capital without losing family control. In 1961, Arthur Sulzberger listed the *New York Times* on the New York Stock Exchange. The power of the family was asserted by issuing dual-class shares, with the trust retaining the superior voting shares, leaving little power in the hands of the new minority investors.

The trust was reorganized in the 1980s (Iphigene was by then in her nineties), when Punch initiated the formation of four new trusts, one for each of his siblings and himself. When the old family trust was dissolved upon the death of their mother, the holding would be distributed to the four new ones, each to remain in effect for 21 years after the death of the last of their 13 children. Furthermore, the family committed to vote unanimously on any matter that could potentially entail the loss of its control over the newspaper. The agreement went into force four years later, when Iphigene Ochs Sulzberger died in 1990, at the age of 97.

Notice that with the new trusts, history repeated itself. Control of the *New York Times* was left firmly in the hands of the four siblings, and would remain there for the next two generations, implying that all 24 grandchildren of Iphigene Ochs Sulzberger had secured an ownership stake in the global media empire built upon the world's most influential newspaper.

The New York Times is a fascinating illustration of how to use a family trust to perpetuate control within the family and to counteract governance problems arising from the natural dilution of ownership. It is also an example of how powerful individuals (Adolph Ochs and Punch Sulzberger) were able to preserve family control for half a century beyond their own lifetimes.

Pros and cons of entrusting controlling ownership

Around the world, service providers promote trust ownership as a powerful solution to almost any challenge that families face with respect to an increasing number of family members, diverging interests, and the issue of careful tax planning. Obviously, it is worth asking if trust and foundation ownership is superior to direct shareholdings by individual family members. In the following paragraphs we discuss some of the advantages and disadvantages of trust and foundation ownership. Through this discussion we will discover that there are indeed many roadblocks that can be mitigated with the help of trusts, but that such ownership structures also have the ability to prolong existing roadblocks or create entirely new ones.

Let's imagine that, as retirement approaches, a founder wants his three sons to take over the family business. He hopes that the brothers will stick together and the family business will not be broken up. How should he transfer the controlling ownership? Should he set up a trust and appoint the three brothers as managers? Or should he divide and distribute the ownership among them?

As mentioned, there are several advantages of giving a trust or foundation a controlling ownership share. First and foremost, it ensures family control of the business. Trusts and foundations are governed by a charter, typically drawn up by the founder (or the current majority owner) who can stipulate under what conditions the trust can be dissolved and/or exit from ownership. Indeed it's possible to stipulate that the trust or foundation will always (or at least for a number of years) be the controlling owner of the family firm.

Second, it opens up an opportunity for the separation of ownership and control, the appointment of non-family professional managers, and the introduction of governance by a board of trustees. This is a powerful mechanism because it allows family members to be beneficiaries without being responsible for managing the firm. Hence, only the capable and interested family members will be selected to manage the trust, and thus control the firm. It is also possible to appoint expert outsiders to be trustees. In other words, the founder may appoint trustees on merit, or from the head, and designate beneficiaries from the heart.

Third, in most countries a family or charitable trust is a powerful tool for tax planning in general, particularly during a succession. If controlling ownership is transferred to a charitable trust or foundation, the transfer is typically tax exempt. Thus, entrusting ownership can be even more attractive in countries with high inheritance tax.

For these key reasons trusts are becoming increasingly popular in many countries. Given that financial advisors aggressively promote them as a solution to almost any roadblock, it's essential that families understand the limitations and constraints involved in entrusting ownership of their business.

it's essential that families understand the limitations and constraints involved in entrusting ownership

The deadlock problem. The first challenge is the lack of flexibility to resolve conflicts. A pre-condition for a family trust to work is for sound family governance to be in place to secure long-term family harmony. A trust prevents ownership transfers between family members as these are restricted. A trust also prevents one family member acquiring the ownership shares of other family members. So if there is conflict the firm and the family risk ending up in deadlock, with it becoming impossible to make changes in the way the firm is operated because any new initiative is blocked by opposing parties within the family. Such situations can have severe consequences for family businesses. The Kwok brothers, who belong to one of the largest property development groups in Hong Kong, offer an interesting illustration.

KWOK FAMILY TRUST AND SUN HUNG KAI PROPERTIES GROUP

Sun Hung Kai Properties (SHKP) is the second largest business group in Hong Kong. From its core business of property development, it has diversified into telecommunications and other non-property ventures.

Kwok Tak Shen, the founder of SHKP, transferred his 43 percent controlling interest to a trust before he died in the 1980s. Four family members – his wife and three sons (Walter, Raymond and Thomas) – were beneficiaries in accordance with the trust deed. The trust was understood to be non-dissolvable and the entrusted ownership non-transferable, apparently in accordance with the founder's wish to ensure perpetual family control and for the three sons to work together to sustain the group. The trust elected, and the board of directors appointed, the eldest son as the chairman of SHKP, while the other two were appointed vice-chairman and managing director respectively.

After Kwok Tak Shen's death, SHKP continued to prosper under the second generation. The business broadened out, taking control of a number of cell phone and transportation companies. Together the three brothers became the third-richest business family in Hong Kong, and duly ascended the Forbes list of the world's richest families.

The peaceful days of the Kwok family ended abruptly in 1997 when Walter was kidnapped by an infamous gangster, Cheung Chi Keung, known as 'Big Spender', and was held blindfolded in a cage for more than a week. He was released without police involvement after the family paid a ransom believed to be around HKD 600 million. After his arrest, Cheung Chi Keung confessed to having held Walter in a wooden cage for several days. The ransom was delivered in HKD 1,000 notes packed in 20 containers.

Walter returned to Sun Hung Kai Properties after his release but was badly shaken. He kept his position as Chairman of the Board and CEO but left much of the day-to-day management to his younger brothers. These traumatic events may have been the incident that triggered the family fight that exploded in public 10 years later. But the origin of the fight relates back to Walter's youth when he felt in love with an ambitious lawyer, Ida Tong Kam-hing. His father disapproved of the relationship and forced him to enter an unhappy marriage that only lasted a year. Walter subsequently married his current wife Wendy Lee.

After recovering from the abduction, Walter brought his former love Ida Tong Kam-hing into the company, where she became increasingly influential and had a large say in management.

On 8 February 2008 the family fight exploded in public when a press release announced that Walter would take a temporary leave of absence for personal reasons. During the following months, the feud unfolded in the media on daily basis. Walter was voted off the board of directors and removed as chairman by his brothers, citing mental issues. He took his case to court in Hong Kong, claiming that his brothers had set him up by luring him to a doctor, who had prescribed medicine that he did not need to take. The court eventually dismissed the case.

Walter was definitively removed from the chairmanship and replaced by his then 78-year-old mother, Mrs Kwong Siu-hing. Shortly afterwards she ceded the chairmanship to the two younger brothers. But the family crisis did not end there. The Hong Kong Independent Commission Against Corruption, tipped off by an unidentified source, prosecuted the brothers in 2012 for corrupt land deals. Walter was suspected of being the person who passed the commission sensitive information.

The outcome of the legal process is still pending. In 2012, Mrs Kwong removed Walter from the beneficiaries of the family trust, apparently unhappy with her eldest son. But given the trust structure, it would prove to be extremely complicated to divide the holdings between the brothers or to buy out the eldest brother since he did not have personal ownership. In the absence of a trust holding, the family could have bought Walter out of the business, or they could have split the business such that he would own his own part and the mother and the two younger bothers the rest. However, this was not possible because ownership was vested in a trust that was believed to be non-dissolvable and to have no legally specified end. The ensuing deadlock during recent years has resulted in enormous loss of value for the owners of Son Hung Kai shares.

Ownership by way of a trust is common property. Family members are no longer the direct owners of the business; they are beneficiaries of the trust. The voting, dividend and transfer rights of the beneficiaries are allocated according to the charter, and enforced by the board of trustees which comprises key family members, lawyers and accountants. Family members do not hold a known percentage of family ownership they receive a set of 're-packaged' non-transferable rights.

The risk of deadlock is especially high when a founder sets up a trust in perpetuity, specifying in the charter that under no circumstances can the trust be dissolved or the assets transferred, which can limit operational freedom. Due to unforeseen circumstances the feasibility of such a provision may be challenged or may need to be reinterpreted. For example, the more than 100-year-old charter of the Carlsberg Foundation stated that the Foundation should always be the dominant owner. If this had been interpreted as meaning that the foundation should always hold at least 50 percent of the shares, it would have blocked the possibility of Carlsberg buying up other breweries and reaching the size it has today. Since the family no longer exists, the Carlsberg company had to challenge the provisions of the charter in court to be able to re-interpret it in a way that did not constrain the expansion of the firm's activities.

Common pool problem.   Trust ownership has a profound impact on the incentives of family beneficiaries. Because they share in a common pool of assets and have no right to sell their shares or to exit, they behave somewhat like employees of a state-owned enterprise; they prefer the business to distribute dividends, employ friends and relatives, sponsor interesting non-business related activities, and so on. Moreover, they may be reluctant to spend corporate funds on investments that do not promise a near-term payoff.

Both the deadlock and common pool problems of trust ownership become more serious when the size of the family increases. In our research on Hong Kong firms controlled by family trusts, we found that among large families, businesses paid 62 percent of earnings as dividends when ownership was held in a trust, compared with only 43 percent of earnings as dividends when ownership was held by individual family members. The family businesses under trust ownership spent 9 percent of revenues on long-term investment, while those under direct family ownership reinvested 11 percent of revenues. When family size was large, trust ownership was associated with slower sales growth and slower growth in job creation relative to that of individual ownership. Thus, this shows that trust ownership in Hong Kong seems to dampen firm performance among large public traded firms.

Trust ownership performance (measured by market capitalized value divided by book asset value) is on average no different from that of firms controlled by individual family members. However, there are specific situations in which trust ownership underperforms, particularly when the family is large and when the business is in financial distress or in a period of turmoil.

Trust governance problem.   Dispute resolution depends on the board of trustees. Since the board is typically dominated by family members, there is a lack of unbiased third-party arbitration. The board of trustees may be dominated by a single family member (typically the manager or a senior member) and his/her allies, and therefore their decisions may be self-serving at the expense of the interests of the family as a whole. Non-transferable ownership heightens the tunneling incentive when disputes go unresolved or when the dominant individual is in a desperate situation.

Who's-the-boss problem.   Over the years, as family members lose interest in running the family business, the managing role is taken over by non-family professionals. Family members cease to serve on the board of trustees and are replaced by non-family individuals with varying degrees of competence in running a business. The family can end up being passive owners, while the professional managers have all the power. In extreme cases, the owners' influence is eliminated and the firm is managed as if it had no owners.

To sum up, entrusting ownership has clear advantages for many families, but there are considerable risks involved. Careful design of trust charters will reduce but not eliminate such risks. Some guiding principles for founders to consider when entrusting the ownership of their firms in this way are:

Flexibility on transferability.   Founders should be aware of the draw-backs of giving a trust or foundation a controlling interest. While the desire to protect assets and preserve control within the family is under-standable, non-dissolvable trusts and non-transferable ownership do not guarantee business continuity, as we have seen. Founders must build in flexibility, for example by making the trust dissolvable in the foreseeable future, say, after 20 or 30 years. Descendants then have the opportunity to form new trusts if they agree to continue the family business venture. *The New York Times* is an excellent example of such flexibility.

Strong family governance.   Good family and trust governance are criti-cal for trust ownership to function. Are there strong family values binding the current and future family members together? Do (and will) they find common ground on basic values? Are they sufficiently loyal to these values to be responsible to the family and the business when making deci-sions and interacting with other members? Do they defer to a common authority to resolve their differences? Are they accountable to future as well as current members? Only with strong family coherence can families survive the roadblocks; formal ownership and governance mechanisms alone won't work. The case of the Kwok Family Trust and Sun Huang Kai Property Group is a stark reminder that a trust cannot save a family busi-ness when family coherence has been blown to pieces. In such cases the trust becomes a roadblock that makes it difficult to rearrange ownership in a way to stop infighting.

Trust governance.   Trust governance needs to be in place to allocate and enforce ownership rights. In principle, cash flow rights are divided among beneficiaries according to the charter, which is enforced by the board of trustees. In addition to implementing cash distribution, the trust board designates corporate directors to exercise the voting rights of the trust, one of whom will serve as the chairman of the board, as well as taking other decisions based on the stipulations of the charter. For example, in the case of the *New York Times*, the charter stipulates that decisions have to be approved by six of the eight beneficiaries. It also sets out the rules regarding subsequent modifications to the charter, such as a change in the beneficiaries. Thus the trust board has real power, so it is indeed crucial to find and incentivize trustees who are capable and engaged in their job.

Let's return to the SHKP-Kwok foundation. After its restructuring in 2012, the new distribution rule was probably divided three ways: a third to Walter's branch (except Walter himself), a third to Raymond's branch, and a third to Thomas's branch. The restructuring in effect deprived Walter of the right to receive cash flow interest from the trust. The board of trustees holds the Sun Huang Kai shares and ensures that income is distributed according to the charter. However, from the actions taking by the family members, it is clear that the board of trustees do not have real power. The real power of control lies with the mother and matriarch, Mrs Kwong. She organized the ousting of Walter and took over as chairwoman. It is interesting to note that officially she is only a beneficiary of the trust, not a trustee, according to information disclosed by the Hong Kong Stock Exchange.

Hence, while control is officially allocated according to the charter, in reality it is essentially in accordance with custom or norms. It is the mother who is the ultimate decision-maker, not the trustees. This is not uncommon among Asian family trusts. But a serious question remains. After the mother dies, who will replace her as the new authority, and upon what rules will that authority be based?

The continuity of the business is closely associated with trust governance. The board of trustees should be structured and should function to ensure decisions are taken in the interests of all beneficiaries. It may be beneficial to appoint neutral non-family member(s) to the board of trustees in addition to family members. All branches of the family should be represented on the board rather than allowing one branch to dominate, just as rules and procedures should be transparent.

The case for charitable trusts/foundations. Transferring a controlling ownership stake to a charitable organization offers the obvious advantage of tax exemption. It also projects a positive image of the family and the business to society. Charitable ownership also has an important impact on business continuity.

In Chapter 1 we saw how Wang Yung-ching, founder of Formosa Plastics Group (Taiwan), transferred his controlling ownership stake to a charitable foundation. He did not write a will before his death at the age of 92; instead he wrote an open letter to his children indicating that he had decided to leave his business empire to the community. Wang's decision was inspired in that it combined a philanthropic gesture and avoidance of the 50 percent inheritance tax rate effective in Taiwan at that time. It was a product of his legendary persistence in 'getting to the root of the problem' by asking the right questions. Whose business is Formosa Plastics? Should I maximize the value of the business or the value of the family? Are the two conflicting? He must have decided that the business should remain within and serve society, and that his children and grandchildren should earn a living elsewhere or prove their ability before being elected to manage the business. Ultimately, he believed that leaving the business to society was best for the Formosa Plastic Group and for his family.

Every successful entrepreneur has to ask and answer similar questions. Wang Yung-ching spent a lifetime building a successful business empire, but his family was built less coherently: he had 4 wives and 13 children. Creating a sustainable family culture and values is very difficult in such a context. Without them, the business would lack the stable foundation to survive after his death, so instead of consigning it to the battleground of a family feud, he left it to the community.

Charitable ownership offers an opportunity to introduce formal governance to family business. The board of directors of the charitable organization can include family members as well as non-family managers and outsiders. By bringing in outsiders with no particular business experience, charitable trusts enlarge the who's-the-boss problem we discussed above. Trusts laws often require a minimum number of outside trustees for a trust to qualify as charitable; these can be prominent individuals, community leaders or charity experts. For example, the board of Chang Gung Memorial Hospital (the institution that controls Formosa Plastics Group) is composed of one-third family members, one-third non-family managers, and one-third outsiders, in accordance with Taiwanese law. Trustees in the Carlsberg Foundation – the controlling owner of the Danish beer group Carlsberg – are for the most part distinguished individuals with a scientific or cultural background but little business experience. As a result, it is often the case that the controlling owner ends up being a passive owner leaving actual leadership to the executive management.

Challenge 4: going public

Many family owners are tempted to float the company (make shares available) on the stock exchange. This may seem an attractive way to raise capital to finance new investment or to generate cash to distribute among family members. However, we have seen many cases of family owners who have been unpleasantly surprised after going public. Some are so disappointed that they end up delisting the family business – a costly process which may require the support of banks or other investors. The process of listing and delisting the family business could in many cases have been avoided if the family entrepreneur had better understood the challenges involved before embarking on the listing process.

Let's begin by looking at some of the many benefits which potentially can be achieved through listing the family business:

First, it can provide a significant amount of cash which can be used to finance larger investment projects in the firm. Raising funds through listing on the stock exchange is often the key to finance future growth. To keep control, families can choose only to list a minority of the shares or use control-enhancing mechanisms such as shares with different voting rights, keeping those with superior voting rights within the family.

Second, going public can also provide a significant amount of cash to increase the personal spending power of family members and allow them to invest in other projects. A related point is that it makes the shareholdings of individual members more liquid. In a growing family there will be diverging opinions about selling shares; listing the company allows each member to make their own decision about selling. Some will want to sell, either to spend the money or to diversify their investments. In private firms it can be complicated to find family members who are capable of and interested in buying other family members' shares, whereas in a publicly traded firm individuals can choose to sell their shares on the stock exchange, which makes it much more flexible.

Third, listing the firm provides the family with a clear valuation of their ownership stakes. Valuation of private firms is difficult. There may be opposing interests in establishing the true value of the company. A lower valuation will be in the interests of those seeking to minimize wealth tax. A higher valuation will be in the interests of those who want to exit the business, but will also drain resources from family members who stay in, or from the company itself if it ends up buying back shares from exiting family members. It is our experience that valuation of shares in private family firms often generates significant conflicts that can tear entire families apart.

Fourth, going public may be a first step towards exit. If roadblocks multiply and family assets are less crucial to the business, then in accordance with the *FB Map* the family will move towards exit. Going public can support that process because it provides a structure that allows the family to gradually reduce its role in the firm both on the ownership and the management side.

Indeed, given the benefits of going public it may be difficult to understand why an initial public offering (IPO) is not the ultimate goal of all family businesses. In a nutshell, there are three main reasons why listing is often a disappointment for the family. First, being a publicly traded firm is very different from being a private firm. Corporate legal requirements are much stricter for publicly traded firms. They need to hold shareholder meetings, appoint a board, deal with minority owners and so forth – all in a highly regulated fashion. If the founder is used to running the firm like a dictatorship or through board meetings over Sunday lunch, it can be a real shock to have to deal with the board of a publicly traded company. In many countries there are strict regulations about what, how and to whom information can be delivered. We have met numerous entrepreneurs who find dealing with the board and the new owners of the business extremely cumbersome. Indeed they often feel that the new owners contribute little on the strategic side but constrain the flexibility of management on the governance side.

Second, even if the family retains a majority stake, the new owners have a voice and will want a say in how the family runs the business. They may start to contest the leadership: Are they managing the firm well enough? Are they working for their own interests or in the interests of the owners as a whole? Are they able to create shareholder value or could others do better? Since publicly traded firms are more visible, unhappy minority owners may use the media to criticize the family. We know many entrepreneurs who have been hugely disappointed with the new investors, including some entrepreneurs who attempt to ignore the existence of those investors and continue to run the firm like a closely held family business.

Third, the family's control of the company may ultimately be challenged. Even when ownership is carefully designed, going public may create long-term dynamics that threaten the family's control – either in the immediate aftermath or years later – but which are not foreseen at the time of the IPO.

going public may create long-term dynamics that threaten the family's control

One illustration of the long-term consequences of going public is the Cadbury chocolate empire, whose Quaker-based family assets we discussed in Chapter 2. As the *FB Map* predicts, over the years the ownership structure was re-designed several times in response to changes in family, market and institutional roadblocks. The first significant change to Cadbury's ownership profile came at the end of the First World War, when Cadbury merged with its main rival for almost a century, the Quaker firm Fry, partly to save Fry and partly to block the entry of Swiss and Dutch rivals into the British chocolate market. Officially it was a merger of equals, but in reality Fry became a subsidiary of the stronger partner Cadbury. The merger had the effect of doubling the number of family members who held shares in the firm but were not actively involved in management.

Fast forward to 1945, when there was growing pressure from the Cadbury and the Fry families to take the company public. The ownership structure was already complicated and there were more than 200 individual family members altogether. True to their Quaker values, the second-generation Cadburys, Richard and George, had given much of their fortune away to charitable trusts that owned most of their shares. Many of the Frys had seen little income from their shareholdings, yet their capital had been tied up in the business since 1919 without a market for the shares. Faced with the challenge of supporting poorer family members (who were only rich on paper) they had three options: (1) they could continue without making changes and leave family members to find their own ways to earn income, (2) the managing family members in Cadbury could prune the tree and buy out family members from both sides who wished to sell, (3) the family could list the company, which would provide an objective valuation of the shares and allow family members to sell at will.

Option (1) was difficult because of the pressure from non-managing family members who wanted to sell and because of real concern for the Fry family's situation. Option (2) was not possible because almost all the wealth of Richard and George had been transferred to charitable trusts, so they did not have the resources to buy out members who wanted to exit. Only option (3) was left. Fortunately, it happened to coincide with the ambitions of the young managing family members who wanted new capital to support additional growth of the company.

Cadbury – or *The British Cocoa and Chocolate Company* as it was officially named after the merger with Fry – was floated in 1962. At that time, little thought was given to the issue of control in the future. After all, the family and the trusts were majority owners with more than two-thirds of the shares, so how could their control be challenged? In 1969, Cadbury merged with Schweppes (partly to protect Schweppes from being taken over by even bigger players), creating one of the largest confectionery companies in the world. Over the decades of rapid global expansion that followed, there was a sharp reduction in the ownership stakes of the family. The charitable trusts and foundations sold their shares to reduce the risk of being over-dependent on one company.

In January 2010, KRAFT bought Cadbury in an uninvited takeover. We describe the process of this takeover in details in Chapter 7. For now it suffices to say that the loss of Cadbury was a result of the dynamic changes in the structure of ownership over a period of 50 years after the firm was listed.

The loss of Cadbury as an independent company was a shock to the family and to the British public. But in retrospect, it was simply a logical consequence of the way ownership had been designed and developed over time. The successful Quaker entrepreneurs in the second generation had given most of their wealth to trusts and foundations. The merger with Fry increased the ratio of passive owners to active managers. Ambitious growth plans had to be financed with new capital – the main reason for going public. Further expansion, seen as a key to staying independent, triggered the merger with Schweppes. When the trusts disinvested to reduce their company-specific risk, the family's direct and indirect control through ownership vanished. Speculative investors forced the de-merger of Schweppes and Cadbury. Ultimately the hedge funds played an active role in the takeover process, paving the way for Kraft's success.

Clearly the Cadbury family could not have foreseen the loss of the company when they took the decision to list in 1962, but the case provides a powerful example of how ownership is a dynamic concept; going public can, over time, set in train unforeseen changes in ownership and control. Having thought that the company was safe in 1962, disinvestment, a forced de-merger, and 40 years of aggressive expansion, made it vulnerable to a hostile takeover.

Could the Cadburys have held on to the company if their ownership stake had not been diluted over time? Probably, but even a big family stake may barely be enough to protect family ownership of a publicly traded company. This is the experience learned by the Hermès family, whose strong family assets we also discussed in Chapter 2.

Like other families in the luxury segment, the descendants of Thierry Hermès chose to raise capital from an IPO in June 1993, in part to enable the company to pursue its own style of vertical integration, but also to allow dissatisfied heirs to liquidate their company shares. Hermès listed all its shares but around two-thirds remained in the hands of the more than 50 family members. The IPO was very successful, and the initial offering was oversubscribed more than 30 times. Since the family still controlled two-thirds of the company, the leadership felt they were safe despite the listing. Surely there was no way an outsider could threaten their control?

They were in for a surprise.

In October 2010, CEO Patrick Thomas was interrupted by a telephone call during a bike ride in the Auvergne. It was Bernard Arnault, head of the luxury conglomerate LVMH. Thomas was shocked to learn that Arnault had acquired a 17 percent stake in Hermès and wanted to buy more, as he was planning to announce at a press conference a couple of hours later. The first thing that went through Patrick Thomas's mind was that this was no way to do business: Arnault had not even requested a meeting prior to the move. It was, he concluded, 'ungentlemanly'.

Most of the family agreed that Arnault was an unwanted interloper whose methods and style would ruin the unique culture of Hermès. He was, they feared, not only ruthlessly aggressive like an 'American businessman', but his formula for success mixed glitzy advertising and outrageous publicity stunts with a continual search for designers with a cult following – a blend entirely unsuited to Hermès. Arnault insisted he was no threat to the autonomy of the company or its brand – he only wanted to help, to make Hermès more profitable.

How could Arnault be a threat to the Hermès family who jointly owned more than 70 percent of the shares? The key to understanding the situation is that ownership was diluted even further after the 1993 IPO and the family shares were now held by more than 70 family members, each of whom had very small shares. Even if they seemed united, Arnault was planning to negotiate with every potentially interested member who would sell. In such a big family, he reasoned, there would always be individuals willing to sell at the right price. Not only did Arnault have the cash, he was willing to be patient. And he was given some encouragement when one branch of the Hermès family publicly advocated collaborating with him.

What could Hermès do to stop Arnault? Since trading in family shares was not restricted, there were two possible actions: either the family could buy up all the outstanding shares and de-list the company, or they could make Arnault a counter-offer and pay him a premium to leave the company alone. Neither option was attractive: de-listing would require a lot of cash, and the family was reluctant to pay Arnault a large premium to leave the firm.

The solution they found centered on the tradability of the family shares. In response to the threat the family created a holding company that had first right to buy any family shares. Through this mechanism they could prevent at least 51 percent of the shares of family members being transferred (to LVMH) for the next 20 years. For the time being, the holding company would keep 73.4 percent of the shares in the hands of the descendants of Thierry Hermès.

But while this solution offered powerful protection of the family's interests, it would be seen as costly for minority investors who might have expected a large premium if Arnault had been successful or the firm had de-listed. Though LVMH appealed against the measure, arguing that it was not in the interests of shareholders, a court upheld the legality of the arrangement.

The Hermès family had protected themselves by creating a holding company. But they (and other family entrepreneurs like them) learned a hard lesson. And although the holding company was legal in France, it may not have been legal in other countries like the UK or the USA. Re-designing the tradability of publicly traded shares has a significant cost for minority shareholders who originally invested under a different set of rules. In this case they were not compensated. Would the French courts have come to the same conclusion if Hermès had not been an icon in the luxury industry of France, and Bernard Arnault's aggressive tactics had not strained his relationship with the French government? This is an interesting question, subject to speculation, but one that we will never know the answer to. What is clear, however, is that the family's control of Hermès would have come under severe pressure if the courts had reached a different conclusion.

It is worth pointing out that the family could easily have protected themselves in 1993 when the company first went public. If the holding company or other control protecting mechanisms had been in place at the IPO stage, new investors would have known this when they invested, and the price of the shares would have incorporated the lack of a potential takeover premium.

The Cadbury and Hermès stories are dramatic illustrations of how going public can have long-term implications for a family's ability to control the business. They teach us how control of even the biggest family businesses can be lost if the listing process is not carefully designed.

Four inspirational cases in ownership design

As indicated at the beginning of the chapter, the goals of ownership design are to secure control, provide incentives, and mitigate conflict. Below we examine several real life cases of ownership partition. We hope these examples provide inspiration for family entrepreneurs engaged in the process of re-designing ownership, as well as an opportunity to learn from their successes and failures.

Case 1: effects of critical minority shares

Founded by Kam Shui-fai (甘穗煇) in 1942, Yong Kee evolved from a modest food stall in to an internationally renowned restaurant in Hong Kong. Famous for its roast goose, it was ranked by *Fortune* magazine in 1965 as one of the top 15 restaurants in the world, and was the only Chinese restaurant on the list. Yung Kee is owned by Yung Kee Holdings Ltd, a private holding company.

Following the founder's retirement, his two sons Kam Kin-sing (甘健成) and Kam Kwan-lai (甘琨禮) took over and successfully ran the business. After the chairman passed away in 2004, the shares were divided among his children. Kam Kin-sing and his younger brother Kam Kwan-lai each received 45 percent, while their younger sister Kam Mei-ling received 10 percent (a share that was first given to a third son who was terminally ill).

The younger brother Kam Kwan-lai was later found to have secretly acquired the 10 percent holding from his sister, thereby accumulating 55 percent to his brother's 45 percent. His attempts to secure control of the company triggered a bitter dispute between the two. In March 2010, Kam Kin-sing applied to the High Court for liquidation of Yung Kee Holdings Ltd if Kam Kwan-lai refused to buy out his stake. In 2013, the Hong Kong courts finally approved Kam Kin-sing's application to liquidate Yung Kee Holdings Limited, ruling that it would not affect the shareholders, customers or employees. However, the court was not able to enforce the ruling because the holding company was registered in the British Virgin Islands. Just weeks before the ruling, Kam Kin-sing suddenly passed away. Press reports claimed that his death was related to the family business woes.

The founder had given 45 percent, 45 percent, and 10 percent to his three children in the hope that the brothers would work together and jointly make business decisions while taking care of the younger sister. This division resulted in an unintended outcome. There are several lessons to be learned here. The first is that (45–45) equal share ownership design does not guarantee family harmony or prevent family fights. The second is that the ownership division weakened the control of the enterprise and exacerbated the effects of the conflict on the family business. Third, minority family owners (like the sister) often have an incentive to sell family shares and exit (as the saying goes, 'a bird in hand is worth two in the bush'). In short, an unbalanced ownership partition like the 45–45–10 split is not sustainable in the long term.

However, there was a positive feature of this arrangement. Family ownership was quickly re-concentrated within one branch of the family (the younger brother). In less than two years of taking the dispute to court, the holding company was liquidated and his ownership of the restaurant was secured. This highlights ownership transferability as an important mechanism for family conflict resolution. The swift conclusion contrasts with the slow progress made by the Kwok family, whose controlling interest in SHKP was held in a family trust, thus preventing resolution by ownership transfer.

The founder of Yung Kee chose not to follow the Chinese tradition of giving majority ownership of the family business to the eldest son, perhaps for good reason. But the cost of the ownership structure, at least in the short term, was soon apparent – disruption of the business by a family feud. If business stability is the prime consideration, he should have given one of his sons at least 50 percent of ownership to secure effective control, for example a 51 percent-39 percent-10 percent split.

Case 2: dual-class family ownership

Before his retirement, a founder divides and distributes his sole ownership of a significant business to his wife and six children. Two classes of shares are created, one with voting rights, the other with no voting rights but rights to cash flow. The only son (and successor CEO) receives 48 percent voting rights and 20 percent dividend rights. The five daughters each receive 7 percent voting rights and 15 percent dividend rights. Finally, the mother receives 17 percent of voting shares and 5 percent of dividend rights.

By observing the pattern of the resulting voting and dividend rights, we can guess that the founder designed the dual-class ownership structures with two considerations in mind: control and equality. The son (and future CEO) has almost half of the voting power. His business decisions are almost uncontestable unless all the other family members unite against him. The allocation of dividend rights is more even among the six children, with the mother receiving a much smaller share. The dividend distribution is primarily based on ensuring equality among the children.

In this example, the dual-class structure enables the founder to separate voting rights from dividend rights, since the two are based on different criteria. Voting rights are allocated to promote efficiency in corporate decisions while giving right of veto to the rest of the family. Dividend rights are allocated such that all family members can obtain enough income from the company to enjoy a decent standard of living. A potential drawback is that the son, as the new CEO, may have an incentive to use his voting power to 'tunnel' cash for his private benefit while refraining from paying a dividend. Since the son is a residual claimant for one-fifth of the value created in the company, he may choose to enhance his private consumption through the company, for instance by letting the company pay for houses, cars or holidays. Or he could make the company invest in other business activities that would give him a larger share of the outcome. Such activities have the potential to create family conflict. Where serious family conflict arises, it may be urgent to re-design the ownership structure again. One possible option would be for the son to buy back the minority ownership of the other family members.

Case 3: interlocking ownership

Now let's consider a family with 80 years of business history, currently managed by the third generation. The founder has four sons, all entrepreneurial. The firm diversified into four different businesses in the 1970s and early 1980s, all under one roof. It was understood by the four branches that each branch owned 25 percent of the business.

It so happened that one branch of the family was more successful than the other three, and that there were disagreements among the four branches. They tried creating a family board in the 1980s, but failed because it was dominated by one branch. Eventually, the family firm was broken up into four businesses and a cross-ownership structure was implemented in which each of the four branches owned 75 percent of the business they respectively managed, and collectively owned 25 percent of each of the businesses run by the other three (Figure 5.2).

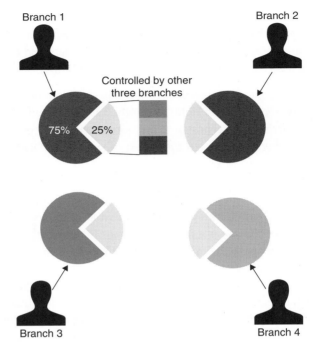

FIG 5.2 / **Cross ownership within a family with four branches**

The family hoped the cross-ownership design would provide autonomy in each of the four businesses while giving all members an incentive to uphold family values and share resources. To date, the family has maintained this ownership structure. We find this is an interesting case of providing incentives for each branch to develop their own businesses while keeping the overall family cohesion. Hence, we believe this cross-ownership model can be an inspiration to other families where different branches are managing separate business divisions in the business group.

Case 4: family holding company

A founder has a controlling ownership of a holding company, which in turn has sole or majority ownership of four subsidiaries, each managed by his three sons and a son-in-law. Neither the sons nor the son-in-law have a stake, or only a minority stake, in the subsidiary he manages. The founding father wants ownership of the holding company to be divided among his four children after he dies.

Under the holding company structure, the sons and son-in-law are in effect subsidiary managers, receiving a salary as compensation. They have an additional incentive to maximize the value of the subsidiary, hoping to get a larger ownership stake of the holding company after the father dies.

One advantage of the holding company structure is that each of the subsidiary managers benefits from a common pool of family assets. They may even enjoy full autonomy if the father delegates decision-making power. In addition, if any family members are in dispute, the subsidiary in question can be carved out from the holding company and sold to the respective manager (a son or the son-in-law). The downside of the holding company structure is the risk of breaking up the business after the father dies, with the four each obtaining their share of the holding company. Therefore, the holding company structure is not a stable structure unless the family shares strong values and has robust family governance.

Discover more

Bennedsen, Morten, Robert J. Crawford, and Rolf Hoefer. Hermes. Case Pre-Release version, *INSEAD*, Fall 2013.

Cadbury, Deborah, and Morten Bennedsen. Cadbury – The Chocolate Factory: Sold for 20p. (Part 2). Case Pre-Release version, *INSEAD*, Spring 2013.

Leung, Winnie S.C. Concentrating Ownership in Family Firms: The Case of Family Trusts. PhD thesis. The Chinese University of Hong Kong. 2010.

Villalonga, Belen, and Chris Hartman. New York Times Co. Harvard Business School Case (207–113; 209–017), 2008.

Highlights

- The ownership structure affects the incentives, behavior and ultimately the performance of family members, family managers and other stakeholders in the firm.

- Sound ownership design is the key to good governance and the most effective way to minimize the impact of roadblocks, whether they arise in the family, the market or the institutional environment. Flexibility is important since it is likely that the optimal structure will have to be readjusted over time as the family and the business grow.
- The four most common challenges in designing ownership structures in family firms are:
  1. to raise capital to expand without giving up family control
  2. to counteract ownership dilution as a result of the power of numbers
  3. to institutionalize ownership using trusts and foundations
  4. to go public, listing the businesses either as a whole or in part
- Given the current popularity of trusts in Europe and Asia, it is important to understand that trusts and foundations can raise additional challenges such as deadlocks and free-rider problems.
- Our recommendations are to have procedures for dissolving a trust and to be careful in choosing competent trustees.

We now turn to the topic of family succession. We will discuss the biggest challenges that family firms around the world face during the transition from one generation to the next, and how long-term planning can help overcome them.

6

Succession

For all family firms there comes a point when the founder or current steward has to retire. In a perfect world, the succession plan will have been communicated to the entire family well before that time comes, after the current family leaders have thought hard about the right model for the transition. They will have chosen the best time to step aside and let the next generation take over. After years dedicated to the family business, they will catch up with life 'on the outside', having no further involvement unless called upon for a historical perspective or advice. The next generation will agree that the chosen model is best for the company and the family, and will happily take up their new roles as owners, managers, or without direct involvement in the firm.

Sadly, succession scenarios often bear little resemblance to the above ideal. Indeed in many cases, the patriarch (or matriarch) makes no succession preparations whatsoever, formal or informal. The warning signs of a heart attack are rarely so clear that they can't be ignored by busy business leaders. Long-term planning is difficult and challenging; it raises so many company, personal and family related issues that many business leaders postpone it forever.

It is a fact that succession is one of the most crucial points in the life of any family firm, be it the first, second or third time. In this chapter we examine succession within the family, that is, where the controlling ownership is passed down from one generation to another. Our discussion focuses on how families can prepare for succession through understanding the most common challenges that they face. We discuss transfer of ownership between generations and the trade-offs embodied in choosing between future managers from within or from outside the family. In the next chapter we will discuss exit, both on the individual owner/manager level and on the level where the entire family leaves the business.

succession is one of the most crucial points in the life of any family firm

Our point of departure is the *FB Map* outlined in Chapter 4 and summarized in Figure 6.1. In an ideal world, family succession occurs when there are strong family assets and few roadblocks. The assets constitute the foundation of a successful business strategy and can simply be transferred from one generation to the next, while efficient governance structures ensure that concentrated ownership does not constrain the growth of the business or present major challenges within the family. In such cases, the *FB Map* predicts that family succession will be the best model for the firm and will deliver value over and above that which alternative models could provide.

However, efficient governance structures and practices are not easy to come by, and they require advance planning and a lot of effort to make them work. Once the assets and roadblocks have been identified, the keys to succession planning are to transfer the family assets to the next generation as efficiently as possible and to design governance mechanisms that minimize the cost of future roadblocks. The focus is on how to integrate the next generation and how to help them develop the ability to exploit the family assets, be they powerful networks, the name and legacy of the company, or the values-based leadership of the old guard. The other imperative is to structure ownership and future management to minimize the cost of future challenges both from within the family and

FIG 6.1 / **The family succession path**

from the business environment. Since the family has decided to continue the adventure together, family governance and communication will be an important element of a successful family succession.

The succession decision, if not taken solely by the founder, will usually remain within the family circle. It will involve a number of soul-searching questions for both generations. For the older generation these will relate to making the succession work for the benefit of the company and the family, for example:

- Do any of the children want to take over the firm?
- How to choose between equally able children?
- Will they make good business leaders or will the company suffer under their leadership?
- Will the heirs collaborate in the future – do their personalities blend well – or descend into sibling rivalry?
- How do we nurture the competencies necessary to take the firm forward?
- And how shall we support others who wish to pursue a career outside the company?

Meanwhile the younger generation will battle with questions like: Do I want to join the family business at all? Shall I begin now or get experience outside first? What do my parents have in mind about the timing of succession and their retirement?

Such questions may seem highly personal and specific to individual families and the countries and cultures they live in. However, we firmly believe that families can learn from the experience of other families and that we can extract common elements from a structured analysis.

A number of our earlier examples illustrate the complexity of finding the right succession model for the individual family firm, as well as how specific models take into account assets and roadblocks. The Ochs-Sulzberger family has designed trust structures with the aim of securing future family control and opportunities for competent and interested family individuals to contribute to the future business venture. When Adolph Ochs was close to retirement as editor of the New York Times, he designated his son-in-law to succeed him. Keen for all his children and grandchildren to have the chance to be involved in the corporation, he set up a trust that would continue well beyond the death of his daughter Iphigène. The trust bound the family together. Indeed the model worked so well that the family chose to replace it (when it expired) with a new one in the 1990s, thereby extending their control for at least another half century.

Wang Yung-ching, founder of Formosa Plastics Group, designed a complex succession model focused on ensuring business continuity. When he died in 2008, de facto ownership and control was transferred to a local hospital that he had founded and supported for decades. He decided that business continuity would require that ownership and management were structured in a form that gave more stability than would have been the case if ownership were transferred directly to his 12 children belonging to three different family branches.

The Mulliez family developed a third model of succession focused on how to provide incentives and common bonds in a very large family. By providing in-house education and training, allowing all family members to hold shares at the group level, and emphasizing the 'tous dans tout' principle, they have forged a unique succession model which is key to their successful business ventures, as exemplified by Auchan, Decathlon and other retail chains that have evolved into local and global business leaders.

The challenges involved in family succession may derive from constraints imposed by society or the prevailing succession culture. For example, while Japanese families adopt sons-in-law to resolve 'manpower' issues, most Chinese families would baulk at the idea. The transfer of family assets such as extended business, regulatory and/or political networks, family values and heritage raises questions such as:

- How should entrepreneurs nurture an interest in the family firm?
- How best to prepare the next generation to take over management and ownership?
- What kind of education and skills will they need?
- What ambitions should they be driven by?
- How do multi-member families provide career opportunities for all interested children?
- How to handle tax issues related to succession?

We group all these questions into six key challenges that families and business across the world face during a succession process. These are (1) the challenge of succession culture, (2) the challenge of transferring family assets, (3) the challenge being competent, (4) the challenge of change, (5) the challenge of planning, and (6) The challenge of institutional roadblocks.

Each of these challenges is analyzed below, showing how family businesses handle them in an effort to create the best possible conditions for the future, highlighting those that we have met time and time again in family firms worldwide. They have convinced us that firms that flourish from one generation to another are those that resolve the challenges of transferring family assets and minimizing potential roadblocks at succession. However, before we engage in what families can do to improve the likelihood of a successful family succession, let us turn our attention to how it is performing today. By observing the outcome of family successions, we grasp the magnitude of the challenge that families face when transferring the business to the next generation.

The economic consequences of family succession

First-generation family firms are successful if they reach the stage of succession. Most do not survive beyond ten years, and surprisingly few flourish after a succession. The American financier and investment guru Warren Buffet once compared family succession to 'choosing the 2020 Olympic team by picking the eldest sons of the gold-medal winners of the 2000 Olympics'. His analogy captures one of the most intriguing questions of family succession: can a company flourish after letting an 'average' child succeed a 'genius' entrepreneur?

Buffet is not alone in his skepticism, which is why in most languages you can find an expression that encapsulates the notion that family firms rarely survive beyond the third generation. The idea that a successful entrepreneur builds up a business only to see it destroyed by heirs with neither talent nor interest is neatly captured in the English expression 'from shirtsleeves to shirtsleeves in three generations'.[1]

---

1   Professor Yupana Wittawangka has collected similar expressions from many other languages including Italian: *'Dalle stalle alle stelle alle stalle'* (*From stables to stars to stables*); Spanish: *'Quien no lo tiene, lo hace; y quien lo tiene, lo deshace'* (He who doesn't have it, makes it and he who has it, wastes it); Japanese: 三代目が家を潰す' (The third generation ruins the house); and Chinese: 富不过三代 (Wealth does not survive three generations).

Indeed, there seem to be as many arguments against family succession as there are in favour. On the positive side, the firm gets a new CEO who, through long-term active ownership, protects the firm's interests as well as having an in-depth knowledge of the firm. Sustaining business strategies based on powerful family assets is easier for family managers than outsiders, hence the return on those assets is likely to increase. On the negative side, it cannot be taken for granted that the best qualified of the founders' children will match the best possible external candidate for the job. Indeed, if there is a flourishing market for talented managers, and the firm itself is attractive, the talent pool of professional candidates may exceed that within the family, so insisting on an internal successor may be short sighted.

Let's look at what the research has to say about the corporate consequences of family succession. The simplest way is to compare changes in a firm's performance before and after the CEO transition in cases where a family CEO was appointed and where an outsider was chosen – what economists call a difference-in-difference estimate.

In a seminal study of large US firms, Professor Francisco Pérez-González of Stanford University Graduate School of Business analyzed the economic consequences of family succession in the 500 largest US firms, around one-third of which were family controlled. He compared average changes in returns between those firms that chose a CEO from the ranks of the family with those who appointed an outsider. The measure of returns was earnings divided by the book value of assets for the three years before the succession compared with the three years after.

What he found was that among the top 500 US firms, succession improved performance. On average, changing to a new CEO increased the industry-adjusted performance by around 1 percentage point. However, this was primarily driven by firms that did not have a family succession. On average, family succession had a significantly negative effect on operational performance. There was a difference of almost two percentage points between firms that chose an unrelated successor and those that appointed a family member.

The study revealed one area where family succession can clearly be improved: the education of successors. Returns were significantly higher in firms where the family successor received an elite business education from a top university or business school. In fact, well-educated family CEOs performed at least as well as non-family CEOs.

Are these results unique to the largest firms in the US? Our research on Asian and Northern European firms suggests that this is not the case. In Asia, where family enterprises are more prevalent than in the US and Europe, we studied the economic outcome of succession in almost 250 publicly traded companies in Hong Kong, Singapore and Taiwan. Almost 65 percent of the events were family successions, about 22 percent were non-family (outsider) successions, and the rest were sell-out cases. Since these were publicly traded firms, we measured performance as the monthly cumulative market-adjusted stock return from 60 months before to 36 months after the year that the chairman stepped down and was replaced by a successor. What we found can only be described as dramatic.

From five years before the succession year to three years afterwards there was on average a loss of 65 percent of firm value. Moreover, this huge dissipation of value was common to all succession types, that is, there was no significant difference between family and non-family succession. It is easy to see why succession is among the biggest challenges faced by large publicly traded Asian businesses. Indeed it's not only firms that suffer when founders have to be replaced; it can reach a level where whole economies are affected – because family firms constitute a very large share of Asia's private and public firms. Add to this the tremendous growth experienced by most Asian economies during the last 50 years – largely fuelled by entrepreneurs who, having started new business ventures, are now on the verge of retirement – and you get some idea of the scale of the challenge for the region's economies as a whole.

Another finding was that much of the value loss around succession occurred before the chairman stepped down and failed to be restored afterwards. This suggests that the timing of succession is a critical issue: either the founders do not exit at the right moment, or they stay on too long in the absence of alternative options. It also suggests that founders embody the all-important family assets, which they are unable to transfer efficiently to the next generation.

Not only does our study highlight the enormous challenges faced by Asian firms when founders reach retirement (or die while at the helm), it underlines the urgency of long-term succession planning as a key in reducing the potential cost of founder retirement and family succession.

Is within-family succession universally costly? The above examples focus on larger businesses in the US and Asia, but the typical family business is much smaller than these empires; most of them are small and medium-sized firms with fewer employees and much simpler organizational and financial structures. In our quest to provide recommendations for the typical family business owner, we took a close look at the economic challenges surrounding succession.

We investigated over 6,000 successions in private firms in Denmark[2] – the largest succession study ever carried out. And since small and medium-sized family firms are similar across countries and cultures, we believe that our insights are representative of family succession worldwide.

Our first insight is that family firms that appoint new managers from within are typically in better condition than firms that are transferred out of the family. We see two explanations for this: First, parents want their children to succeed so they do everything they can to boost the firm's business and financial standing before they leave it in the hands of the next generation. Second, children prefer to take over a firm that is doing well – if they have a choice between joining the family business and pursuing a career elsewhere. For small and medium-sized firms, parents often must make a real sale to convince their children to continue the business. Naturally joining the firm is a more attractive proposition if the outlook for the business is bright.

Our second finding was that industry-adjusted operating performance declined after a family succession at the *managerial* level. We estimate that a family CEO costs approximately EUR 8,000 per million euros in assets compared to a non-related CEO. In the event of transfer of *ownership*, we found that a family successor had a similarly negative effect on firm performance. On average, firms that transferred ownership within the family experienced a decline in performance over the three years following succession, whereas those that transferred ownership out of the family saw no change in performance. In short, whether on the managerial or ownership level, family succession hurts firm performance when measured against succession involving outside managers or owners.

---

2   See Bennedsen, Morten, Kasper Meisner Nielsen, Francisco Pérez-González, and Daniel Wolfenzon. Inside the Family Firm: The Role of Families in Succession Decisions and Performance. *Quarterly Journal of Economics*, 122(2), 647–691, 2007.

When you consider that firms choosing family successions are generally in better shape than those who choose alternative models, the true cost of family succession is likely to be larger than the figure estimated above (EUR 8,000 per million euros in assets). Children do not only look at the current status of the firm before deciding to join or not, they also evaluate the opportunities for growing the business. Thus, a child will be more eager to take over a firm with a strong future, and less keen if they expect it to suffer. Potential business opportunities – even if they can't be measured – include future product development or entry into new markets. If there is no obvious way to improve future performance, capable children may prefer to make a career elsewhere, so their parents will have to find an outside manager or sell the firm.

Why are we so concerned that our difference-in-difference method does not capture the cost of future business opportunities? Because if it is indeed the case that firms which choose family succession have better business opportunities, we are likely to be underestimating the cost of family succession, since these firms not only do worse in measurable terms but they fail to capitalize on the superior opportunities they started out with.

Fortunately, we can use modern statistical methods to measure the cost of family succession while taking into account differences in firms' business futures. To understand how, an analogy from the medical world may be useful. Assume we were medical doctors measuring the effect of a new 'pill' dubbed 'Family Succession'. In the medical world we would take a sample of 100 firms and toss a coin to determine which of the firms would have a family succession and which an external manager. It is neither possible nor very useful for a researcher to buy 100 family firms and do such a randomized experiment, but we can do something which is a good approximation. We look for natural events that randomly allocate the firms to the two succession models. By randomly assign, we mean any event that affects the choice of succession model and which is not dependent on performance, personal interest or future business opportunities.

Our starting point is the observation that families where the first-born child is a girl are 10 percent less likely to have a family succession a generation later. Given that the gender of the first-born in the eyes of an economist is almost the same as tossing a coin in the eyes of a medical researcher, we can use this randomness together with advanced statistical methods to capture the real cost of family succession for a randomly chosen firm. In this way we can answer the question of what the performance difference would be if the two succession models were applied to firms in similar condition.

What we find is that when firms are randomly allocated to family succession or non-related succession, the cost of family succession is *significantly higher* than we initially estimated. Our best estimate is that a family successor will generate zero surplus for a period of three to four years after succession in the average small or medium-sized firm, whereas an unrelated successor will neither harm nor improve performance. Not only is this a significant effect, but the only reason it is not more visible is that firms who appoint a family successor are in better condition to start with.

To sum up, studies of management and ownership succession across three continents suggest that there is a significant corporate cost to letting a family member take over at the helm. Although it's not always the case – many heirs deliver impressive results in terms of performance and growth – on average a family succession will not deliver results on a par with the average outside successor. Indeed it is often a value-destroying process.

How do we reconcile these observations with previous research that suggests family businesses outperform non-family firms?

In fact, comparative studies have produced conflicting results: some family firms thrive; others underperform. One reason for this discrepancy may be the different definitions used to classify family businesses. Most studies of US family firms define family firms as those that have a founding-family member on the board of directors, even if the family no longer has meaningful ownership; whereas in the rest of the world (including Asia and Europe), family firms almost always have concentrated ownership and/or employ multiple family members.

More importantly, many studies fail to address the fundamental question of why family ownership and/or management is value-generating in some business activities but not in others. As our *FB Map* highlights, it's a question of opportunities and constraints. Firms that are able to exploit the strategic advantages of their family assets and reduce the cost of roadblocks tend to prosper; others who have fewer family assets and more roadblocks will do worse.

While this may make depressing reading for many entrepreneurs and families, we are convinced that the key to a successful family succession is to understand the 'caveats' that too many business families ignore. It takes long-range planning and robust governance for any family to own and manage a company on a long-term basis. Only by learning how other family firms have built business and governance strategies to face the succession challenge can owner-managers and their families increase their chances of success.

In the remainder of this chapter we discuss the major challenges that collectively explain the poor economic performance of the average family succession. We present the six most important succession challenges identified in our research on three continents, from our interactions with families in more than 20 countries. Our aim is to provide a toolkit to improve the transfer of family assets and to avoid the most threatening roadblocks during the succession process, and thereby increase the number of successful family successions.

The challenge of the succession culture

'Succession culture' refers to the set of common practices and traditions that shape the distribution of ownership and management positions in a family business across the generations. To understand its importance, it may help to look again at an extreme case: the 46 successions in the Höshi Ryokan we first met in Chapter 2.

The succession model used for centuries by the Höshi family (and in other old Japanese family businesses) is tailor-made to mitigate family roadblocks. Think about the challenge of a small family firm going through 46 successions and the sheer 'power of numbers' if each generation was to have an average of two children who reached adulthood, who in turn had two children, and so on. After 46 generations, the family would be counted in millions! Even if there was a mechanism to operate a small hotel with thousands of owners, there would be overwhelming problems at the management level: who should be allowed to make a career in the firm? Who should be the next leader? and so on. It would be impossible to offer everyone a fair chance.

The question of equal treatment evokes other challenges. Imagine that in each generation, ownership and management are conferred on one heir while other offspring are compensated with an equal share of the family fortune. The likelihood of the business surviving on half or one-third of the family resources is small, but its chances of surviving being cut down 46 times would be zero since it would drain the hotel's resources to the point where long-term survival would be impossible.

So what type of succession has sustained the family firm through almost 1,300 years and 46 generations? Our interviews with Mr. Höshi revealed a fascinating succession process which, despite its drastic implications, focuses on transferring powerful family assets and eliminating roadblocks related to the power of numbers. Ownership and management responsibility is given to one individual in each generation according to the following criteria:

- The first-born son is considered the natural successor to the ryokan.
- When there were no sons, the husband of the eldest daughter has been adopted into the Höshi family and became the next Zengoro Höshi.
- Most marriages are arranged (they are not love matches).
- If there are no children in one generation, the Höshi will adopt a successor who will carry the family heritage and the ryokan forward.

Let's explore the implications of these rules. First, the model is focused on producing one clear successor and avoiding dilution of ownership. Second, as there is no guarantee of transition from father to son, and since Japanese traditional culture favors male business leaders, the model resolves this dilemma via points two and three (above). As the Höshi family is an old prestigious family in Japan, marrying into the family is an attractive prospect. Typically, the eldest daughter will marry into another old family. Third, there is a tradition among business-owning families of adopting capable male heirs. Examples include such well-known family names as Toyoda, Misui and Suzuki.

How does the Höshi family deal with the increasing number of offspring, who mostly live locally? The following steps in the succession model deal with this aspect:

- When the old Zengoro Höshi retires from business, the chosen successor (who carries the Höshi name either from birth or by adoption) will change his first name to Zengoro. So for 46 generations, the owner-managers of the ryokan all have the same name: Zengoro Hōshi.

- Daughters become part of other old Japanese families through arranged marriages, thereby giving up the Hōshi name.
- Younger sons likewise marry into other old Japanese families. They are adopted by the wife's family and take her family name.
- As a majority of the family fortune is tied up in the ryokan, the successor is the exclusive heir; other offspring receive no share of the inheritance.

According to Zengoro Hōshi, the name is an integral part of the heritage. Essentially it secures the stability of the succession. Beyond its symbolic value, in our view, the inn possesses the most powerful family asset we have ever seen: 46 generations of history and heritage. The selection process and the name offer the most efficient transfer of this asset across the generations. Imagine if the Hōshi Ryokan were managed by the husband of a Hōshi daughter with another surname; not only would the magic disappear, but it would do so for good, since future generations would no longer bear the Hōshi name.

These rules may seem blatantly unfair, but the current Zengoro Hōshi is candid about their necessity. They are a cornerstone of the business model and simply cannot be challenged. When we asked how he catered for his other children, he said he focused on investing in them so they could achieve the best possible education to prepare them for life outside the ryokan. He acknowledged the dilemma between wanting to support them and having to preserve the family's wealth exclusively in the ryokan to ensure the optimal future for the inn.

He also expressed concern about the 'americanization' of many old Japanese family businesses since the Second World War, particularly the tendency to support all children financially by dividing ownership or by removing wealth from the firm to compensate non-successor offspring. In his view, this is one reason why a number of old families have been forced to exit their companies in recent decades. However, he recognized that culture can change and that keeping the strict male- and firm-oriented succession model described above may be difficult in the future.

There are many variations of the traditional Japanese succession model. The Kyoto-based Gekkeikan Sake Company has brewed sake for almost

400 years and has been transferred through 14 generations of the Okura family (including sons, adopted in-laws, and adopted sons) according to a similar model. However, ownership has been diluted. The current president, Mr Haruhiko Okura, together with his four brothers, owns less than 10 percent of the shares. Other examples include the distinguished tea school Enshu Sado and the 350-year-old Okaya trading group.

Traditional Japanese succession culture is an extreme version of primogeniture – the right (by law or custom) of the first-born son to inherit the entire estate to the exclusion of other siblings – and is still observed. Many old European families followed the principle for centuries, and to this day it remains the dominant succession model within royal families. But while Japanese culture has been 'westernized' in the post-war era, there are still major cultural differences. Divorce rates in Japan are very low, gender roles in the division of family responsibilities are still strong, as is loyalty towards parents. Surveys have shown that this sense of family as a unit is stronger among people that have a livelihood to pass down, such as business owners. Such social trends are important inputs to designing the right succession models.

In France, established dynasties followed succession models introduced in the Napoleonic era, based on *la dote* or dowry. There are many versions of dowry in family businesses, but in its purest form it may include the following provisions:

- Two-thirds of the estate is divided equally among the males of the next generation.
- The rest is divided as the predecessors decide. Typically it is given to the eldest son, who will be the future president of the family business.
- Daughters do not share in the estate but receive a dowry equal to the wealth of their fiancé at the time of marriage.

Like the strict Japanese model of succession, the dowry model also focused on securing the business through transfer to male heirs (with the family name), while securing the livelihoods of daughters and younger sons. However, the practice of setting dowry in proportion to the status or wealth of the fiancé obliged families to raise financing outside the corporation to an extent that could limit the growth of the family firm in the future.

In many large European family firms, ownership is divided equally among the heirs. So as the family extends it is diluted among hundreds of members, as we saw with the Wendel family, with over 1,000 owners of Wendel Participation, which owns 38 percent of Wendel Investissement. And in the even bigger Jannsen family behind the Belgian Solvay group. As indicated, with this succession model comes the challenge of incentivizing a vast number of owners and separating family and business interests.

Whereas the giving of a dowry is less common in Europe today, it is practised in many Asian and Middle Eastern families. Succession culture is very different in Middle Eastern countries such as Saudi Arabia, the United Arab Emirates and Kuwait, where it is strongly influenced by Sharia law. Many family businesses are managed by first- or second-generation children, and family structures can be complicated including many siblings in the first generation and thus several branches in the second generation

Where Sharia law does not prevail, it is often assumed that the male heirs will share ownership, all next generation family members will have some form of work or engagement in the firm, and the family has a responsibility to take care of female members that do not end up as owners. Thus ownership is diluted and rarely renegotiated. The oldest son will run the firm together with the father, will take over after the father's death, and will have the ultimate say in discussions between brothers and cousins, often backed by a powerful matriarch.

Whether a succession culture is explicit or not, for most family businesses around the world there will be norms or rules which determine the model followed. Indeed it's tempting to assume that the absence of a succession culture may make for a better outcome. Sadly, our experience suggests otherwise. Indeed, the absence of inheritance customs can be an even bigger headache. It is often the case in developing countries with weak social and political institutions that there is no established culture of transferring wealth from generation to generation. The case of Chief Abiola, Nigeria's most influential entrepreneur since independence, is a reminder that the absence of succession culture can destroy a business empire.

The Nigerian constitution recognizes the legitimacy of both civil law and custom for the country's 250 ethnic groups. A man may have only

CHIEF ABIOLA OF NIGERIA

Chief Abiola stands out as a pioneer entrepreneur at a time when the Nigerian economy had begun to recover from the global downturn of the early 1980s. He started out as an importer but quickly moved into shipping, newspaper publishing, telecommunications, aviation, agriculture, banking, real estate and oil services. Significantly, the rapid growth of his business was facilitated by his closeness to the military–political establishment, which guaranteed him access to highly lucrative contracts and subsidies from the government. From an outsider perspective, there was no evidence of a holding company; he simply had interests in various companies or full ownership.

As the twenty-third child of his father and the first to survive infancy, it is perhaps not surprising that Chief Abiola went on to father over 40 children. But there was no documented evidence that his children were directly involved in the business. He was relatively young and his eldest son was probably in his early 30s when his multiple businesses began to expand. A lack of consolidation and management style may explain why most of these early ventures failed – his brothers and wives were made CEOs of some of the businesses, including Abiola Farms (a brother) and the Concord newspaper (a wife).

In early 1990, he turned his attention to politics, winning the presidency in 1992. But his mandate was withdrawn when the election results were annulled. Subsequently the government began to systematically refuse operating licences to his various businesses, starving them of funds and leading to an eventual collapse.

For his offspring, there was nothing to succeed to as there was no consolidation of his interests and assets into a holding company in which the family had a controlling share. The existence of multiple wills compounded the issue of 'asset succession' – which is still being contested in the courts today.

one wife according to civil law, whereas customary law allows multiple wives (generally up to four). High rates of infant mortality mean that large families are the norm. Succession planning is therefore a complex predicament. Although it is traditionally assumed that the first son will inherit all or most of the assets, this is often contested in a polygamous household, particularly where conflicts arise between wives (and in turn their children). Upon the death of the patriarch, informal and formal wills are often contested. In many cases disputes continue long after the assets have deteriorated. In the largely Muslim north, such disputes are less prevalent, or at least less public, due to Islamic dictates concerning inheritance. However, the majority of businesses exist in the Christian south.

Lack of succession planning is a common feature of Nigerian family businesses. How to plan in such extreme conditions in the absence of any kind of succession culture? How to align different family branches which neither love nor respect each other? How to ensure the 'best' heirs for the firm based on skills rather than power? How to instil drive and discipline in the younger generation to manage the family business?

With westernization and falling rates of infant mortality, the younger generation tends to have one spouse and far fewer children. As such, it is hoped that the effects of large families will decline with successive generations. However, the desire to have male children to whom one's assets can be passed is still as strong.

The above examples remind us that succession cultures vary significantly from one country to another. Likewise, there are different notions of respect for the older generation. In Thailand and India, children rarely go against their parents' wishes, whereas it is more common in the USA. Primogeniture is still practised in Asia and Africa. A willingness to discuss personal, family and business issues is less developed in China and Latin America than in Western Europe. These variations in turn have a huge impact on the success of succession.

Understanding the specific succession culture surrounding the family and the firm is crucial for the success of long-term planning. The diversity of succession cultures implies that long-term planning has to be context specific. It is unlikely that a succession model that works well, say, for a 40-year-old US family business, can apply to a Chinese Confucian-based family firm in Malaysia.

The challenge of transferring family assets

Successful family business strategies are based on powerful family assets. According to the *FB Map,* strong family assets are predictors of successful family succession. So a key challenge is how to nurture and transfer existing family assets to the next generation. Will the next generation be able to extend and exploit the network the founders had? How can they capitalize on the family heritage as a future business strategy? How do they develop the values-based leadership that their parents were so successful with?

Figure 6.2 illustrates the essence of transferring family assets from one generation to the next. Whether in the form of the firm's heritage, powerful business networks or core values, what it boils down to is finding common ground between the two. But how does it work in practice?

Initially, the older generation serves as role models – they inspire, teach and communicate. Common ground is created from shared values and activities that extend beyond the corporate sphere, for example, family involvement in social or religious groups, specific projects that unite the family or simply spending time together. Ultimately, the transfer process can be based on a structured or unstructured apprenticeship model, or it can take place in the family sphere outside the business context.

A good example of the informal apprenticeship model comes from a young French sixth-generation entrepreneur who recently took over the family business, a world leader in frozen herbs. He talked enthusiastically about

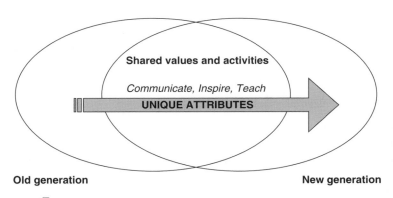

Old generation   New generation

FIG 6.2 Transferring family assets through generations

touring the fields with his father from a very early age. From the age of 6, he recalled how on Sundays mornings he could choose between going to church with his mother or visiting the fields on his father's tractor – an easy decision for a 6-year-old boy. The memories of riding the tractor with his father served several functions. It was a father/son bonding experience that the son still remembers. It was an early introduction to the firm and which gave him an appetite for being involved in the herb business when he grew up. And it was also the beginning of a transfer of the strong family assets that had been nurtured.

Taking a more structured approach to learning, we have observed that many business families introduce character-building obligations for children, such as having to work once a week in the firm or imposing duties to be performed in or outside the business. The purpose is to instil entrepreneurial discipline, and through it to transfer important family assets. A popular approach among western business families is to give children age 10–14 the task of arranging the next family holiday. It is a fun project for the kids and it teaches them about budgets, planning and implementation, thereby building their entrepreneurial skills from a very early age. The reactions of other family members also teach the children about family values and interests.

The transfer of family values is often most powerfully done outside the business sphere, where its impact on children is more authentic. One Chinese entrepreneur told us how his father would donate money to charity every month, insisting that he remain anonymous and that nobody except his sons and wife should know. The fact that he did so from personal conviction rather than to promote his business interests had a profound impact on the young boys, and made him a role model for both their personal and professional personal lives.

We have met second- and third-generation heirs from family businesses in South East Asia who recalled how they would be taken by their parents to orphanages or local hospitals on Sundays to visit the poor. The parents would typically donate money to these institutions, but it was the allocation of their time and the personal encounters that made the strongest impression on their children.

One of the biggest challenges is how to groom the next generation – to give them opportunities to be involved in the firm and to develop their skills so that those who are interested can one day take over. Talking with families and entrepreneurs across several continents, we have observed many different ways of doing this. Some opt for learning by observing and following their parents; others combine grooming with formal education; while yet others prefer their children to find their own path in life.

Most rely on some variation of the apprenticeship model. The children are exposed to the firm from a very early age by helping out in the 'back room' when they have spare time after school. They learn everything about the business from numerous discussions around the dinner table. If the firm is big enough, they may spend their entire career in the family firm, working their way up the corporate ladder until the parents are ready to retire and they can take over.

In addition to providing the younger generation with a strong platform from which to take over, the apprenticeship model also prepares the older generation to let go. At some point, the parents cease making the phone calls and the younger generation have direct access to business partners. The more common ground there is between the generations, the easier this will be.

The apprenticeship model is good at aligning the interests of generations and hence does a good job of transferring family assets. It also has its shortcomings since it tends to groom the next generation to continue along the track laid down by the founder, and does not prepare them for changes in the business and economic environment. So while we recommend some version of the apprenticeship model as a powerful means to transfer family assets, as a stand-alone model is has deficiencies. It is vitally important that children get educational and working experience outside the family firm, as the next section explains.

The challenge of being competent

Founding entrepreneurs are often individuals who have done things differently and are good at 'thinking out of the box'. Research shows that, on average, they have less education and less formal training than other business leaders. They tend to be creative, pushy types who have little respect for formal structures. Those who get as far as a succession often have a limited understanding of the value of formal education and little experience outside the family business.

Most are self-made individuals with strong egos and a firm belief that the apprenticeship model is the right way to prepare children to take over. They nurture their children's involvement from an early age, bring them to the business when they are small, give them character-building tasks after school, and take them to meet customers and suppliers when they are in their teens. Since they themselves have often succeeded without the benefit of an elite education, they tend to underestimate the value of formal (measurable) skills.

But as we saw earlier, while the apprenticeship model addresses the core challenge of transferring family assets and ensures a sound knowledge of the business, the next generation often lack formal education at a higher level – a pattern we have observed on every continent and among small, large and even very large firms.

We wanted to know how far this lack of formal competence prevails in family firms, and whether it's possible to demonstrate a link between the CVs resumés of successors and the outcomes for the companies they take over.

To answer these questions we conducted a study of the importance of education and experience for successors to small and medium-sized family businesses in Denmark. We investigated the background of successors in 11,026 management successions and in 3,739 ownership successions. We divided the sample into two: in the 'family group', the departing manager or owner was replaced by a family member (most often a child), whereas in the 'external group' the new manager or owner was not related to the family.

When we looked at the formal education levels of both groups and their leadership experiences at the point when succession took place, our first insight was that the family successors were younger than the outsiders. But although they inherited responsibility earlier, the parent(s) definitely exited the business at a later date. In other words, the departing entrepreneur was more likely to stay involved when the successor was from the family, remaining on the board of directors in nearly four out of ten successions (or twice as often as for outside successors).

The most striking contrast between family and non-family successors was observed when we compared differences in education and job experience. Figure 6.3 highlights the differences in education levels and relevant business experiences. Column 4 shows that whereas four out of ten non-related successors have relevant managerial or leadership education from a university or a business school, only one out of five family successors has such a background. On average, family successors have almost one year less schooling than external successors.

This lack of education among family successors is not limited to small and medium-sized family companies. Recall how in the previously cited study of the largest US family businesses, one explanation for the cost of family succession is that heirs were significantly less likely to have an MBA from an elite university than external successors.

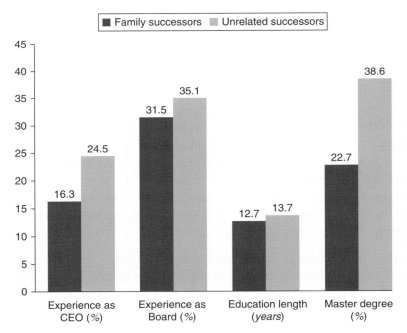

FIG 6.3 / **Comparison of formal competencies between family successors and unrelated successors**

Note: Based on 11,026 CEO successions in small and medium-sized Danish family businesses.

Source: Morten Bennedsen and Kasper M. Nielsen "Family Firms in Denmark", 2014.

Not only are family successors less educated, they also have a less impressive track record in top management before they take over the family firm. As per Column 1, approximately 16 percent have previous experience as a CEO, whereas among non-related successors the figure is approximately 24 percent. However it is worth remarking that among those with previous CEO experience, family successors had on average spent the same amount of time in their previous job (around four years) as unrelated successors.

Their lack of managerial experience is not compensated by experience on the board. Column 2 indicates that family and non-related successors have almost the same length of director experience before joining the family business, suggesting that family successors are not appointed to the board at the earliest possible opportunity.

Overall, our findings suggest that family successors have fewer measurable competencies compared to unrelated successors. While the apprenticeship model provides detailed insight into the day-to-day running of the firm and a relationship-based experience, it is seldom supplemented with formal business education or work experience outside the family business.

Is the lack of measurable competencies a problem for running the family business in the second, third or fourth generation? To answer this question we looked at the resumés of new CEOs and new owners in firms that prospered after succession compared with firms that suffered after succession. Specifically, we identified the 25 best-performing family firms and the 25 worst-performing firms after succession, and compared the resumés of the successors in the two groups, focusing on their respective education and relevant business experience.

We begin by comparing owners' backgrounds between successful and suffering family succession. Figure 6.4 compares the resumés of the new family owners in firms that did worst and best during the family succession. Most strikingly, from Column 1 we see that the share of new family successors that had managerial experience prior to being appointed was three times higher among successful firms: 36 percent compared to around 12 percent for the worst-performing firms. They were also significantly more likely to have had experience of sitting on the board of the family business or another relevant firm before they took over the family business, as illustrated in Column 2. In Columns 3 and 4 we notice that that family successors in the best-performing firms had experienced a considerably

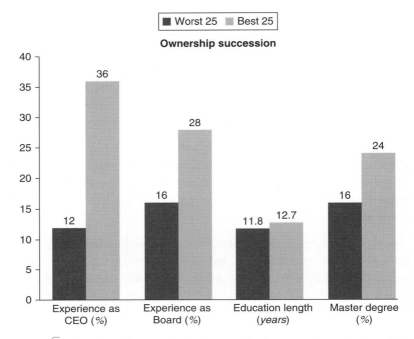

FIG 6.4   **Comparison of measurable competencies between the 25 best- and 25 worst-performing family ownership successions**

Source: Morten Bennedsen and Kasper M. Nielsen "Family Firms in Denmark", 2014.

longer education – on average almost a year longer – and were much more likely to have obtained a relevant university degree.

Figure 6.5 provides a similar comparison based on CEO competencies. It confirms the insight from the ownership analysis: family firms suffer after a succession as the heir has less experience of being a CEO, less board experience, and is less well educated.

A lack of education and formal leadership training characterizes many struggling family firms worldwide. While entrepreneurs increasingly acknowledge the importance of education outside the family business, we still encounter a strong bias towards in-house training.

In our view, grooming competent heirs requires a blend of planning and training. While the apprenticeship model indeed allows children to learn the ins and outs of the family business as an integral part of their upbringing, creates common ground between the generations, and is an effective

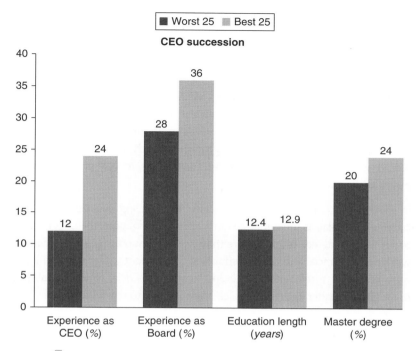

FIG 6.5 Comparison of measurable competencies between the 25 best- and 25 worst-performing family CEO successions

Source: Bennedsen and Nielsen 2013.

way of transferring family assets, the importance of measurable competencies should not be underestimated by any entrepreneur. It is vital to provide the next generation with the best possible education and let them gain experience and inspiration from other companies in other industries, other countries and other cultures. In this way they will be equipped to cope with the changes required when they take over.

We end this section with a caveat. Family succession can sometimes be more difficult when children have *too much education*. In our MBA classes we see more and more heirs to businesses in Asia, Africa and South America who have been educated abroad, are accustomed to living in a metropolis in Europe or the USA, and then are reluctant to return to the provincial setting where the family business is located.

In one case, in which a father had created a successful seafood business in a coastal town in mainland China, the only son was sent abroad to get the best possible education from top MBA schools in the US and Europe. Not daring to admit that he did not want to return home to work in the seafood business, the son's strategy was to found a software company while he was overseas, hoping to grow it to such a size that the father would agree that it made more sense for the son to stay in the software business than to go home.

In another case, the founder of a successful tire retailing business in a provincial town in Malaysia sent all six children to either Singapore, the UK or the US to get a graduate education, where they were very successful in their careers, working in financial and other companies. Subsequently, five of the children were no longer interested in returning to that provincial town in Malaysia, leaving the founder with little choice when it came to the succession.

The challenge of change

The above insights reveal a paradox in the way that many entrepreneurs prepare the next generation. They themselves are living examples of creative 'uneducated' risk-takers, as illustrated by the many 'rags to riches' stories like the late Wang Yung-ching of Formosa Plastics Group or the recently retired Ingvar Kamprad of IKEA. Coming from poor backgrounds, these individuals tend to believe that the most important aspect of preparing the next generation is to teach their children everything they know; they have little time for formal education.

This can work well if the firm continues along the same track as before the succession – a stable business that generates enough cash by continuing on the path laid out by the founder, particularly if it has a well-defined niche and can protect itself against competitors. We have seen several examples of this in previous chapters, including Henokiens such as the Japanese Hōshi Ryokan and the French spice company Thiercelin. But paradoxically, bringing up heirs as a carbon copy makes it difficult for them to implement fundamental changes in the business. When a successful firm has been around for 30 years or more, it is no longer a start-up.

So whereas the founder tended to centralize decision-making and kept everything 'in his or her head', the situation is very different for the next generation.

Sadly, we've met far too many small and medium-sized family enterprises that stopped growing after 10, 20 or 30 years. Two of the most important barriers to growth are a lack of ambition and an inability to manage change, which can be extremely challenging for the successors. The older entrepreneurial generation (where successful) discovered a well-defined niche and produced significant results for a generation. But taking the family business to the next level almost always signifies major changes – to the business strategy, to the organization of production, as well as geographical changes in markets, supply lines, plant facilities, and so on.

This has two major implications. First, there will be more formal requirements to deal with from employees, suppliers and stakeholders in general. For example, as the average age of the employees rises, they become more focused on pension plans and job security than on climbing the career ladder. Second, the company may have developed to a stage where it has to go to a new level. For example, a family firm that has been producing and selling in Europe may want to explore new markets on other continents, to become a regional or global player, or to outsource production to Asia where labour is cheaper. Managing such changes is always hard. A prerequisite for being able to do so is to learn from other businesses, which is why the apprenticeship model alone will not suffice. It is through business education that the next generation acquires the management tools that enable them to implement change. It is business experience acquired from other companies in other industries, other countries and other cultures that gives them the inspiration to invest in new markets or to move production facilities to trim labor costs.

At the beginning of this chapter we discussed how businesses often fail to thrive after a family succession. Our research shows that the cost of succession is particularly high in companies where changes are needed. The succession challenges are greater for firms operating in a competitive industry where a new business model is required, and for those in industries that rely on product development through investment in R&D, and for fast-growing companies that must respond to new markets and new customer demands.

The challenge of change is often amplified when the owner-manager is reluctant to delegate or let go. When we asked owner-managers of small and medium-sized firms to cite the biggest obstacle to long-term strategy planning, they often said they were simply too busy with day-to-day management to plan ahead. Not only do they work more hours than most, they tend to be indispensable to the day-to-day management of the firm; every decision, no matter how big or small, is referred to them – simply because they have an intimate knowledge of everything to do with operations. The cost of this level of control and involvement is that there is no delegation. Inevitably, these owner-managers spend their entire time managing.

Ultimately, the organizational structure is the responsibility of the owner-manager. Too often, the firm's growth is constrained for want of an overhaul in production or strategy because no time is set aside time to be creative and contemplate major changes.

The previous discussions provide a strong message for succession planning. Owner managers must take a balanced view on how to groom successors. On one side it is important to transfer family assets through the apprenticeship model; on the other, it is equally important to equip the next generation with measurable competencies derived from a combination of the best possible education and leadership experience outside the family business.

The challenge of planning for succession

Succession planning involves answering a number of difficult questions. How to choose one or more successors – on what principles – and what happens to 'non-chosen' family members? How to give heirs the right education and competencies? When should children be sent abroad to get new inspiration from other businesses? How is next generation introduced into the firm? How best to structure family careers inside the family business?

The truth is that few family firms have a formal response to such questions. Plans tend to stay in the head of the older generation and are rarely communicated. Meanwhile, the questions of the younger generation themselves – as well as their expectations and aspirations – go unanswered. Not surprisingly, a whole industry has grown up dedicated to helping families engaged in succession planning – consultants who specialize in succession planning, books on planning, business schools that offer courses to help families identify the right succession model – all based on the premise that they enable families to communicate.

So which option should they choose?

Our advice to families who talk easily and have a shared interest in planning for succession is to use consultants as part of the planning process. Creating time and space away from the all-consuming day-to-day business of the firm is often the best way to start working towards succession. A second recommendation is to get inspiration from successful models used in other family businesses, such as older firms that have been through multiple successions.

What is special about the centuries-old Henokiens companies is not only their longevity, but also the fact that they have been continuously owned

DE KUYPER ROYAL DISTILLERS

The De Kuyper family business was established in 1695. Its main business at the time was manufacturing barrels used to transport spirits and beers. By 1702, the family had bought its first distillery and was a leading producer of Dutch gin. Early on, the business focused on exports, and by the 19th century De Kuyper products were present in the European, UK and Canadian markets.

By the end of the prohibition era in 1934, De Kuyper had partnered with distillers in Canada and the United States. Over 30 years later, the firm partnered with Jim Beam brands to manufacture and market their products in the United States, as of 1966. Fast forward another 30 years, and the business was granted 'Royal' status in 1995 by the Queen of the Netherlands on its 300th anniversary. Henceforth it was known as De Kuyper Royal Distillers.

The main family assets of De Kuyper are its expertise in distilling and its focus on quality and reputation. De Kuyper has strict principles that regulate family involvement in the business. The main one is that there is only 'one captain of the ship' – all members must follow the vision of the family leader. A second is to keep the family business out of family life and avoid business discussions around the dinner table (although this is about to change as the younger generation seeks more discussion and information exchange).

The De Kuyper family has an independent supervisory board responsible for selecting family members who want to work in the company. To ensure that only competent family members can be hired, candidates must:

- Have completed higher education.
- Have worked for five years outside the company.
- Have a real interest in the family business.
- Undergo psychological testing and interviews by professional headhunters.
- Be willing to accept annual evaluation assessments if they pursue a career in the business.

by the same family, as well as managed and/or controlled by members of the founding family. How do they last so long and provide opportunities for each generation to contribute to the business? Let's look at some inspiring examples.

Currently, Bob De Kuyper is the captain of the ship. In the past, the company has had both external and family CEOs – they found the interaction between family and external managers inspiring. Bob De Kuyper has had a crucial role in implementing the succession rules and his son Mark is now involved in the business and being groomed as a possible future leader. He has completed higher education, has worked in the food industry outside De Kuyper, and has a genuine interest in making a career in the business. He has gone through external evaluations and testing and is a great supporter of the annual evaluation program. Ultimately, the supervisory board (with a majority of outsiders) will decide if he is the next captain of the ship.

Not all companies have such formal guidelines, but this example serves to underline how important it is to ensure that the family members have the right skills and drive, and that non-family managers do not see the family as an obstacle to their own career progress.

In Italy, the Monzino family insists that those who want to work in the company sign a protocol before joining. The current head of the family business, Antonio Monzino, told us that the protocol serves two major purposes. First, it aligns the expectations of all interested family members – by signing it they accept that they will most likely never take a large salary or

M O N Z I N O   G R O U P

The Monzino group's roots go back to 1750, when Antonio Monzino established a workshop for the production of musical instruments in Milan's historical Via Dogana. Since then, the Monzino family has continued to operate in the music business, making instruments, publishing music, and lately producing audio equipment.

The main family asset is a passion to share music with the public. Its *raison d'être* is to pass on the joy of playing music – which they firmly believe no one can resist. This passion has always been linked to another major family asset: a commitment to spreading the culture of music in society. All activities, from the production of instruments to the distribution of music publishing and its expansion into the school curriculum, are underpinned by this shared family vision.

These assets are the foundation of its strong relationships with suppliers and dealers, and its focus on people in all of its activities, which adds to its credibility. Given the enormity of the task and resource constraints, management takes a medium/long-term vision of the business, which provides both coherence and drive. By adopting a low profile and a humble approach, the group retains a realistic, down-to-earth perspective, which has allowed them to remain close to both the artists and the music-lovers who are their customers.

On the 250th anniversary of the birth of the Monzino group in June 1999, the family established the Antonio Carlo Monzino Foundation. Its mission is to preserve and embellish the family's artistic heritage and the promotion of musical education as a basic element of the cultural upbringing of the individual from infancy.

other monetary resources from the firm. As his son Francisco (who decided to join the business in his late twenties by operating some of its Spain-based activities) puts it: 'I have signed that I will never drive a Ferrari.'

Second, it helps select family members who share, and are most suited to nurturing, the most important family asset: a passion for music. Family members must have a good knowledge of music from learning to play an instrument over a long period of time. While this may seem purely symbolic, we see it as highly innovative and extremely useful. For a 250-year-old family business working in a competitive industry selling musical instruments, scores, books and audio equipment, to survive the Monzinos must keep their reputation and their history alive and be recognized for their passion for music. By signing the protocol they pledge to transfer this most important family asset and base their involvement on sharing and nurturing that passion.

We saw earlier how the strict rules of succession of the Höshi Ryokan, based on traditional Japanese culture, have endured for 46 generations. The Monzino case offers an alternative model for transferring family assets across generations. Clearly there is no single way of planning for succession – each family has worked out a way of meeting the challenges. But although models differ (as do family firms), those that succeed somehow manage to align the interests of the family members as the best possible basis for transferring the most important family assets to future generations.

Explicit planning gives clarity and transparency to the parties involved. Where few models make all family members happy, clarity reduces uncertainty. Transparent processes reduce the risk of conflict that arises from misunderstandings or from family members clashing as they try to chart their own career in a cloud of uncertainty.

The challenge of institutional roadblocks

Inheritance laws and inheritance taxes create specific challenges for business owners where most of the family's wealth is tied up in the firm. Inheritance laws place a limit on how both corporate and non-corporate wealth can be transferred to the next generation. Regulations on distributing ownership and wealth vary significantly across countries and continents. We have seen a huge variety in succession models, from the old Japanese model of giving everything to the first male heir to the French model of distributing everything equally among the descendants. To simplify the discussion we now look at the size of the share of a family's wealth that can be given to a single child – which will depend not only on the law but also on the surviving spouse and number of children.

There is, for example, a huge discrepancy in the transfer of wealth between the US and Italy. In the US there are no restrictions on the share that can be given to a single child; it is possible to leave one's whole estate to a single son or daughter, regardless of the number of siblings. In Italy the law is much less flexible: the widow(er) of the founder will receive at least one-third of the estate, hence the heirs receive a maximum of two-thirds. If the founder leaves a wife and three children, no single heir can receive more than 40 percent of the estate.

Interestingly, the ability to transfer the estate to a single heir is greater in countries where so-called common law prevails. Countries such as the US and UK impose few restrictions on the distribution of the estate, unlike Italy and France where there is a more equal distribution of ownership of the business among heirs in accordance with civil law. Basically, the law confers more rights on heirs who have less interest in and/or less talent for running the family firm. Since non-controlling heirs are entitled to a higher fraction of the founder's assets, the fraction given to the designated successor is lower, which reduces the incentive as well as the firm's ability to invest.

Ultimately, firms may have to liquidate a profitable business, but even where this is not the case, the ability to grow the family business following a succession may be limited in countries that restrict the division of the estate among the heirs. Research suggests that this is indeed the case. Investment in family business around succession tends to be lower in countries where the law prescribes the equal distribution of wealth compared to those where ownership can be transferred freely. Indeed some countries which have traditionally regulated the transfer of wealth have recently made moves to loosen the restrictions. In France and Italy, for example, there are proposals to make it easier for families to transfer the estate without incurring major costs.

For many retiring family entrepreneurs inheritance tax is a significant roadblock. The level varies widely – in some countries it is zero, in others it can run up to a significant fraction of the total sum to be transferred. In some cases it will depend on whether the entrepreneur left a will; it can exceed 50 percent if the entrepreneur dies intestate. Many European countries have reformed their inheritance tax system over the last two decades. Where once it was very high in countries like Greece, Sweden and Denmark, in recent years it has been either been significantly reduced or eliminated for corporate transfers.

While the challenge of inheritance tax is undeniable, there are – for most firms – ways to avoid it having negative consequences for the business. For example, families can choose to transfer the estate to a foundation or trust that uses part of the income for charitable purposes. Ownership may be transferred to more tax-friendly countries such as Lichtenstein, the Cayman Islands and other tax havens, or structured through a number of holding companies whereby the parents retain ownership during the succession as a means to eliminate or postpone payment of inheritance tax.

There is one caveat to designing succession in a way to mitigate inheritance taxes. Whereas it is *technically* possible in most cases, it relies on a fundamental premise: that the family have shared interests and are good at communicating and finding solutions. If these criteria are fulfilled, then tax consultants and accounting firms can be employed to mitigate the cost of inheritance taxes – which is, after all, how they make a living, and they are generally clever at finding solutions. But families who do not share common goals or communicate easily (due to a history of squabbles or diverging interests) find it harder to implement tax-efficient ownership and succession strategies. In cases where solutions cannot be found, inheritance tax will often undermine the growth of the company following succession.

How big is the tax challenge of succession? Do most firms avoid paying it? Any casual reading of the business press (as well as conversations with family business owners) will reveal that it is a widespread preoccupation. This was recently confirmed by a research study of succession in family firms in Greece by Professor Tsoutsoura at Chicago Booth School. Greece cut the inheritance tax rate for family successions from 20 percent to less than 2.4 percent, while leaving the tax rate for unrelated successions unchanged.

The reduction in inheritance tax in Greece boosted the number of family successions from around 45 percent to almost 75 percent. Most privately held family firms in Greece are owned by a single person or a single family. The tax reduction led to a more than 60 percent increase in family succession – a dramatic rise which suggests that inheritance tax had formerly been a significant roadblock. Furthermore, family successions after the reform were found to invest more and to hold more cash to finance these investments.

To sum up, the challenges created by laws of succession and inheritance taxes are particularly testing in countries that impose restrictions on wealth transfer and high tax rates. Given the prevalence of family ownership around the world, this has major policy implications. Laws that stipulate that a founder's assets must be divided equally among heirs (ostensibly aimed at ensuring equal opportunity) would seem to limit the choice of inheritance model for the business, jeopardizing future investment as well as family harmony. Similarly, succession taxes tend to discourage the perpetuation of wealth within a few dynasties, drawing on the equality-of-opportunity principle that every individual should start out with a similar endowment of resources. They also lower investment around succession, therefore curbing the firm's growth and limiting investment opportunities.

Discover more

Bennedsen, Morten, Joseph P.H. Fan, Ming Jian, and Yin-Hua Yeh. Family Firm Succession: the Role of Family Assets and Roadblocks. Forthcoming in *Journal of Corporate Finance*.

Bennedsen, Morten, Kasper Meisner Nielsen, Francisco Pérez-González, and Daniel Wolfenzon. Inside the Family Firm: The Role of Families in Succession Decisions and Performance. *Quarterly Journal of Economics*, 122(2), 647–691, 2007.

Bennedsen, Morten and Kasper Meisner Nielsen. Report on Family ownership and succession in Denmark. 2014.

Pérez-González, Francisco. Inherited Control and Firm Performance. *American Economic Review*, 96(5), 1559–1588, 2006.

Tsoutsoura, Margarita. The Effect of Succession Taxes on Family Firm Investment: Evidence from a Natural Experiment. Forthcoming in the *Journal of Finance*.

Highlights

- Evidence from three continents shows that succession is very challenging for business families, regardless of size, country and culture.
- The *FB Map* predicts that succession is most likely to succeed when family assets are strong and roadblocks can be minimized.
- The most common succession challenges include:
  - To plan the best possible succession model given the cultural reality the firm and the family live in.
  - To transfer intangible family assets across generations.
  - To equip the next generation with the best possible skills for taking over the responsibility, including nurturing, education, and relevant experience outside the family firm.
  - To plan for changes to business strategies, organizational structure and governance often associated with the transition from one generation to the next.

- To work around institutional barriers such as inheritance laws and taxes.
- Transparent long-term planning which is communicated and shared among family members increases the likelihood that the firm will prosper after succession.

In the next chapter we discuss exit from two angles: the challenge for owner-mangers around their own personal exit, and how the *FB Map* can help a family plan a collective exit.

chapter

7
Exit

In our experience, exiting the family firm is perhaps the most difficult decision an entrepreneur has to take. For decades the firm has been the centre of their existence, the embodiment of their dreams, and the focus around which the family has developed. In this chapter we consider both types of exiting – collectively by the family, and individually by the entrepreneur.

The outright sale of the firm (whose new owners then put in place a new management team) constitutes the most definitive form of exit. But, as we have seen, there are other ways of relinquishing control. For example, the family may retain ownership but exit at managerial level, or it may decide to list the business through an initial public offering and only relinquish control afterwards. Some exits are swift and definitive, others can take years and be more reversible in nature. The Toyoda family, for example, continued to be Toyota's largest strategic shareholder (with a 5 percent shareholding), but stayed out of top management for 14 years until Akiro Toyoda became CEO in April 2009. In some instances the family is ultimately pushed out as a result of an ownership structure created many years earlier, or because over time they gradually allowed their control to be eroded as the firm grew.

Our starting point for discussing exits is again the *FB Map* as illustrated in Figure 7.1. The *FB Map* predicts that families will investigate exit options where there is a combination of *declining* strategic value of the assets that built the company and *increasing* roadblocks related to family ownership and control. In the planning process, a number of key issues must be resolved such as the timing, the exit model, and what the family will do afterwards.

We begin with a classic case: an exit from a 100-year-old family business. Although the firm never grew big, the family did. And this, combined with shifting market forces, ultimately pushed them into selling the business. We then describe the exit of the founding partners of Little Sheep, a successful franchise-based restaurant chain in mainland China, showing how ownership dilution can be a double-edged sword. In this instance, a governance mechanism that had initially served to finance growth and incentivize key personnel and franchisees ultimately drove the founder and his long-time partners out of the chain. Finally, Kraft Foods' take-over of the long-established UK chocolate firm Cadbury in 2010 provides a cautionary tale of a family driven out of a publicly traded company because its early growth strategy and ownership design decisions unwittingly left it vulnerable to an aggressive raider.

We then consider exiting from the perspective of the individual. Asking tough questions that (for good reason) have been postponed and coming to terms with the psychological aspects of retirement is difficult for entrepreneurs whose entire existence has revolved around the firm. The notion of life without work is hard to accept. Many entrepreneurs don't know how to relax – to spend their days playing golf or looking after grandchildren. When these personal challenges are added to professional decisions such as the choice of exit model, of successor, and how to organize future ownership, no wonder they postpone thinking them through.

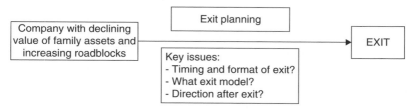

FIG 7.1 The *FB Map*: the exit path

We have already seen how Wang Yung-ching, founder of Formosa Plastics, spent decades organizing the succession to his corporate assets, but left no will concerning the distribution of his personal fortune. Also how Ingmar Kamprad left the daily operations of IKEA to a non-family management team, having initially wanted one of his three sons to succeed him. And even how Sir Run Run Shaw, who chaired the publicly traded company Television Broadcasting Limited in Hong Kong until he was 103, chose his 79-year-old wife as his successor, and finally sold the business entirely.

Based on a survey of around 2,800 owner-managers in small and medium-sized companies, we explore the issues involved in planning personal exits as well as ways to fill the vacuum when the firm is gone.

Exit forces

Selling the business after decades of family involvement is a very big change. It is not an easy decision: it takes time and energy and raises multiple questions about life after the firm.

As indicated by the *FB Map*, exit is a natural solution when the strategic value of family assets is declining and the roadblocks associated with family ownership are on the increase – be they from increased competition, technology or market-driven industry concentration, or from an increasing number of family members with diverging opinions.

All three of those forces were in evidence at the Vordingborg Lumber Yard, presented in Chapter 3. The Brorsen family, who had owned and managed the business for almost a century, sold it in 2007. The story of their exit illustrates how family and market roadblocks ultimately left them with no other viable solution.

You will recall how the dilution of ownership among the burgeoning family created a series of increasingly challenging roadblocks. In the second generation a son was removed from management, and in the third and fourth generations his family challenged the way the company was run. The managing heirs consistently refused to pay dividends in order to reinvest profits in the firm, prompting dissatisfaction among those who were less involved. Until the fourth generation, everyone had known the founder Phillip Brorsen, or at least had childhood memories of him. Conflicts were manageable; disagreements about corporate policy or strategic decisions never got out of hand out of respect for the grandfather. After his death, conflicts escalated with the branch that included the descendants of Karl, the son removed from management in the 1930s. They demanded bigger pay-outs, then asked to be bought out, and ultimately insisted the company be sold. Hence Tim Brorsen – third-generation steward – decided to prune the tree in 2001 and buy out the dissenting branch.

Beyond the mounting family roadblocks, the market was also changing. Ownership was concentrating in chains – companies that bought up several yards across the country (and sometimes in neighboring countries). But Vordingborg Lumber Yard did not have the capital to invest and grow. It became clear at a family shareholders meeting in 2005 that the non-managing members had coordinated their interests, sending a strong signal that a majority wanted to sell. Added to the prevailing economic situation and the changes in the market, the writing was on the wall. The lumber yard was sold, at a good price, to a chain of lumber yards in 2008. After almost a century in business, the Brorsen family venture was over.

Their case is typical of small and medium-sized family businesses around the world in a number of ways. First, the firm was not big enough to make an impact on the life of non-managing family members. When the ratio tipped in their favor, the roadblocks (diverging family interests) escalated to a point where exit was the only realistic solution. Second, without the capital or the growth potential to become a big player, market concentration can force a family out. It was not economically viable to sustain a two-plant lumber yard when other yards were becoming franchises of larger chains. The Brorsen story thus serves as a reminder that smaller family firms don't always decide their future: external and internal pressures can make selling the only reasonable option.

This in turn generates another insight. In a fast-evolving industry, families should always be prepared for a sale, or at least to discuss exiting. Many refuse to discuss the possibility when a potential buyer shows up, and the acquirer ends up buying their local competitor instead. If no further buyers arrive and the competition intensifies, the family will end up in an even worse situation. So we urge families to always be ready for exit, even if they dream of handing the firm on to future generations.

One of the biggest obstacles to selling a small family business is its valuation. Indeed in our experience, it is the main reason why negotiations break down. It's unlikely that a formal valuation will have been made when a potential buyer arrives. The entrepreneur may have a gut feeling and can put a figure on the company – one that relies heavily on intangible assets. For the outsider this seems opaque. Moreover, they will not be willing pay for value linked to non-transferable family assets.

LITTLE SHEEP: THE SHEPHERD'S EXIT

Born in Baotou, Inner Mongolia, Zhang Gang made his fortune from scratch. After a short stint as a factory worker in Baotou Steel Factory, he ventured into clothes retailing. In the early 1990s, Zhang entered the cell phone business, eventually becoming the sole distributor of cell phone equipment in Inner Mongolia. He founded Little Sheep on 8 August 1999, with co-founder Chen Hongkai, who had a 40 percent stake. Its Mongolian lamb-based hot pan cuisine was an instant success. Little Sheep quickly became a franchise group with hundreds of outlets.

Zhang believed in sharing ownership to attract and incentivize key people. 'I was born an "Alpha Man." My management philosophy is human-based. Most of my partners and I have been old friends for many years, and we trust each other deeply ... I want Little Sheep to be "Chinese Yum," a great company that lasts a century'. Zhang shared the ownership with long-term employees and franchise owners who deeply respected his leadership: 'Our chairman is a visionary and intelligent man. He is an expert in gathering talented people by sharing shares', said Wang Daizong, former Chief Financial Officer of Little Sheep. After five years there were around 50 owners, but the way ownership was designed left the founder in control.

Little Sheep partnered with the 3i Group Plc and Prax Capital Fund ILP in June 2006, and went public on the Hong Kong Stock Exchange in June 2008, raising about HKD 460 million. On 25 March 2009, 3i and Prax Capital sold their stake to YUM.

On 2 February 2012, Little Sheep Group Limited was privatized and sold to US fast-food giant Yum! Brands Inc, three years and seven months after being the first mainland China catering business listed in Hong Kong.

Little Sheep is an interesting case of an ownership design that ultimately led to the exit of the founder and his long-term partners. It's a fascinating story because the founder strove to build for the long term together with a nucleus of long-term partners including his co-founder. In developing Little Sheep, he faced two roadblocks: how to finance the fast-growing franchise chain without losing control, and how to incentivize and forge long-term bonds with key investors, franchise owners and core employees. He resolved both of them via an innovative ownership design.

Zhang solved the incentive challenge by giving shares to loyal employees, franchise owners and investors. (Figure 7.2 illustrates the evolution of ownership over time). He and co-founder Chen Hongkai remained the sole owners up to 2001. Zhang invited franchise owners and key personnel to share ownership, and four years later there were almost 50 owners. Furthermore, to finance growth he invited in two private equity firms and eventually went public. To keep control he used a pyramidal structure. He organized the nucleus of long-term investors into the controlling holding company, Possible Way, and organized other smaller individual share-owners into the non-controlling company, Billion Year. Zhang Gang controlled the nucleus through a passive investor (Li Xudong – a major franchise owner) whose votes he controlled. But by 2008, when Little Sheep went public, Zhang's share was diluted to 12.93 percent.

The innovative ownership design was hugely successful in resolving roadblocks in the form of finance, incentives and loyalty. However, opposing management philosophies emerged: the private equity funds pushed for professionalizing, whereas the old nucleus wanted to keep the old ways. Outsiders were appointed to top positions and tried to professionalize management and structure the organization. Tensions grew. The private equity firms sold their stake to Yum! and exited. Yum! in turn pushed for privatization, hoping to buy out the other owners to refocus the organization.

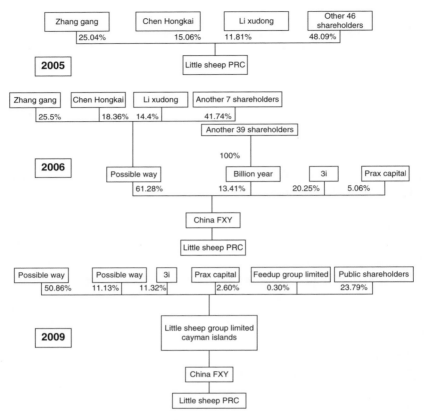

<figure>FIG 7.2 Evolution of ownership structure in Little Sheep</figure>

The case highlights how the management and ownership model that had worked so well during the expansion of Little Sheep ultimately became too big for the founder to keep control and impose his ideas on the business. Ownership dilution made it harder to implement the overall strategy. It was only through the exit and the sale to Yum! that ownership and management became re-focused.

The Little Sheep example shows how ownership dilution can be a double-edged sword. On the one hand it was key to building incentives, loyalty and remunerating key franchise owners and personnel, as well as financing the growth of the young company. On the other hand, the dilution led to differences in management views about strategy. With its radical expansion, Little

Sheep's brand value was heavily undermined. There was little coordination between branch offices or control of franchise restaurants. In response to a call to focus ownership and control to streamline the organization, the solution was to sell to Yum! and for the original 'shepherds' to exit.

While Vordingborg Lumber Yard shows how family and market roadblocks can force a family to exit even after 100 years of successful ownership, Little Sheep's explosive growth created so many organizational challenges that the founding nucleus exited within 15 years of starting up. The long-term consequences of growth and ownership design are also key elements in our next exit case. This time the family did not leave voluntarily but was forced out by an aggressive raider, ending more than 170 years of principled capitalism.

THE END OF QUAKER CAPITALISM KRAFT TAKES OVER CADBURY

In 2007, the 64-year-old American billionaire Nelson Peltz bought 3 percent of the shares of Cadbury Schweppes. He insisted that the combined company was worth around GBP 12 billion, but was not realizing its true value. In an open letter dated 18 December 2007, he said that the current management's credibility among shareholders was so low that they had nowhere to hide.

In the spring of 2008, Peltz was happy to see a de-merger of Cadbury and Schweppes, although the cost soared to almost 1 billion pounds, even if most financial analysts agreed that it significantly increased shareholder value. Cadbury was now smaller, valued at around 8–9 billion pounds, and vulnerable to a takeover, since the Cadbury family and its Quaker trusts no longer had a controlling ownership stake.

In late August 2009, Cadbury chairman Roger Carr received a voicemail, which began: 'This is Irene Rosenfeld. I'm in the UK next week and wouldn't mind coming by for a cup of coffee ...' Rosenfeld was the chairman of Kraft Foods, America's largest food giant. She made an offer to buy Cadbury in a shares and cash deal worth GBP 10.2 billion.

Carr's response was: 'First of all, this is something I want to discuss with the board. Secondly, Cadbury is a very good business, it's doing very well as an independent and certainly doesn't need Kraft'. Subsequently the board declined the Kraft offer, but Rosenfeld went public with the offer via the press – a so-called 'bear hug'. The Cadbury family, employees and the British public were shocked, but its stakeholders finally woke up to the long-term consequences of being a public company with a diluted shareholder base.

The very public pursuit of Cadbury prompted hedge funds and short-term investors to buy shares in Cadbury, hoping for a premium if the company were indeed sold. By January 2010, hedge funds, which had owned less than 5 percent of Cadbury in August 2009, now held a 30 percent stake. It was rumored that most institutional and financial investors would sell if the offer was just 20 pence higher than they had paid for the shares only weeks before.

Running out of options, Cadbury tried to bring in a 'white knight' – other buyers to bid for the company or agree to merge. The candidates were the usual suspects: Mars-Wrigley, Nestlé and Hershey. Kraft then sold its pizza business in the US to Nestlé, which provided GBP 3.7 billion in cash and made Nestlé's interest in Cadbury disappear.

In the first week of January 2011, Rosenfeld met with Carr again, this time offering GBP 8.50 per share. At that point Carr knew that Cadbury would be taken over.

Source: 'The Chocolate Wars' by Deborah Cadbury and the two-part INSEAD case 'The Chocolate Factory' by Deborah Cadbury and Morten Bennedsen.

The Kraft offer was based on raising an estimated GBP 7 billion of debt and on the premise that there would be efficiency savings of more than GBP 400 million per year. The takeover was not only a shock to the family, it sparked enormous public debate in the UK about the choice between 'principled capitalism', as the Cadbury family called their values-based leadership, and short-term shareholder interests. It was also about the ability to keep British firms under British ownership in an ever more globalized world.

The Cadbury exit underscores the challenges of keeping control in large publicly traded family firms. In fact, the explanation for it originated with the merger of Fry and Cadbury and the resulting distribution of shares between the respective families. A series of events subsequently reshaped the ownership structure of the company, ultimately making it vulnerable to a hostile takeover.

As we saw in Chapter 5, the listing of Cadbury was driven by at least three roadblocks: the rich-on-paper but cash-poor members of the Fry family, the increasing ratio of non-involved Cadbury family members, and the charitable trusts set up by the Quaker founders in pursuit of social objectives.

It is intriguing that 40 years later the listing would prove to be the mechanism through which the family was ultimately forced out. There were two reasons for this. The first was that the family listed the firm without building in any further protection to prevent the transfer of their remaining shares. Any member could, in principle, sell his or her shares on the open market. Nor did the family's shares entitle them to more control than non-family shares. This is common in family firms but potentially dangerous. The Cadbury family assumed that they were protected since they held a majority of the shares and that the charitable trusts had so many shares that an outsider could never secure a controlling interest. In contrast, when Nestlé listed in Switzerland, voting shares could only be held by Swiss investors – an arrangement that protected the company from takeover, allowing it to grow into the giant it is today.

The second reason was that the company partly financed its ambitious growth plans by issuing new shares. In this way the family- and trust-owned shares were proportionally reduced. Henceforth the majority were held by diffuse shareholders and institutional investors. The firm was safe during the decades when Cadbury and Schweppes merged, since the combined company was so big that no outsider could buy it.

Those who originally took Cadbury public could not have foreseen the way that investors (hedge funds and other short-term investors) would ultimately put pressure on management to maximize shareholder value.

The American billionaire Pelz was pivotal in splitting up Schweppes and Cadbury, and the moment that happened, it was clear that the ownership design had left Cadbury extremely vulnerable. Thus the Cadbury case is also a lesson in how difficult it can be for publicly traded family firms to defend the family's control (as well as its values). As soon as Cadbury was put in play, hedge funds bought 30 percent of the firm in expectation of a final offer from Kraft that would give them a 20 pence margin. With 30 percent of shares in the hands of hedge funds ready to be transferred, it became clear that Kraft would win.

One obvious insight here is that ownership design is crucial to the long-term survival of families in business, and that ownership and governance decisions can have an impact on control many years later. Cadbury is not alone in this respect. Many families do not understand the long-term consequences of going public or how listening the shares can be a threat to their future control. As we saw earlier, the Hermès family's control was contested after going public. Indeed they could have lost the firm had the French government not allowed them to put their shares into a trust without compensating minority owners.

It is our experience that the growth of the family and the increasing ratio of uninvolved to involved members are the most common reasons for exit. As the family grows, members lose interest in the company and disengage from the business. As they disperse (sometimes across the globe), it becomes more difficult to impose shared values, presuming they share the entrepreneurial talent of their elders.

Changing family culture also plays a role in exit decisions. In the West, families are becoming more democratic in the sense that the older generation respects the free will of the next generation. The ability to say 'no' to parents may be greater than in the past. Indeed we have met many second- and third-generation entrepreneurs who refuse to force the family business upon their children (unlike their own parents). Many of them had other dreams when they were young – about seeing the world, doing something different – yet they sacrificed these on behalf of their parents' desire to see the family business continue. They learned that the family business brings obligations as well as opportunities – and refuse to impose these on their offspring. The dream of seeing the kids

families are becoming more democratic

involved increasingly gives way to letting them make their own choices in life. Whereas this tendency is less developed in other parts of the world, we believe it will become more common in Asia, Africa and Latin America in generations to come.

We saw in the previous chapter that the decision to pursue a family succession is affected by socio-economic trends. With families producing fewer children, we can expect to see a higher rate of exit. Birth rates in Europe and the US have declined significantly over the last 40 years, the divorce rate is increasing, and traditional family structures are being challenged.

Cultural factors can also affect exit decisions. As the flow of people and information around the world continues to accelerate, the idea of staying in a small town and taking over the family business loses its lustre. Children of highly successful business families may be more tempted by a life of luxury, fast cars and good wine than to stay in a backwater and run the family business – particularly in countries such as mainland China.

In addition to these family roadblocks, family assets can be made redundant by new technology developments. Whereas families used to transfer a set of unique skills from father to son over centuries, new materials and new machines can revolutionize the system. Remember how Hermès, which proudly refined its craftsmanship over 150 years, went through a serious crisis in the 1970s when plastic and nylon suddenly became hip in the clothing industry. When demand for Hermès leather bags and silk scarves declined sharply with the introduction of plastic and polyester, Robert Dumas-Hermès halted production rather than break with tradition. Though this impacted profitability for over a decade, a taste for the original products revived and its reputation remained intact. Hermès was right to stay faithful to its values and quality, but many other families have been forced out of business.

Changes in the structure of the market can affect whole industries. The luxury industry is a powerful example of this. In the beginning, the market revolved around skilled artisans, many of them located in central Europe, serving a local elite. A hundred years ago, when the market extended to the US, meeting customer needs on the other side of the Atlantic was a challenge for these established family businesses, and even more so when Asia took off and the Middle East became a huge market. In the coming decade, mainland China is expected to be the fastest growing market for the industry.

Since changes on this scale were too big a roadblock for many small and artisanal family businesses (some of them over 100 years old), an alternative organizational form evolved to cope with the market changes, expanding swiftly by mergers and acquisition to enjoy the scale effects of geographic and product diversification. LVMH and Kering (who we met in Chapter 3) are two such conglomerates.

Similarly, 100 years ago there were more than a 1,000 family owned newspaper companies in the US. With the advent of new technology and the globalization of news, many families were forced to sell. Today there are only a handful left in the media industry.

Institutional roadblocks can be a major driver of family exits, as we have already seen, including China's one-child policy, which may account for a wave of exits from the private sector in future, the liberalization of the banking sector in Hong Kong, where the number of family banks has shrunk from 150 to less than five in 30 years, and South Africa's empowerment of the black population.

Exits can also be due to a lack of ambition. A family may have reached the pinnacle of its ambition by building a thriving business in a local market that provides income to the family, job security to workers, and recognition in the local environment. They may decide to sell the business simply because they don't want to take it to the next stage, as that implies investing in new markets, moving production out to low-wage countries, and reducing family control over the day-to-day running of the business.

To sum up, many factors can push a family to exit, whether as a result of previous governance decisions, family or cultural developments, or market/industry evolution.

Exit models

All over the world, a common model for exiting the family firm is to sell the firm to existing managers who are interested in continuing the enterprise after the family has left – a so-called management buyout (MBO). This is a relatively simple way of exiting and can be administered with a minimum of external help from accountants, lawyers or corporate finance specialists. It is typically the outcome of a long process where the senior managers and the owners have been talking and planning for some time. The senior managers have an interest in continuing the firm and may dream of being captains of the ship. The advantages are many: the new owners know the business inside out, they have a good relationship with the employees, customers and suppliers and the bank knows them well. When family assets are an important factor in the firm's business strategy, an MBO provides a special advantage. Since family assets are difficult to transfer, there will always be some loss, but the loss will be smaller if senior managers continue running the firm – they have typically worked closely with the family, can exploit the same business and political networks, and understand the importance of the heritage or values underpinning the business model. Thus a major reason to choose this exit model is to have new owner-managers in charge who understand the DNA of the firm and can minimize disruption on the operational side.

Structuring the deal is the main challenge in MBOs. How can managers finance the purchase of the company? As salaried employees they tend not to have accumulated a large fortune that can be used to buy out the family, so they need the backing of banks or equity investors. Part of structuring the deal is to put a value on the company that both the family and the senior partners can agree upon. In our experience, this is not a major stumbling block – typically the buyer and the seller have a common view of the firm, so the risk of negative surprises after the sale is small. However, they may want to have an external valuation by a trusted third party as part of the process.

A close cousin of the management buyout is the management buy-in (MBI), where the family sells to one or more *outside* investors who are looking for a firm where they can be owner-managers. Although initially this will not change the firm significantly – the continuation of business and employees is the focus – there are important differences. First, it is harder to transfer family assets since the new owner-managers typically have no relationship with the firm before the purchase. Thus their business strategies will be less anchored in the previous strategy and over time there may be changes. The new owner-manager may be less attached to existing employees and/or the environment where the firm is located, so again changes in employment or operational geography may be more likely in a MBI.

Second, valuation may be more challenging. Many family owners have unrealistic expectations about the value of their company. It is not easy to value a privately held family business. Much of the value may derive from intangible family assets and goodwill. As they have little incentive to seek a formal valuation, they base their estimate on their personal view (typically undocumented), often failing to understand that the family assets are worth much less when they are no longer around.

A third exit model is to sell to a strategic buyer – a firm or owner-manager that sees the family business as a strategic asset to add to its existing assets with the aim of expanding. It could be a local competitor who knows the family and the business well. It could be a national competitor that buys up many firms as a way of consolidating its industry position, or a foreign player that wants to establish a market presence in the country. The negotiation of the deal will be very different in each of these cases.

If the local competitor is the only buyer, the situation can be psychologically challenging, especially if buyer and seller have been competing for years – creating a sense of winner and loser. Negotiations can be difficult and driven by idiosyncratic issues. They will often include discussion of how to secure jobs and how to keep operating the facilities. Valuation tends to be less complicated because both buyer and seller have a clear view of the firm's potential.

Selling to an outsider who is using the acquisition to grow has its own challenges. The first is to be ready for sale when the right buyer arrives. Most families assume they can choose the timing of their exit. While in principle this is true, a buyer may not be ready when they want to exit; and potential offers will vary over time. The right buyer may only arrive once-in-a-lifetime or after years have elapsed. If the family is not ready, and the (national or international) player that could have bought them buys the local competitor instead, it can be a costly mistake, especially if the competition intensifies and no alternative buyer shows up. This may significantly reduce the price they get when they are eventually ready to sell. If the strategic buyer is not a local competitor, valuation may be the biggest obstacle. Again it's a case of exaggerated expectations that are rarely related to the tangible assets or formal evaluation.

A fourth exit model is to sell to a private equity fund or a similar financial investor. This option is one that many entrepreneurs find attractive, partly because they assume they will get a good price, but also because they avoid selling to their rival, and they may even get to serve on the board or in some kind of managerial position after the sale. There are many cases of successful sales to private equity firms, as the following examples illustrate.

As incomes rose in the 1960s and 1970s, people in the Nordic countries increasingly bought second homes – vacation properties that were used for a few weeks every year. A handful of visionary entrepreneurs made a business out of renting out such houses when the owners weren't using them. After 20 years of steady growth, they had made a fortune and vacation home rentals were an established business. But it had become clear that the market for renting vacation homes in Scandinavia was in need of consolidation. There were too many players, as well as room for synergies – from merging IT platforms, achieving scale economies, and brand recognition. A consolidated company could become one of the industry leaders in Europe.

The major roadblock to this process was the egos of the strong-minded entrepreneurs who could not agree on a consolidation model, in particular who should buy whom. In 2001 and 2002, the private equity fund Polaris bought up the two biggest players and through a series of acquisitions became a major European player. In the end, the PE fund exited through a sale to another major European player at a very good price. It had been able to catalyze the consolidation process in a way that the original founders could not do on their own.

Our second example, Kompan, is today a global market leader in playground construction. When artist Tom Lindhardt in the beginning of the 70s discovered that kids loved to climb on his colorful sculptures, he began constructing playground equipment in strong colors. It was hugely popular and the company went public 16 years later. His vision was simple: to change the way kids played and to keep production and headquarters in the small town where he grew up. Having fulfilled his ambition he had no urge to grow bigger.

In two rounds of funding, private equity invested in the company and in the end it was taken private with the aim of making it a global leader. The PE fund bought up competitors in the Nordic countries, Europe and Australia, moved the production facilities to the Czech Republic, and the original factory was ultimately sold. In sum, private equity was able to exceed the founding family's ambitions and take the firm to the next level. Indeed PE funds are often prepared to pay a high price for firms with potential they can unlock.

Exiting through sale to a private equity fund may be hugely attractive to entrepreneurs but very few family firms ever get this option. PE funds buy up firms of a certain size, within certain industries, and with a clear potential for expansion. Given their urgency to exit the investment within a relatively short time, they look for targets that can be taken to the next level relatively fast. The traditional old family business that has relied on organic growth for decades rarely fits this case. Selling to private equity funds is an option only for a select few. Most family firms have to rely on other forms of exit.

A fifth model is a gradual exit (upper left corner of the *FB Map*). The first step is typically to professionalize the company, that is, to hire more professional managers and make the organizational structure more transparent. The next step is to dilute one's ownership and over time become a minority owner with a hands-off approach to management.

We have already seen how the founder Zhang Gang of Little Sheep exited gradually. He used ownership dilution as a governance mechanism to expand the restaurant chain. This reduced his own stake but for years he kept control through a clever ownership design. Then he brought in professional managers to cope with the expansion and organizational complexity of Little Sheep. In 2004, he hired Lu Wenbing who worked on changing the culture of the franchise chain. Lu brought in other external managers and was pivotal in enlarging the ownership base, first through private equity funding and then through an IPO. During this period, Zang Gang took an increasingly hands-off approach to management. After privatization and the sale to Yum! he ultimately became a minority owner with little managerial engagement.

A specific model of partial exit is through going public. Listing the firm is a natural way to professionalize the firm and to reduce the dependence of the family behind the business. As we observed in Chapter 5, it can be an efficient way to finance growth of the family business and provide cash to individual members.

Exit planning

Our first story illustrates how difficult retirement can be for a hardcore entrepreneur, to the point where it dragged down a business empire and the family that built it.

Herbert H. Haft was born in 1920 in the USA. Son of a Russian immigrant pharmacist, he became a successful businessman who developed a number of discount store chains in the drugstore, bookstore and auto-part businesses. Haft created the first Dart Drug discount store in 1955 and sold the chain in 1984 when it had 75 outlets. He invested the proceeds in other businesses such as alcohol, books and auto parts, and aggressive raids on Safeway and Stop & Shop, aiming at taking partial control. In the end he was bought out, in the process earning 250 million dollars.

Herbert was married to Gloria. Their eldest son, Robert, was groomed to be the successor and always showed a keen interest in business, unlike his younger brother, Ronald, and sister, Linda. In 1977, Robert wrote a business case at Harvard Business School and, together with the father, used this to develop Crown Books, which went on to become the third-largest bookstore chain in the US.

In 1993, in an interview with the *Wall Street Journal*, Robert, age 40, stated that a change of guard in the family business venture was imminent. Having never consulted his 72-year-old father prior to the interview, the news came as a shock since Herbert had no plans to step down. The day after the interview was published, Robert was fired.

This triggered a very public family battle which made national headlines. Gloria, who supported her son, was removed from the board for being disloyal to the business. She filed for divorce on grounds of infidelity, physical abuse and wrongful discharge. The family now openly at war, Herbert turned to his younger son, Ronald, whom he had hitherto spurned because of Ronald's openly gay lifestyle. Ronald played along and became the new CEO of the group.

To dilute the share of ownership of the other family members and to reduce the divorce settlement with his wife, Herbert gave Ronald a very generous stock allocation. Initially, the younger sister Linda supported her father, but later aligned with her eldest brother and mother. After one year in charge, Ronald was fired by his father over a disagreement about real estate. Now there was a full-blown legal battle between Herbert and all the other family members.

Not surprisingly, Crown Books fell into decline. It filed for bankruptcy in 2001. At the start of the millennium, Robert built a dot.com pharmacy, which again upset his now 80-year-old father. Still spoiling for a fight, Herbert started a competitor. Both firms crashed when the IT bubble burst in 2001. Herbert remarried at the age of 83, a few months before he passed away, which embroiled the family in further disputes over his estate with his young widow.

From the outside, it is not easy to understand Herbert Haft's decisions – why did he not take up the role of the retired founder of the family empire and creator of the family fortune? Equally, why did Robert tell the *Wall Street Journal* that his father was retiring without having asked him? Few business people would be happy to learn of their unplanned retirement in the *Wall Street Journal,* even less via an interview with their son. And why did Herbert escalate the conflict to include his wife, his second son and his daughter, squandering a huge amount of money in the process as well as family harmony? The Haft debacle underlines the difficulty of reaching the exit decision for entrepreneurs, and the irrational path they may take.

To get further insight into the role played by family psychology and preferences in determining the succession model, we interviewed almost 2,800 owner-managers about their plans for exiting their family firms. The firms were mostly small and medium-sized incorporated stock companies, a majority of them in the first generation.

A large fraction of all family and other non-publicly traded corporations will be exited through either succession or sale during the next decade. To verify the number of approaching succession cases, we asked business owners when they expected to exit the company.

As can be seen from Figure 7.3, many expect to exit in the near future. One in five expect to exit within the next two years, and three in five within the next decade. Given that remarkable number, and the impending decisions about the future of their firms and their own future, we assumed that most family business entrepreneurs were deeply engaged in the planning process. We were wrong.

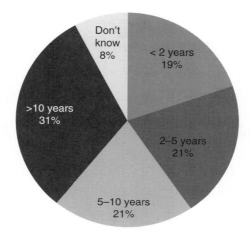

FIG 7.3 How many years to succession?

Note: based on 2,747 responses.

Figure 7.4 shows that for those who plan to exit within the next two years, 10 percent have not started planning for exit yet, half have finalized their exit plans, and 40 percent are still in the planning process.

For those who plan to exit from two to five years hence, almost one-third have not started planning yet and only one quarter have finalized their plans. Lack of preparation is even more dramatic in the group that plan to retire in five to ten years. Two-thirds of this group have not done any planning so far, and only one in eight has finalized the succession plan. Of those who foresee at least ten years to succession, almost 90 percent have not started the planning process.

These numbers underline how hard it is for owner-managers to work on succession planning ahead of time. Most wait until very close to the actual succession point to decide on a succession plan.

Figure 7.5 looks at anticipated exit models among family business owners according to whether they already have a plan, are engaged in the planning process, or have no succession plan.

For those who have a finalized exit plan, the two dominant forms are a family succession or a sale either as a management buyout or a management buy-in. These account for six out of ten cases. Notice that almost

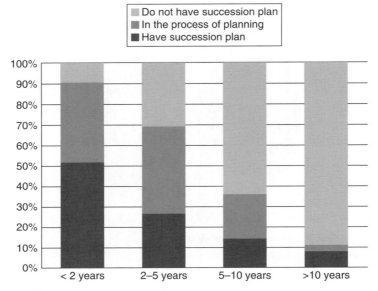

FIG 7.4 / **Do you have a succession plan?**

Note: Based on 2,747 responses.

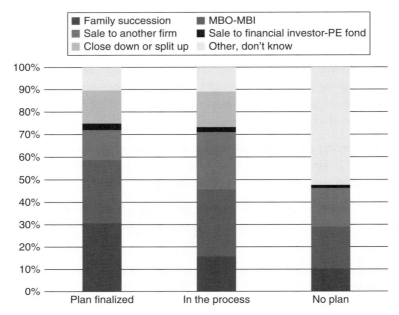

FIG 7.5 / **Expected exit model**

Note: based on 2,891 responses.

15 percent of firms plan to close down or split up the firm when the owner-manager exits. It is also worth remarking that few firms plan to sell to a financial investor such as a private equity fund.

There is a significant difference between the exit model favoured by entrepreneurs who are in the planning process compared to those without a plan. The 'planners' are less likely to implement a family succession and more likely to eventually sell. Those who have not yet started naturally have less clear expectations – essentially they are postponing the issue.

Given that many family firms reach the point of exit with no model in place, we sought to identify the personal or family roadblocks that constrain the process. From the many cases described above it is clear that personal, family and psychological factors are important determinants of the exit model, but we wanted further evidence that these case-based observations have a more general application.

As illustrated in the Haft case, lack of communication between a dominating business owner, the successor and the rest of the family can have devastating consequences. We therefore asked the owners if they had communicated their exit and/or succession plans.

Among those who had completed or were developing an exit plan, the vast majority had informed other people about the plan – so there was definitely *some* communication about the choice of succession model. But did this mean that families and successors in particular had been informed about the plan? In fact, less than 10 percent of entrepreneurs had informed their family. Even more surprisingly, almost none of the successors had been informed. Despite many owner-managers expecting family to take over the firm, very few of them had discussed this with their successors.

Instead of communicating with the family, most of them had discussed exiting with the board or chairman. It is difficult to judge what the consequences of such patterns are, but lack of communication obviously increases uncertainty and may postpone decision-making about future ownership and management structures. In the presence of risk and uncertainty, uninformed family members may choose other careers or decide to give up the family firm. It can also induce opportunistic and strategic behaviour among family members that can jeopardize future harmony and collaboration.

A second important roadblock in family succession concerns the role of the retiring business owner after succession. Will he/she be involved in the firm? Will he/she still exercise control and challenge the new management team by exploiting his superior knowledge of the firm and longstanding relationships with customers, employees and others? To find out, we asked the business owners that were actively planning for exit or had a finalized plan about what they expected to do after they had left the top job.

According to Figure 7.6, less than one out of five owners plan to retire after exiting the top job. Aproximately 30 percent plan to stay on in the firm after succession. A large fraction hope to engage in other business activities such as starting up new companies or sitting on corporate boards, and 27 percent 'don't know'.

The founder's future involvement can potentially be a roadblock to the succesful implementation of the succession. Many retired business owners make a valuable contribution to the family firm after succession – they are, after all, the most important of the family's assets and can smooth the transition of family assets. But they can also become a serious roadblock

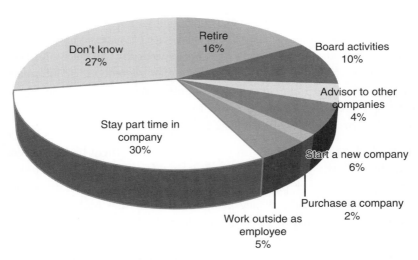

FIG 7.6   What does the entrepreneur plan to do after exiting the family business?

Note: Based on 1,395 responses.

if they hamper changes to the existing business model. Uncertainty about the owner-manager's future position can also delay succession planning and be a major impediment to family communication.

To understand the importance of such constraints, we asked the owner-managers who were actively planning or had a finalized a succession model to identify the biggest roadblock they had faced during the process. More pointedly, we asked if the connection between exit and retirement – either for others or for themselves – was an impediment in this sense.

Figure 7.7 indicates that the three biggest roadblocks in the planning process are the economic crisis, lack of buyers and the valuation issue, all of which are are linked to some extent. The economic crisis implies a decline in the number of potential buyers and in the price they are willing to pay. (Our interviews were done in late fall 2009, three months into the global financial crisis). It is worth emphasizing that valuation is a significant roadblock to successon planning. Again, we would strongly recommend having a transparent valuation of the company done by an independent third party.

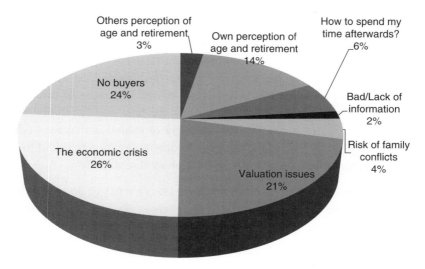

FIG 7.7 / The biggest challenges that the entrepreneurs face during the exit planning process

Note: Based on 1,395 responses.

It is interesting that, beyond the market roadblocks, many owner-mangers find it hard to accept retirement. One in five owner managers said that growing old and deciding how to spend time after retirement was a significant roadblock to planning. This confirms that personal and family psychological influences are crucial to understanding the succession process in family firms.

If personal and family issues are major roadblocks for owner-managers who are already involved in succession planning, they may account for the fact that so many family owners postpone thinking about how to exit the firm. Hence, we asked those who had indicated that they had not started succession planning why they did not have a plan, with a number of possible answers along the lines of 'being too busy' and 'not relevant at the present point in time' among others.

Almost 80 percent said that they had postponed thinking about succession issues. Part of this may be because exit is too far ahead in the future, but it may also be because these issues are difficult to confront. The concrete demands of the business leave little time to reflect on the future of the company, own's own future, and the many family interests involved.

Life after sale

For many families, life after sale is a new challenge. It may sound easy – no more work and lots of cash to finance a comfortable life – but the business has been the centre of the universe for decades. For as long as anyone in the family can remember, every dinner has had its share of business talk. For the next generation, the business is the only way to achieve real recognition – status in the family is strongly correlated with how much individuals are involved in the business. Suddenly the glue that had tied the family together is gone and it is not clear what replaces it.

We have seen that entrepreneurs often are unsure what to do after exiting. But beyond the individual challenges there is also the issue of what the family can do to continue the entrepreneurial ventures.

The most common and simplistic model is to split the surplus of the sale and let family members get on with their lives. A more ambitious strategy for good communicators is to stay together and invest the proceeds in new business ventures. The family becomes a private equity investor after selling the core business. We see this as a growing trend, particularly when the sale of the core business generates a relatively large amount.

One early example of rethinking the business venture after a forced exit is the Wendel family, who were in the steel business for more than 300 years before a crisis in the European steel industry triggered nationalization by the French government in 1978. The 300-plus family members decided to use the (modest) proceedings to invest in other private companies. Ernst Antoine Sallière led this new venture for almost three decades with extraordinary success. The investment company was ultimately listed on the French stock exchange, and at its peak was worth more than EUR 7 billion. The family has now grown to more than 1,000 family shareholders who together own 38 percent of the public company.

Today, none of them work for Wendel Investissements, but their business heritage continues to unite the family. To incentivize family members, an entrepreneurial prize is awarded every year to a member who starts up a new business. The family uses its network as a way of helping and grooming talented young entrepreneurs arising from within the large family.

One way to structure the future ventures of a family that exits its traditional business is through the creation of a family office. A family office can be the centre of their shared activities after exiting the businesses. The role of the family office can vary significantly depending on the size of the family fortune and the size of the family. Its typical functions include family and wealth management services.

For individual family members, the family office can help with legal and financial issues, such as filling out tax declarations, taking care of legal affairs and supporting educational activities. Some family offices are also responsible for governance activities including organizing family boards, social events and philanthropic activities. For the family as a group, the office can be in charge of wealth management including investments and property management.

Very few family offices around the world provide all the services listed above. Most formalized family offices are in the US or in Europe; they are less common in Asia, Latin America and the rest of the world, mainly because it is expensive to operate a full-service family office and only very wealthy families can afford one.

Discover more

Cadbury, Deborah. Chocolate Wars: The 150-year Rivalry between the World's Greatest Chocolate Markers. Public Affairs, The Perseus Books Group. 2010.

Cadbury, Deborah and Morten Bennedsen. Cadbury – The Chocolate Factory: Principled Capitalism (Part 1) and Sold for 20p. (Part 2). Case Pre-Release version, *INSEAD*, Spring 2013.

Gordon, Grant and Nigel Nicholson. Family Wars: Stories and Insights From Famous Family Business Feuds. Kogan Page Limited. 2010.

Highlights

- The *FB Map* predicts that families will investigate exit options when there is a combination of *declining* strategic value of the assets that built the company and *increasing* roadblocks related to family ownership and control.
- Exit can take many forms including going public and hiring external managers to outright sale to for example long term employees, new investors that want to manage the firm themselves, competitors or private equity funds.
- Exit planning is challenging and owner-managers tend to postpone it. Lack of preparation creates unclear transition models and that many companies suffer during and after the exit process.

In the final chapter we return to the foundations of the *FB Map* and look at further applications with a focus on how to integrate family and corporate governance into the long-term planning tool.

8

Beyond the Family Business Map

In the preceding chapters we have identified the core of every family firm that we have encountered: family assets and roadblocks. At their best, families manage their assets in ways that create exclusive business opportunities that are not available to non-family firms. In this final chapter we suggest a number of additional applications for the *FB Map*, and extend it to issues such as family governance and corporate governance.

To Build a sustainable family business is like making a clock – it's not enough to have the right parts, they must be perfectly coordinated so that we can tell the time. For this we need a well-designed blueprint that shows not only each of the parts but how they should be connected into a whole. Only with the blueprint can we confidently assemble the parts into a functioning watch. This analogy should help families, consultants and other service providers understand that what families need is a roadmap (blueprint) with suitable governance institutions (parts) to help the family and the firm advance to a pre-determined destination (telling the time).

In this chapter we explore three critical institutions: (1) family governance, (2) ownership design, and (3) corporate governance. While these are common to all family businesses, they are differently designed according to the family's particular roadmap and goals. First let's revisit the foundations of the *FB Map* and look at further applications.

The foundations of the *FB Map* revisited

The first dimension of the *FB Map* considers family assets. In Chapter 2 we saw many examples of powerful family assets which have become the foundation of successful business strategies.

The Höshi family enshrines the magic of the oldest family managed hotel in the world. When the 80-year-old Zengoro Höshi greets his customers as they drink cups of foaming green tea in the tearoom behind the reception, overlooking the beautiful 500-year-old Japanese garden, they have the unique sensation of being taken back 46 generations to AD 818, when the first Zengoro Höshi cared for the community in what is now the village of Awezu Onxen near Kamatzu in the Ishikawa district of Japan. It is a unique story that has made this little inn world famous, even if Zengoro Höshi (for good reason) has not exploited the full market potential of this family asset.

The Ochs-Sulzberger family's 100-year control of the *New York Times* is the foundation of the high-quality journalism for which it is renowned, enabling it to win more Pulitzer prizes than any other newspaper in the US. Its adherence to the basic principles of good journalism – the protection it gives to reporters and a willingness to stand by their stories at all times – is the enhanced value that it brings to the paper.

The work ethic of Formosa Plastics Group was forged from the hardship that Wang Yung-ching experienced during childhood, inspiring his values-driven leadership with its emphasis on hard work, cost savings and rigor. His philosophy, summed up in the phrase 'Get to the root of the issue', has remained anchored in the firm since his death.

The core of the *FB Map* is to recognize that the enhanced value provided by family assets is delivered through the *management* of the firm. It is the top manager whose values affect day-to-day corporate strategy; it is their connections that are used to improve business operations; and they who safeguard the firm's heritage and reputation over the decades. By management we mean the people involved in making key strategic decisions. In a western setting it will typically be the CEO and the chairman of the board. In Asia it tends to be the president of the corporation, who is often also the chairman.

Figure 8.1 represents this first dimension of the *FB Map*. The enhanced value of the family assets is correlated with the identity of the top manager. It follows that where there are sizeable family assets, there will be strong economic reasons to appoint management from within the family. When assets such as political and marital networks or reputation are embodied in the family and optimized by their day-to-day decisions, it makes sense to have family members as top managers.

Conversely, when such assets are less important, there is a stronger case for appointing management from outside. First, the 'gene lottery' leaves only a small probability that the best successor from a limited number of heirs will be more talented than the best external manager on the market, particularly for prosperous family firms which offer attractive career opportunities to experienced outsiders. Second, as a general rule, external managers are better educated and have more business experience at managerial and director level.

The second dimension of the *FB Map* concerns roadblocks. Family firms must build solid governance strategies to sidestep obstacles that originate within the family, the market, or local institutional environment. We have seen how, following the merger between the two British chocolate firms Cadbury and Fry, there were over 200 family owners. The major shareholders transferred their shares to charitable trusts, but there came a time when the firm needed capital to finance an ambitious growth strategy. Like other family firms, Cadbury chose to go public in 1962, allowing individual family members to cash in their shares as well as financing the company's expansion.

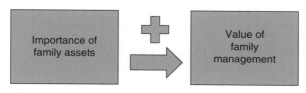

FIG 8.1 **Family assets and family management**

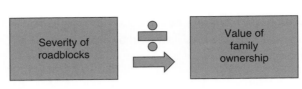

FIG 8.2 / Roadblocks and family ownership

Market concentration and lack of government protection changed the landscape of banking in Hong Kong. Sixty years ago there were more than 100 relationship-focused family banks; today the market is dominated by a handful of large listed banks.

In South Africa, the Black Economic Empowerment Programme created since the 1990s meant that white families had to develop structures admitting non-whites to partial ownership if they wanted to compete for government contracts.

The above examples highlight the various roadblocks that can emerge at the ownership level – the need for external capital, dilution in the absence of succession rules or control-enhancing mechanisms, a founder's desire to treat children equally – all of which may mean that resources are taken out of the firm to compensate family branches that have no management or ownership stake. Further constraints such as inheritance tax may mean that well-performing parts of the business have to be liquidated when the succession occurs.

Figure 8.2 represents this second dimension of the *FB Map*. Roadblocks generate specific constraints, hence exclusive family ownership becomes more costly. In other words there are economic arguments for giving up family ownership. In its most drastic form this could mean the outright sale of a company that has been in the family for generations. Less dramatic alternatives include inviting in new minority or majority owners, an over-the-counter sale of family shares that reduces its stake significantly, diluting family ownership through an initial public offering, and so on.

Locating family firms on the *FB Map*

In Chapter 4, we saw how the *FB Map* can be a powerful planning tool for individual family firms (be they owners and/or managers) and for outside analysts. Below we illustrate a number of other applications. We begin with how it can be used to understand and develop key governance structures, and then extend the analysis by showing exactly how the *FB Map* intersects with family and corporate governance.

First, let's apply the model to understand why firms end up with a particular governance structure, that is, a particular configuration of family involvement in management and ownership.

A number of prominent family firms are shown in Figure 8.3. In the bottom right quadrant we have the proud members of the Henokiens. For centuries these 38 companies have deployed strong family assets – focused on tradition, heritage, reliability and reputation – to survive and prosper in various industries around the world. By exercising prudence and focusing on organic growth they have avoided the constraints of being family owned. Hence, they have been able to keep ownership within the family and deliver generation after generation of family managers.

Moving upwards, we have classified the *New York Times* as a company with family management and to a large extent family controlled ownership. As described above, the Ochs-Sulbergers have delivered significant family value

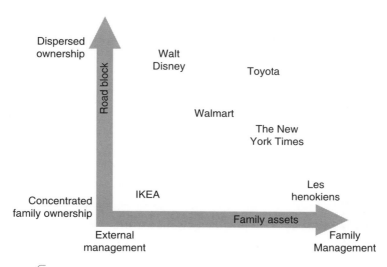

FIG 8.3 / **Locating a firm in the *FB Map***

to the media corporation. Until recently the constraints of family ownership have not been a major brake on its expansion or prosperity. For these reasons it has been an optimal governance structure, albeit the need for external capital has diluted family ownership over the last four decades.

Toyota is located in the top right quadrant. Clearly the Toyoda family name and reputation still represent a valuable asset for the firm, even if an increasing number of external investors have taken ownership stakes as a result of expansion so the family is no longer the controlling owner. Admittedly, times are not easy in 2009 and 2010: Toyota had recalled millions of cars and major strategic changes needed to be implemented. Having a Toyoda at the helm sent a clear signal to placate worried workers and other stakeholders.

Walmart is one of the largest family businesses in the US today. Again this is a 'mixed' case where the family – now in its second and third generations – still represents a valuable asset to the corporation but there is a blend of professional management and family influence on the board. The family continues to be an important owner but the need for external capital has diluted the nominal size of its stake.

The Walt Disney Corporation is one of the largest US corporations where the family has almost entirely exited, retaining only a symbolic ownership stake. After the death of the founder, none of his heirs were able to deliver significant value to the management of the corporation. An ambitious expansion into new domains in the entertainment industry on a global scale made the constraints of family ownership too heavy to be sustained.

At the Swedish company IKEA, we saw how following CEO Ingmar Kamprad's retirement, in the absence of significant family assets within the next generation, professional management was brought in at the top. Since no major constraints have arisen from the family's ownership, IKEA's ambitious global expansion has been achieved without diluting it. This combination of a lack of family assets in the second generation and a lack of ownership constraints puts the firm in the lower left quadrant.

The *FB Map* allows us to put the governance structures of family businesses into four major groups, whereas most family business research has hitherto focused on a binary classification (family/non-family firms). We have provided case-by-case evidence in support of this categorization, showing that governance structure is related to the nature and extent of family assets and roadblocks. But are these simply isolated cases, or is there systematic evidence for this categorization on a larger scale? What follows suggests that this is indeed the case.

Figure 8.4 depicts 193 Japanese firms listed on the nation's stock exchanges in the years after 1949. We tracked changes in their governance structures over time, counting the years from the day of listing. The lowest segment of the columns represents classic family firms – equivalent to the bottom right quadrant in the *FB Map* – where the family controls both ownership and key management positions in the corporation. The second lowest segment are those firms where the family still controls ownership, but the CEO and the chairman are 'salary men' – the term used in Japan to signify that the family has relinquished control of management but kept control of ownership. The second segment from the top are mixed cases of family

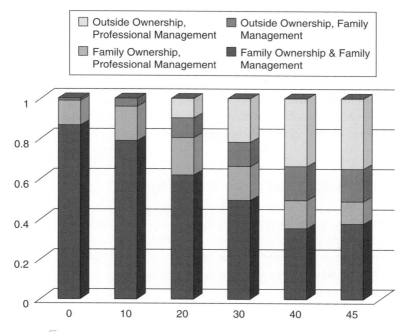

FIG 8.4 **Evolution of ownership and management in Japanese firms after IPO**

Source: *Exit and Transitions in Family Control and Ownership in Post-War Japan* by Morten Bennedsen, Vikas Mehrotra, Jungwook Shim and Yupana Wiwattanakantang. 2014.

involvement where only management control is still in the family's hands, like Akido Toyoda at Toyota. Finally, the top segment reflects family exits – where the family has relinquished control of both management and ownership, either by an outright sale of their stake or by a more gradual dilution of ownership to the symbolic level.

Note that 44 years after listing their family businesses, only 30 percent of the listed firms still have close family involvement with both a controlling ownership stake and family management. Around 40 percent of the families have exited the firm at both ownership and management levels.

The most interesting revelation is that 40 years on, around 30 percent of all Japanese firms have changed their governance structure to one of the two mixed cases described in the *FB Map*. Around 15 percent of family firms have retained family ownership while introducing professional management on all levels. And in even more cases the family has given up controlling ownership but is still active in management. The case of Akio Toyota is therefore far from unique – many families relinquish control on the ownership side but keep control on the management side.

The figure highlights the importance of the model's predictions for the four broad types of ownership and management structures. It is worth emphasizing that cases of mixed family ownership/salary management and non-family ownership/family management are not insignificant in Japan. In 2000, mixed cases constituted almost 20 percent of all corporations listed on the country's stock exchanges.

The *FB Map* and corporate governance

In the last couple of decades, corporate governance has become a key topic for large firms worldwide. The collapse of business empires such as Enron and WorldCom in the US, Parmalat in Italy, and others, has sparked a global debate about forms of governance.

Looking across diverse countries and cultures, we have been struck by the difference in focus when it comes to governance. We argue that the *FB Map* explains why the governance debate in

USA, Europe and Asia is so different. In the US and Europe, the debate is centered on the accountability of corporate governance institutions. Issues such as how to make boards accountable and how to select the ideal board are at its heart, including individual directors' backgrounds, competencies and (not least) independence from management, as well as how best to equip board members to oversee and steer a modern corporation.

A second hot topic on the western governance agenda is the compensation of managers and directors. Recent years have seen an explosion in executive pay, generating a heated debate about whether executives are worth the salaries they earn, and to what extent their compensation reflects actual performance. The reform of compensation is seen as a way to make board members more accountable in modern corporations.

However, these concerns come much lower on the agenda in Hong Kong, Japan, China and other Asian countries, where the governance debate centers on issues such as ownership of family firms. What is the right ownership model? How should families concentrate their control through control-enhancing mechanisms such as trusts and foundations? What model of succession should family firms choose when the older generation retires?

Whereas the variation in focus may seem puzzling at first, the *FB Map* offers an explanation. When family assets decline and roadblocks proliferate, the model predicts that we should see families relinquish control of management and reduce their de facto ownership. Once ownership is dispersed (there is no single controlling owner), a key governance issue is how do 'weak' owners ensure that management works in their interests. The problem of incentive alignment has been debated for decades. How can owners secure a return on their investment when power is delegated to powerful agents at the executive level? Another issue is how to get representatives on the board who are independent from management yet sufficiently competent to direct a large modern corporation. A related issue is how to align the incentives of powerful managers with those of weak owners to ensure a favorable return on investment, such as structuring remuneration in a way that makes managers internalize the owner's interests.

We observe that a majority of large US family firms fall into this segment of the *FB Map*: their family assets are not significant enough to outweigh the constraints of family management and so professional management has been installed. At the same time, the need for external capital to finance expansion has diluted the family's ownership stake, so questions of governance inevitably revolve around issues like accountability and remuneration. There is also the issue of how rich families should spend the wealth that they receive from their shares in the corporation, given that it is no longer a major source of capital for the firm, which may explain why we see an increasing focus on family investment offices in the debate on family firms in the US.

Conversely, where firms derive enhanced value from strong family assets and there are no significant constraints from family ownership, the model predicts that the family will remain in control, hence management accountability and remuneration issues will be of second-order importance. When the family CEO is also the owner, the structure of his or her remuneration will not be a major incentive, as the example of the UK-based Indian tycoon Lakshmi Mittal, CEO and owner of 41 percent of the Arcelor Mittal empire (and the richest person in Europe) illustrates. He took a salary cut in 2008 and 2009, leaving his base salary at USD 1.49 million. While this would seem a huge salary by ordinary standards, it was a fraction of his total wealth, estimated at USD 45 billion in January in 2008. As the majority owner of the corporation, the major part of his income derives from dividends and payouts, not salary.

In this instance, the *FB Map* predicts that the prime governance issues will focus on the optimal ownership structure within the family, particularly when the power of numbers tends towards ownership dispersion.

- How can ownership and management be transferred through the generations in a way that maximizes the potential of the firm and minimizes conflict within the family?
- What control-enhancing mechanisms can be used to implement an optimal ownership structure?
- How can such a structure leave control in the hands of family yet satisfy minority owners outside the family?

From these considerations, a number of issues arise in the classic family firm with concentrated ownership and management.

- What are the economic consequences of introducing control-enhancing mechanisms, such as trusts or foundations, dual-class shares or voting agreements?

- If the family occupies the most powerful executive positions, what is the role of non-family managers in the corporation?
- How can non-family managers be incentivized to pursue a career within the firm when the top positions are closed to them?
- How to design fair and transparent career paths for family members within the firm?
- What are the criteria for making it all the way to the top?
- How to select from among several qualified family members?

Again, we can use the *FB Map* to predict the orientation of governance issues in 'mixed' cases. When the family is still the dominant owner but has exited from the executive level, the focus will be on the incentive and entrenchment aspect of the relationship between managers and owners. In cases where the firm is wholly owned by the family, we rarely observe major incentive issues – the family closely monitors executive management and is often involved in important decisions. Hence a key governance issue is how to confer upon the professional managers enough freedom and trust to pursue long-term strategies that benefit the firm on a day-to-day basis. Even if the family has exited from management, family members may be reluctant to accept that they are not the best executives and that they no longer have the power to overrule the professionals. Thus the challenge for the governance structure is to put some distance between family and management such that competent professionals can focus on the prosperity of the company, rather than subjecting the firm to the idiosyncratic preferences of individual family members.

Perhaps most challenging from a governance perspective is where family managers prevail at the executive but not the ownership level, not because the family refuses to relinquish its power but because the value of its unique assets is recognized by the controlling non-family owners. Often such family managers are more powerful than their professional counterparts and have strong ideas about how to move the firm forward. The model predicts that the relevant governance questions in such cases will be:

- How do the owners structure governance to get most out of the assets that the family possesses?
- How do the owners incentivize family managers such that they defend the interests of all the owners, not simply those of the family?

The *FB Map* and family governance: keeping the family together

From the above discussion it's clear that a family must have the means to make critical decisions and resolve conflicts if it is to preserve its assets and manage the business on a long-term basis. Much has already been written about the importance of effective communication, team building, and conflict management. Our main preoccupation here is to emphasize how forms vary – despite the fact that many aspects of family governance are universal – mainly because of cultural differences.

Learning by example

How can a sense of governance be instituted among family members? For a small family, it could be as simple as the day-to-day education of children by the parents doing things together such as going to church (or temple), paying respects to ancestors, or engaging in educational, cultural and philanthropic activities.

Wang Yung-ching, founder of Formosa Plastics, whose philosophy was 'getting to the root of the issue', asked his children to detail their daily spending down to the cost of a toothbrush while studying overseas.

In Beijing, we met a successful Dutch third-generation business family member. When we asked how he had inherited his family values, he answered that when he was in college his father provided only basic funding and asked for spending reports, so he had to work part-time to cover his cost of living and education.

When an 80-year-old businessman in Hong Kong finally decided to retire, his children unanimously decided to continue their father's business. It was clear that they did not lack alternative opportunities; they were well educated and had successful professional careers. When asked why they were coming back to the family business, they answered that it was out of admiration for their father, who had donated one-tenth of his profits to church for the past 40 years on an anonymous basis. Although no one else knew the source of the donations, his children were well aware of the values underpinning his generosity and were deeply inspired. They wanted to keep the business and generate profits for that good cause.

Making decisions

For large families, more explicit forms of governance may be needed in addition to informal communication and inspiration. The family might consider holding formal meetings to discuss issues and make decisions. If there is a lack of consensus, decision-making rules should be laid down to resolve differences. Majority rule (with one person one vote) may work for families of a protestant background, which stresses equality and respect for independence of thought. It may work less well in families influenced by other cultures that do not embrace equality.

For example, Chinese culture promotes harmonious family and society. Interestingly, for thousands of years Chinese emperors and philosophers taught that harmony in the family and in society could be achieved by music and good manners rather than verbal communication and voting. In China there are principles governing relationships between superior and subordinate, father and son, husband and wife, siblings, and friends. A traditional Chinese family has a clear hierarchy: the father, the eldest son, the second son, and pre-marriage daughters. And the mother? She has no formal power but acts as a family coordinator behind the scenes. Daughters lose their position in the hierarchy after marriage when they join another family, albeit compensated by dowry. It goes without saying that in-laws have no power in the family. Ultimately the head of the hierarchy decides how family property is divided and how conflicts are resolved.

Indeed, on a scale of 0 to 100, sociologists have shown that the United State's score for individualism is almost 90, whereas China scores only 20. Today many Chinese families are not only influenced by tradition but by other cultures. Since traditions are deeply rooted, they often reject the notion of majority rule. Every family will go through some 'soul-searching' according to its cultural origins. It will design and implement family decision-making rules consistent with the family culture, as the following hypothetical example illustrates.

A Chinese family of five, composed of parents who can be described as traditionalists, and three adult siblings who have been exposed to protestant influences via Western friends and their education, may find that a 'mixed' form of decision-making works: they adopt majority rule but the head (the father) will have two or even three votes instead of one. Alternatively, the father may have one vote like everyone else, but he also has power of veto, which can be used once every three years. Another possibility is to let the head make decisions but allow the rest of the family to veto those decisions.

Regardless of which form of decision-making is adopted, it will usually take several years and numerous meetings for family members to learn to respect the rules and the decisions taken. For complex business families it is an effort worth making since it can help avoid costly conflicts in the future.

Separating family from business

Another feature of governance of large, multi-generational families is the separation of family and business decisions, whereby different decision platforms are created to resolve family and business issues as much as possible. For example, they could establish a family board represented by different branches and generations of family members to resolve family issues, whereas business decisions could be delegated to a separate corporate board.

The personal demands of individual members may be met by institutions outside the business so that the firm's operations and performance are not hindered. For example, if an entrepreneurial member wants to start their own businesses but is short of finance, a fund separate from the family corporation can be established to finance new venture activities, subject to evaluation and approval by an investment committee of the family board. Similarly, the family may choose to establish a fund outside the corporation to sponsor family members' education and emergency needs.

Of course, business issues should be under the purview of the family – after all, some of them will be significant shareholders so they may end up sitting on the family and the corporate boards. The key is not to fill the corporate board with family members. Rather, the family board should elect just enough family members to serve on the corporate board as their representatives and monitor the business. To achieve additional professionalism and proper checks and balances, the corporate board should include non-family managers and independent third parties.

Despite the family's best efforts to delegate business decisions to the corporate board, there will always be overlapping family and business issues, such as how much dividend to pay, whether members can buy and sell business shares, whether they can work in the business, whether they can start their own businesses, etc. Hence the need for guidelines defining the division of responsibility between the family board and the corporate board.

For example, whereas the family board determines a range of annual dividends that the business should distribute to shareholders in the next three years, the corporate board decides the specific annual dividend level within that range. The family board sets guidelines to evaluate and monitor family members' employment qualifications and performance, while the corporate board will set and execute performance evaluation and compensation for both family and non-family employees.

Family constitution

Large multigenerational business families should consider integrating their family governance efforts. A family 'constitution' is commonly used to integrate various forms of governance. The typical constitution will define the members, values, and goals. To unify these across the family, the constitution will include guidelines to regulate members' behavior and relationships. The constitution is not a legal document; its 'enforceability' depends on consensus and cause and effect. All family members should believe in the values and goals set out in the constitution, and be willing to bear the consequences of any violation of the rules. Of course, good behavior should be rewarded just as bad behavior should be punished.

The family constitution may establish additional governance institutions such as a family council and family board. Composed of all adult family members, the family council elects family board members, and organizes family educational, cultural, entertainment and philanthropic activities. The constitution should lay down the rules to be followed by them both.

Shareholder agreement

A large multigenerational business family should establish a family shareholder agreement. This defines the share of business ownership by individual members, and the specific rights associated with the ownership shares, such as voting rights, receiving dividends, and transferring shares. For example, the shareholder agreement may deviate from the one-share-one-vote rule by requiring that the family vote en bloc, or by according higher voting rights to some shares. It may restrict the transfer of shares to within the family and set share prices.

Application: how family governance shapes the succession path

We have discussed the effects of family assets and roadblocks on succession for family firms. The simple framework presented in Figure 8.5 serves to emphasize the importance of planning. However, family assets and roadblocks are not independent; they may affect each other and in turn a family's succession path and specific governance tasks. For example, we already know that the power of numbers tends to diffuse family ownership. In addition, as family size and complexity increase it becomes more difficult to maintain consensus and harmony, and the family risks losing its critical assets. If problems go unattended, they may eventually break up the family and the business altogether. Ultimately, it depends on whether the family can enhance family governance and design ownership to cope with the power of numbers.

Figure 8.5 illustrates how the ability to enhance family governance affects the succession outcome. Faced with increasing numbers and complexity of family members, the long-term outcome will depend on how well it improves governance within its cost limits. For simplicity, assume that family governance does not substantially affect near-term family asset levels (not a realistic assumption but let's bear with it because it should not affect our conclusions). Where a family has abundant family assets and is able to install robust family governance (the upper-right quadrant), then the succession mode is 'unify': the family will continue to own and manage the business under one roof. By contrast, if a family does not have significant family assets in the first place and its family governance is poor (the lower-left quadrant), then the 'sell-off' mode makes sense – sell the business and distribute the cash – although they may seek legal assistance in the process.

There are two additional in-between cases. If a family makes little unique contribution to the firm but its governance level is expected to be strong in the future, then it could continue to unify and own the business while delegating business decisions to non-family professionals (the upper-left quadrant). Lastly, if a family has abundant family assets yet is not able to boost family governance from its current low level, then the optimal

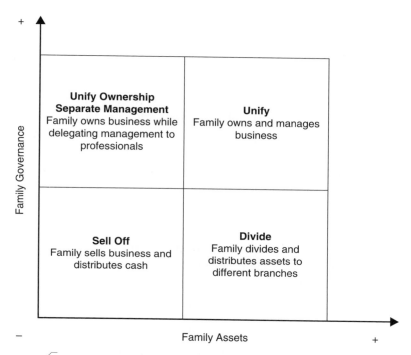

FIG 8.5 Family governance and succession mode

succession mode could be 'divide' – split the business and distribute the assets to different branches of family members. Short of a complete separation, the family may choose to design cross-shareholding structures to share family assets such as names, legacy and networks.

The *FB Map* and ownership design: sharing family assets while preserving control

Ownership is the interface between a family and its business. The quality of ownership design affects the smooth running of both the family and the business. Ownership arrangements should not be made 'last-minute' by the patriarch. To return to the clock analogy, it should be designated once the family is confident that its 'part' works well with other parts of the family clock to tell the time (achieve the family's long-term objectives).

Ownership is a set of rights: the right to make decisions, the right to share profits, and the right to exchange. Ownership design is not just about cutting and dividing the family pie, but also assigning these three specific rights. Below we summarize several important principles in designing ownership.

The first is control. How concentrated does ownership need to be to control a business effectively while fulfilling other needs? For example, more concentrated control is necessary in hostile business environments. But we know that environmental roadblocks tend to diffuse family ownership, so the family might create ownership-enhancing mechanisms such as dual-class or pyramid share structures to reinforce their control, and improve corporate governance to mitigate side effects of these ownership structures on outside investors.

The second is balance. To whom and to what extent should ownership be distributed to induce a sense of responsibility, promote collaboration, and share intangible assets? The family will design rules to distribute shares to family and non-family managers and employees. In many cultures, distribution is governed by tradition and occurs once in a life time – upon the death of the head of the family. However, with due respect to culture and tradition, a family should consider distributing ownership earlier rather than later, because the ownership arrangement helps stakeholders form reasonable expectations about their relationship with the family and the business. In the absence of such expectations, we have seen many family businesses suffer from free rider problems, infighting, and ultimately destruction.

Alternatively, a family can estimate the level of control required based on roadblocks, and distribute shares to stakeholders without sacrificing effective control. This gives priority to family members, managers and employees who are important to the long-term success of the business. It would be a mistake to distribute business ownership primarily for the purpose of subsidizing the livelihoods of family members. Remember, ownership is for sharing family assets, not material, wealth. The more a family is able to capitalize on its family assets, the more it is able to create material wealth.

The third is liquidity. To what extent can ownership be traded within the family and with outsiders? Many families believe that ownership should be tightly held by few, if not just one entity, and that exchanges should not be allowed even among family members. This is a mistake. Transferring ownership is an important means of realigning interests and resolving

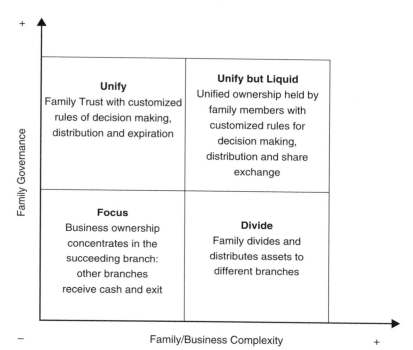

+

Family Governance

| Unify
Family Trust with customized rules of decision making, distribution and expiration | Unify but Liquid
Unified ownership held by family members with customized rules for decision making, distribution and share exchange |
| Focus
Business ownership concentrates in the succeeding branch: other branches receive cash and exit | Divide
Family divides and distributes assets to different branches |

−   Family/Business Complexity   +

FIG 8.6 Ownership design subject to family/business complexity and family governance strength

conflicts. If a family restricts or prohibits exchanges of ownership, it will require very robust governance mechanisms in both the family and the business to perform those functions. Families must weigh up the costs and benefits between the ownership approach and the governance approach. Often both are used to complement each other. For example, if the family has a complex family and business, it will not depend on internal rules to regulate family owners' behavior, and will design share exchange mechanisms to allow family shares to be traded in an orderly manner.

We prefer to offer guiding principles here rather than ready-made solutions because ownership issues are complex and will be affected by various family, business and environmental factors. Rather than suggesting that ownership is largely an emotional choice, we would encourage families to make ownership choices based on their specific constraints.

To put this in perspective, let's imagine a family preparing a succession of the business. They identify family governance and business complexity as important variables in the future. To enhance their chance of success, they are contemplating potential ownership structures, as in Figure 8.6, which presents possible scenarios and their respective ownership choices.

1. If the family expects to invest to establish strong governance, it will consider unified ownership. If it anticipates that it will maintain small family size and/or a stable business, then it may establish a family trust and transfer family ownership to the trust, while designing rules for business decision-making, dividend distribution, and expiration within the trust framework (upper-left quadrant).
2. If the family anticipates a more complex family and/or business situation in the near future, then it might let family managers own a majority of shares and gain effective control, while allowing regular share exchanges to help them adapt to changes (upper-right quadrant).
3. If the family estimates that family governance will be weak despite its best efforts, then its ownership design will focus on effective control and conflict avoidance.
4. If the family structure and the business environment are stable, then the ownership mode is 'focus': transfer the controlling ownership to a designated family successor while other family members receive cash and exit from the business (lower-left quadrant).
5. If the family and/or the business are complex, then the best ownership mode is 'divide': the family divides and distributes assets to different branches of the family (lower-right quadrant).

The *FB Map* and incentivizing managers and directors

The third category of tasks that a business family should conduct is delegating business decisions to managers, and incentivizing and monitoring them so that they act in the best interests of the owners.

Family or non-family managers?

We have stressed the need for business families to have an employment policy for family members. In Chapter 6 we report statistics that family members do better as business leaders when they have proven abilities from elite schools and work experience, or a long tenure in the family firm. Yet from a governance standpoint, family members could be more reliable managers than non-family professionals. Professionals may not appreciate the family values as much as family members, and may be driven by self-interest. This concern is real in emerging markets where the legal enforcement of private property rights is weak, as illustrated by the story of Huang He Group in China (Chapter 3) and the marriage networks in Thailand (Chapter 2). Even in developed countries such as Japan and the United States, a long string of corporate scandals have involved professional managers: Toyota, Olympus, Xerox, Enron, Tyco, AIG, etc.

If a family sees itself running a small and stable business and is not short of manpower, it can afford not to have non-family professionals. Yet more and more families encounter various roadblocks and family 'brain drain' issues, hence they create a pool of human capital incorporating both family and non-family members.

Collaboration between family and non-family members

The first issue a family should consider when mixing family and non-family members is their different roles and responsibilities and how the two can collaborate. We have observed several approaches. The traditional approach is when family leads, professionals assist; the family makes critical decisions, the non-family managers execute them. This is commonly observed among businesses at the founding stage requiring very specialized family inputs. It may also be used by multi-generational families with robust family governance and a rigorous system of cultivating family successors. However, the key weakness of this approach is the risk of family brain drain and environmental changes. For example, the family leads approach is difficult to sustain in China because of its one-child policy and highly volatile business environment.

Another approach is when professionals lead and the family takes a back seat. The family delegates business decisions to non-family managers, while incentivizing and monitoring them to ensure their decisions are consistent with the family's values and interests. This relieves the family's manpower concerns in the face of new challenges and opportunities. Families that eventually exit from the business entirely may also choose this approach. The key risk here is the typical problem of 'other people's money'. The family must learn to be a responsible yet non-intervening owner, professionalize the business and implement a robust governance system so that professional managers can make value-enhancing decisions efficiently.

The third is a *team* approach: family members work side-by-side with non-family managers. An advantage of this approach is objective decision making that avoids risk due to mistakes or self-interest. We have seen it adopted by Formosa Plastics to fill the managerial vacuum left by founder Wang Yung-ching. It creates a healthy turnover of key executives and mitigates the risk of an unexpected executive departure, be it due to health problems or death. The team approach is suitable for families that contribute unique assets yet are facing increasingly large and complex business operations which are becoming too complex to run themselves. An important weakness of the co-managing approach is that family managers may not be able to resist the 'owner manager' mindset and dominate the decision making. This tendency can be mitigated by dividing decision areas and/or increasing the size of the decision team, although it will obviously incur additional coordination. To mitigate such issues the family should install a system to cultivate healthy working relationships with non-family managers.

Paying and promoting managers

It is a myth that family businesses underpay their managers; indeed it is hard to believe that they can be successful if they exploit managers in this way. The reality is that successful family businesses reward their managers handsomely, and even pay a premium over non-family firms.

Consider CEO pay. In family firms the CEO is often not at the top but comes second to the chairman of the board, who is typically a family member. Given their different responsibilities, people might think that CEOs of family firms should not be paid as much their counterparts in non-family firms. In fact, they should receive as much if not more; the additional pay compensates for the lack of promotion opportunity, even if they are not the top decision-maker. High salary is not just about retaining the CEO and rewarding performance, but about motivating the managers below to work hard to move up the corporate ladder.

An owner must know his business objectives and design appropriate pay structures to induce managers to achieve them. We know that cash and bonuses alone do not induce long-term incentives or the transfer of values that are often important to family firms. Equity ownership is an important means of inducing these incentives but family firms often prefer not to award stock for fear of dilution. They should reconsider. The key is allowing an exchange and thereby establishing a fair value for the shares. The dilution issue can be mitigated by customized rules such as phantom stocks, non-voting stocks, and/or restricting share trading within family members and employees. In designing the ownership mechanism, remember that the more we restrict ownership transferability, the more the business will be run like a communal enterprise – everyone wants to have a say and a good salary, but no one really cares.

Building a robust board of directors

Business families need a place to discuss and make business decisions. Often it's the family dinner table. However, as the family and its business grow, they should create a separate platform to deal with business affairs – typically a board of directors. Similar to a family board that consolidates family interests, the corporate board consolidates shareholder interests and monitors business decisions in the best interests of all the owners, family or non-family.

In a first-generation family firm, the board is often dominated by the family head while other members have only a nominal role. This is fine when the business is small and the family head is the only owner, but as the business becomes more complex there is a need for additional brain power and checks and balances. With new generations and new demands to raise capital, the number of owners increases over time, and new owners need to learn how to make business decisions together. Unfortunately, many families are ill-prepared to make the transition, often resulting in the decline of the firm.

Many business founders find it difficult to give up even a fraction of control because they attribute their past success primarily to their monopoly on power. Since they suspect that their children or professional managers can never be ready (or trusted), they have to keep working and controlling the business as long as they can. Obviously they will have to let go one day – inevitably leaving behind unprepared children and a vulnerable business. Indeed the most important requirement for creating a functional corporate board is that the head of the family firm acknowledges this risk and loosens his or her grip.

A functioning board must be able to make sound decisions based on collective wisdom but not driven by self-interest. To achieve this it should incorporate talent from within the family and within the market, delegate power to the board and design the rules for its functioning. To make room for professional managers and outside directors there should be rules to allow only a small number of qualified family members to be elected to the board. When making decisions, board members should speak with one voice to represent all the family owners. The family should voluntarily give up some of its power to make room for professional advice and monitoring.

Discover more

Bennedsen, Morten, Vikas Mehrotra, Jungwook Shim, and Yupana Wiwattanakantang. Exit and Transitions in Family Control and Ownership in Post-War Japan. Working Paper. 2014.

Hofstede, Geert, Gert Jan Hofstede, and Michael Minkov. Cultures and Organizations: Software of the Mind, McGraw-Hill, Third Edition, 2010.

Highlights

- The two fundamental premises for the *FB Map* are that (1) strong family assets increase the value of family management and (2) severe roadblocks increase the pressure on keeping ownership tight in the family.
- The *FB Map* is a powerful analytical tool by which to understand the ownership and management structure of family firms across the world and to explain the different corporate governance agendas in East and West.
- The strength of family assets and family governance interact to shape the optimal choice of succession model. Strong family governance with few family assets provides space for future family ownership, whereas weak family governance with strong family assets makes it challenging to continue as a united family.

Epilogue

A final word

Throughout this book we have engaged research evidence and case examples from around the world to convey key messages about the sustainable prosperity of families and their businesses. Ultimately, these messages are universal in that they apply to business families from Africa and Asia to Europe, Latin America and the US. Sustainable family firms have succeeded in developing business strategies supported by strong family assets and efficient governance strategies that reduce the cost of roadblocks.

At the heart of this sustainability is the understanding of family assets and how they are preserved and shared within the family, the firm and society at large. Successful business families know how to strengthen family assets and how to cultivate and inspire family members and professional managers to overcome internal and environmental obstacles. They also know their limits, and rationally plan the ideal route to their destinations 20 years ahead. Once their goals are set, families bind themselves together with customized governance mechanisms to steer the family firm to success. Along the journey, each individual is willing to sacrifice their own interests for the common good, and in this way feels fulfilled.

We leave the last word to Zengoro Höshi. When we interviewed him for this book in his idyllic ryokan in the Ishikawa prefecture of Japan, we asked what message he wished to pass on the many owner-managers who devote their lives to family firms around the globe. With 1,300 years of owner-management, the Höshi Ryokan's experience of long-term planning is second to none and it enshrines the most impressive family assets we have ever encountered.

Mr Höshi thought about our question for a long time and then gave us a surprisingly short answer: 'Study water', he said. 'Water has a well-defined mission and constantly invests in improving the efficiency of its path.'

The fundamental truth of this Buddhist-inspired wisdom is echoed in the advice extended throughout this book to families hoping to create a lasting legacy. Start by developing a clear mission for the business. Optimize business strategy by exploiting family assets, and finally minimize costly roadblocks through active governance design.

Index

Printed and bound by CPI Group (UK) Ltd, Croydon, CR0 4YY